The Ultima PAGAN ALMANAC

2019

NORTHERN HEMISPHERE
EUROPE & EASTERN EUROPE

Lustre 4
MMDCCLXXII a.U.c.
2446 A.P.
Olympiad 699, 3rd year

Published Under the Direction Of

Jean-Louis de Biasi & Patricia Bourin

Theurgia Publications
www.theurgia.us

Publishers: Jean-Louis de Biasi - Patricia Bourin

Contributors: Orestis Sakellaropoulos, Mark Todd, Pedro
Mouro, Sophie Watson, Klaytonus Silvanus, Andre Dollinger,
John White, Jean-Louis de Biasi and Patricia Bourin.

From Archives: Vivian Godfrey White (Melita Denning) and
Gemistus Plethon.

Theurgia Publications © 2018
2251 N. Rampart Blvd #133, Las Vegas, NV 89128, USA
secretary@theurgia.us
Made in the United States of America
ISBN: 978-1-926451-18-3

Discover our other publications: www.theurgia.us
and Amazon: goo.gl/RP4RdJ

CONTENTS

Introduction _____ 5

Deciphering the Pagan Calendar _____ 9

Lunisolar Calendar _____ 9

Druidic Calendar _____ 16

Roman Calendar _____ 20

Pletho's Calendar _____ 24

Athenian Calendar _____ 28

Egyptian Calendar _____ 32

CALENDAR _____ 37

JANUARY _____ 39

FEBRUARY _____ 54

MARCH _____ 70

APRIL _____ 85

MAY _____ 99

JUNE _____ 114

JULY _____ 128

AUGUST _____ 143

SEPTEMBER _____ 157

OCTOBER _____ 172

NOVEMBER _____ 188

DECEMBER _____ 201

About the Western Tradition _____ 217

About the Articles _____ 217

Body and soul in Ancient Egypt _____ 219

The four kas: Human happiness as a gift from the gods _____ 231

Heka: The magic of ancient Egypt _____ 236

3

Druid Musings _____ 253

The Lore of Incenses _____ 272

Neoplatonist and Pagan views in the late Byzantine era _____ 290

The Moon within the Hermetic Tradition _____ 297

Harmonization with the planetary days _____ 300

The numinous experience and the archetype of the *teophoros* ___ 306

The Decans _____ 309

Hermes _____ 311

The Mysteries _____ 315

The Afterlife _____ 317

Christian Persecutions against Pagans _____ 322

An interpretation of Plato's Cave _____ 331

Creed of the Ecclesia Ogdoadica _____ 345

Hymn to the Gods _____ 346

Orpheus _____ 348

Tradition of the Aurum Solis _____ 353

Notes _____ **359**

Discount _____ 359

Submissions _____ 359

Press _____ 359

INTRODUCTION

Time is a fascinating subject. For hundreds of years, philosophers, mathematicians, and astronomers have approached it in multiple ways. Astrologers, priests and priestesses, along with initiates, have tried to decipher the mysterious bonds that make us sons and daughters of the earth and the starry sky.

Each day, we witness the cycles of the sun and the moon. Each day, our calendar and clocks try to give us markers to help us in our daily life. However, it is common knowledge that our modern calendar is artificial and deeply disconnected from the real visible and invisible cycles of the cosmos.

One of the greatest mysteries is hidden in plain sight and today you can unveil it. You should know that whoever controls the calendar, controls the time, the mind, and the daily life of every individual. An invisible power, likely political, decides whether you wake up during the night or at daylight. The same entity dictates whether you live your daily life in connection with the sun or disconnected for obscure economic reasons. Although you may or may not like the modifications of the time in Summer and Fall, you will have to accept them, even if they go against your inner cycles.

Some religious leaders understood this power on people a long time ago. For this reason, they recycled ancient festivals while progressively twisting their meaning. They cleared out these essential celebrations from their real astral and natural power. This manipulation happened progressively. Most of the time nobody noticed them, and when ancient believers continued to bring offerings to the altars of Gods and Goddesses, they were simply jailed or killed.

Fortunately, three main things never disappeared.

First, the cosmic cycles continue and they still affect us in the same way they did our ancestors, hundreds of years ago.

Second, ancient beliefs never disappear, as Gods and Goddesses are immortal.

Third, initiates continued to maintain the sacred fire of knowledge. hidden from intolerant powers. This heritage helps us today to rediscover the truth of the western pagan tradition and reconnect it with its real source.

However, don't be fooled by appearances!

Keep in mind that the Western heritage has been twisted and disconnected by very smart people. Never underestimate the winners.

The first thing you need to know if you are interested or involved in Western pagan traditions, is that all calendars were lunisolar. You are the connection between the earth and the stars. As such, both are essential and must be followed if you want your energy and spirituality back. If your celebration is planned according to the civil calendar, you should immediately know that you have been fooled, and you are on the wrong path. Obviously, equinoxes and solstices are specific days that are different every year. So why should Halloween/Samhain be a fixed date, October 31st in the USA? The same question applies for Imbolc, Beltane, and other festivals.

This consideration is even worse if you consider a more astrological and magical approach. If someone tells you there are specific powers associated with the days of the week, believe it. But have you considered that the days of your calendar are totally arbitrary regarding celestial movements? Have you realized that they have been disconnected from their real invisible and divine power? For example, without knowing when the real Monday is, you cannot connect with the power of the moon this very day. This is the same for the other days of the week.

A very ancient tradition associates 36 decans to the year. According to the time you were born, this divine celestial power is different. Knowing its name is essential so you can pray the correct decan at the right time of the year.

To go even further, we have added several pieces linked to the main pagan traditions. They will allow you to learn more about this heritage.

This almanac is a guide that gives you all the information you need to walk with the immortal divinities.

We have been lucky to receive some of the most ancient Western initiations and teachings. From this heritage we have unveiled a definitive way to cross the wheel of the year in connection with the real powers at the right time! It doesn't matter if you are Wiccan or practicing other Western traditions because you will find here the utilmate guide that was missing.

Our goal is simple: Give you the keys to reconnect with the cosmos, the Gods and Goddesses as proud heir of a very ancient and respectable tradition called Paganism!

Jean-Louis de Biasi & Patricia Bourin
Las Vegas December 2018.

DECIPHERING THE PAGAN CALENDAR

Lunisolar Calendar

Wheel of the Year

It is obvious that traditional pagan festivals marking the calendar are linked to the seasons and the cycles of the moon. Almost all the ancient calendars were based on these natural cycles.

The start of the year was also chosen according to the way the world was seen.

Everyone knows that the dates of the seasons were not chosen arbitrarily, but according to the actual movement of the earth around the sun. Consequently, we cannot rely on the civil calendar to learn about the real dates of the eight annual festivals.

Astronomy gives us a precise indication of the time of the Equinoxes and Solstices. It is generally easy to find this indication for your own location. This is not the same, however, for the four other dates you can find on the wheel of the year.

These intermediary celebrations were traditionally calculated by religious authorities. In the Celtic world, druids oversaw this determination, priests or priestesses in Egypt and Greece, etc. In the theurgic tradition of the Aurum Solis, for example, the Collegium Cathedrarum proclaims these festivals according to a simple rule. The time between a solstice and an equinox is divided by two. If there is a phase of the moon in a time frame of two days (one day before and one day after the date), the day of the lunar phase is chosen for the festival. If this is not the case, the real astronomical day is maintained. This calendar will follow this process and of course not the arbitrary choices without spiritual interest you can find in the civil calendar.

The tradition of the Aurum Solis has maintained four characters associated with the seasons. They are called:

9

Tempus Sementis (Spring), Tempus Messis (Summer), Tempus Consilii (Fall), and Tempus Eversionis (Winter). They are indicated in this calendar along with a few comments.

YEAR 2019

NORTHERN HEMISPHERE
Tropical Zodiac - Europe

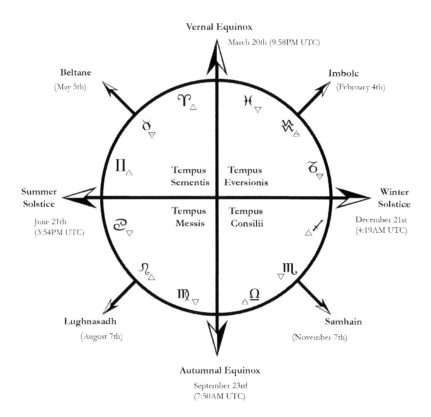

It is well known that what we call today the Western pagan tradition comes from the Mediterranean Sea and more generally, Europe. Consequently, the characters of the eight festivals are very closely linked to the seasons in the Northern Hemisphere. The energies involved in the rituals are an expression of these periods of the year. For this main reason, this almanac provides a wheel of the year in which the traditional festivals match the seasons in this part of the globe. A different edition of this

A "Lustre" is a period of 5 years, each one having 12 months. Consequently, even if the "Lustre" always has the same number of days, this is not the case for the years.

There are two theories about the starting of the month. One claim is that the year starts in Spring and the other one during the Fall. The latter is the most accepted today, as the cycle always begins with the "shadow period," the night for each day. Other interpretations linked the month of Samonios with the celebration of Samhain which adds credit to this hypothesis. This is the method we have adopted.

The century used in our calendar starts, as in antiquity, at the first quarter of the moon previous to Samhain (end of October, beginning of November). The first "Lustre" starts at the same time. It is necessary to have Saturn in Taurus in retrograde movement, and the Sun between the Virgin and Libra. We followed the choice by scholars to start the Gaulish calendar according to these astronomical values at the peak of Druidism which is 150 BCE. However, as this calendar is a stable succession of centuries of 30 years, a clear identification of the beginning of the calendar is not so important.

Festivals

The eight celebrations summarized in the wheel of the year were the main part of this civilization. They are not explicitly mentioned in the calendar because they are associated with the solar cycles and not the lunar cycles.

Besides these eight markers, Celts and Gauls worshiped an endless number of deities. Some specific dates are indicated from archaeological discoveries and others by oral tradition. We have associated these specific days of offerings in the following calendar.

Roman Calendar

For this first edition of this Almanac we decided to follow the usual calendar of the Roman Republic mainly used by pagans today. Even if the prehistoric Roman calendar was probably based on the real lunar cycles, this third version followed the seasons instead.

The Months

Much of what we know about the names of the months comes from two authors: Ovid, a Roman (1st century BCE) and Plutarch (2nd century CE), a Greek. The names of the months are linked to Gods and the numerals as follows:

IANVARIVS (Jan.): Mensis Ianuarius; Month of Janus (Roman god of doors, beginnings, sunset and sunrise, had one face looking forward and one backward); 29 days.

FEBRVARIVS (Feb.): Mensis Februarius. The name of this month comes from the Latin word *Februare* meaning "To purify." It is during this month that the Roman festival of purification, called *Lupercalia,* is held. Duration: 28 days.

MERCEDONIVS (Intercalary month): Mercedonius; Mensis Intercalaris; Month of Wages; 23 days.

MARTIVS (Mar.): Mensis Martius. Month dedicated to the God Mars (the Roman god of war). Duration: 31 days.

APRILIS (Apr.): Mensis Aprilis. Uncertain meaning. This Month is sometimes dedicated to the Goddess Venus. Duration: 29 days.

MAIVS (May): Mensis Maius; Uncertain meaning. This Month is sometimes dedicated to the Goddess Maia. Duration: 31 days.

IVNIVS (Jun.): Mensis Iunius. This Month is dedicated to the Goddess Juno, wife of Jupiter. Duration: 29 days.

IVLIVS (Jul.): Mensis Quintilis (Mensis Quinctilis), changed to "Julius" in the *Julian Calendar* in honor of Julius Caesar. July was the month of his birth. It was originally the Fifth Month. Duration: 31 days.

AVGVSTVS (Aug.): Mensis Sextilis, changed to "Augustus" in the *Julian Calendar* in honor of the Emperor Augustus. It was originally the Sixth Month. Duration: 29 days.

SEPTEMBER (Sep.): Mensis September. It was originally the Seventh Month. Duration: 29 days.

OCTOBER (Oct.): Mensis October. It was originally the Eighth Month. Duration: 31 days.

NOVEMBER (Nov.): Mensis November. It was originally the Ninth Month. Duration: 29 days.

DECEMBER (Dec.): Mensis December. It was originally the Tenth Month. Duration: 29 days.

MENSIS INTERCALARIS called MERCEDONIUS: This is an intercalary month inserted when needed between February 23rd (a.d. VII Kal. Mart.), and 24th (a.d. VI Kal. Mart.).

From the Months to the Days

Months have three main markers called in Latin the Kalendes (*Kalendae*, abbr. "KAL."), the nones (*Nonae*, abbreviated "NON."), and the ides (*Idus*, abbr. "ID."). The Kalends were always the first day of the month. The Nones were usually the fifth but sometimes the seventh day. The Ides were the fifteenth but sometimes the thirteenth day. All the days after the Ides were numbered by counting down towards the next month's Kalends. Because of that the words "Ante Diem" (abbr. "A.D.") were used before the number in numerals. This rule applies to every day except the day before the reference day. In this case the word "Pridie" (abbr. PRID.) was used.

The days were identified with these codes and Roman numbers. To give you an example for January 1st, 2019, the Roman day is: "A.D. XIV KAL. IAN." That means "Ante Diem fourteen Kalendas Ianuarius," "fourteen days before the 1st day (Kalendes) of January."

The days can be associated with letters placed between brackets at the end of the date, for example A.D. IV NON. IAN. (B.F.). To follow what we explained before, this date should be read "Ante Diem four Nonae Ianuarius B.F.," meaning "four days before the Nones of January."

The first letter indicates a market day. This letter is called the "Nundinae" (nine-day) or the "Nundinal letter." Usually the markets were held every nine days. As the length of the year was not a multiple of 8 days, the letter of the market day changed every year. Consequently, different letters were used between A and H. The second letter is the most important for spiritual and religious purposes. They indicate the type of religious or legal observance of the day. They are also called "Characters of days."

Here are the main meanings of these letters:

F (*Dies Fasti*, "allowed days," *fastus*, "permissible"): It was legal to initiate action in the courts of civil law.

C (*Dies Comitiales*): They are fast days during which the Roman people could hold assemblies.

N (*Dies Nefasti*): Political and judicial activities were prohibited.

NP (uncertain): These days are like the *Dies Nefasti* with some modifications. For example: slaves are allowed the day off work; ordinary citizens should avoid any physical labour except what is urgent; etc.

QRCF (uncertain): These days are the same as *Dies Nefasti* until the "king" (rex sacrorum) appears in the comitia.

EN (*Dies Endotercisi* (or *Intercisi*), "halved"): Most political and religious activities were prohibited in the morning and evening due to sacrifices (offerings) being prepared. However, activities were acceptable during the middle of the day. To summarize: Same as *dies nefasti* in the morning, same as *dies fasti* in the afternoon, and same as *dies nefasti* in the evening.

Other combinations of letters exist but are less common.

The Year

Following the Roman use, we count the years from the foundation of the City of Rome which was placed by the Roman writer Marcus Terentius Varro at 753 BCE according to our modern and civil system. The letters a.U.c. are associated with the year. They stand for *Ab Urbe Condita* and mean "from the foundation of the city."

Consequently, the Roman year that corresponds to 2019 is MMDCCLXXII a.U.c. (2772 *Ab Urbe Condita* – 2772 from the foundation of the city).

In 46 B.C.E., Julius Caesar initiated an important reform that resulted in the establishment of a new dating system, that was eventually called the "Julian calendar." This is the one we have used here.

Festivals

The number of festivals is important and usually well documented. The days were carefully chosen and linked to the countless divinities. They are indicated in the calendar after the name of the day. As you will discover in the calendar, the Roman months do not match with our civil months. You should keep in mind that our current calendar has been modified from the time of ancient Rome. For the reasons explained in a previous part, we have used the real dates to give you a genuine calendar.

Pletho's Calendar

Origin of the Calendar

Georgius Gemistus Pletho was one of the most renowned philosophers of the Byzantine era. Raised in a Christian family and well-educated, he became a philosophy teacher. The Emperor sent him to the city of Mistra (Greece) where he taught, and wrote extensively about philosophy, astronomy, history, etc. His visible life was very much focused on classical philosophy (Platonist) and theology. However, a rumor of heresy emerged, although he was not condemned, mainly because he was under the Emperor's protection.

Under the veil of secrecy, he had organized around him a small circle of pupils to whom he taught a different view of history and philosophy. In fact, Plethon rejected Christianity and advocated a return to the worship of ancient Hellenic Gods. Along with Neoplatonism, his teaching focused on Zoroaster and the Magi. This secret group and teachings are not mere speculations: a book written by Plethon, called *Nomoi (Book of Laws)* was circulated among the members of this circle. It was never published, but after Plethon's death, a copy was discovered, and Princess Theodora sent it to the Patriarch of Constantinople. Realizing the extent of this heresy and the danger for Christian institutions, the Patriarch burnt this unique full copy. Just before carryout out this detestable act, however, he wrote a letter detailing the book, providing chapter headings and brief summaries of its contents. Later, another summary written by Plethon himself for his student Bessarion was discovered.

In this fascinating book, Plethon provides several indications about time, and an original calendar.

In 1438, he traveled to Florence (Italy) to participate as an expert on a council between the Greek and Latin Churches. Besides this council he created a small school (the Careggi circle) that would eventually become the Academia Platonica - protected by Cosimi de Medici and headed by Marsilio Ficino. This discovery of the pre-Christian heritage (including the theurgic lineage) led to the rebirth of Neoplatonism, which launched the vital movement called the "Renaissance."

As the theurgic Order of the Aurum Solis comes from this lineage, the main calendar used in the Order comes from Plethon, adapted to the hermetic curriculum. Since other initiatic degrees of this Order are based on Celtic, Greek, and Egyptian festivals, these other calendars are also utilized without rejecting Plethon's heritage.

Structure of the Calendar

It is not surprising that Plethon's calendar is luni-solar.

For reasons not explained in the existing parts of his book, the months are not named.

The structures of the months are documented. According to Plethon, the first week (Histamenou) of the month extends from the first day to the eighth; the second week (Mesountos) from the seventh day to the second (regressively); the third week (Phthiontos) from Dixoumenia, to the eighth, and the last week (Apiontos) from the seventh to the second (regressively). Each week has seven days, even if the number eight is highlighted by Plethon.

This can be confusing, and you can see below a representation of it:

1-2-3-4-5-6-7
8-7-6-5-4-3-2
1-2-3-4-5-6-7
8-7-6-5-4-3-2
29-30

Monthly Holidays

The monthly holidays fall on: the first (Noumenia), the eighth, the fifteenth (Dixomenia), the eighth before the end of the month, the twenty-ninth in a full month (Ene), and the thirtieth in a full month or the twenty-ninth in a hollow month (Ene Kai Nea).

This structure of the month follows the traditional phases of the Moon.

Noumenia: The first day of the month, mainly dedicated to Zeus. We can remember that Plato declared every beginning to be divine. Apollo, Artemis, Hera, Hermes, and Hecate were also worshipped on this day.

This is also a day to honor the household Gods. Among them are Hestia, Zeus Ktesios, Hermes, Hekate, Apollon Agyieus, and one's ancestors.

On the first noumenia of the year, there was a yearly festival in honor of Zeus (Helios) celebrated in Rome to commemorate his triumph over winter.

Eighth day: the sacred day of Poseidon, son of Zeus.

Dixomenia: The fifteenth day of the month is the day sacred to Athena and other offerings linked to the full moon.

Ene: Worship of the God Pluto, chief-god of the underworld. It is generally used for the twenty-ninth day of the month or the intermediary days until the new moon.

Ene Kai Nea: ("the old and the new") the last day of the month, a day of self-examination and analysis. This day should be devoted to leisure, contemplation of the work of the previous month and preparation of the month to come.

Agathos Daimon: Histamenou 2, the day following the Noumenia, is dedicated to Agathos Daimon (Good Spirit).

Days of the Month

Besides the monthly holidays and following the classical tradition, the Aurum Solis associates with this calendar the correspondences to the real planetary days calculated from the day of each new moon. You can check the part about the planetary days to know more about it.

The Year

For symbolic reasons, Plethon chose to start the new year from the midnight which follows the first new moon after the winter solstice. This is different from the Athenian convention of starting the year with the new moon after the summer solstice.

The Careggi Circle, following the Neoplatonic tradition, used years linked to Plato, called Anno Platonis. The number 427, the year of Plato's birth, is added to the find the date of the Platonic year. Consequently, for 2019, the Anno Platonis is 2446 and the 1st day of Anno Platonis 2446 is Sunday, January 6th (2019).

Athenian Calendar

First, we must realize that a country called Greece didn't actually exist in ancient times. The country we know today was a web of independent cities with specific deities and festivals. Consequently, the "Grecians" developed original calendars, sometimes based on different principles. The start of the year could have been different, the names of the months, the days, etc. One major element, however, was always the same: the luni-solar character of the calendar.

In this almanac, we choose to provide the Athenian (Attic) Calendar., which was widely used in the past, and progressively became a reference for anyone practicing or just interested in this rich heritage.

Structure of the Year

This calendar was introduced by the astronomer Meton in 432 BCE. It seems that Meton followed earlier Babylonian astronomers with a 19-yearcycle of 235 synodic months (6,940 full days).

Following the calculation of Meton, the 19-year cycle is divided as follows:

1) Eight years of 354 days (12 months)
2) Four years of 355 days (12 months)
3) Seven years of 384 days (13 months with the addition of Poseidon 2, a month of 30 days.)

This is a festival calendar of twelve months based on the cycle of the moon.

Like the Delphic calendar, it begins with the first New Moon after the Summer Solstice, with the month called Hekatombaion.

The names of the months are linked with events and festivals.

Below you will find the months of the calendar, the seasons, and the meaning of each one.

Summer

- *Hekatombaion* (July/August), named after the sacrifice of a hecatomb (100 oxen).
- *Metageitnion* (August/September), named after a cult title of the god Apollo.
- *Boedromion* (September/October), named after the festival in honor of Apollo Boedromios (the helper in distress).

Autumn

- *Pyanepsion* (October/November), named after the festival in honor of Apollo. The name comes from a meal made of fava beans served on this occasion.
- *Maimakterion* (November/December), named after the festival in honor of Zeus (God of storms).
- *Poseideon* (December/January), named after the festival in honor of Poseidon.
- *Poseidon 2* (Intermediary month every three years to calibrate the lunar and solar cycles)

Winter

- *Gamelion* (January/February) is a "wedding month."
- *Anthesterion* (February/March), named after the festival in honor of Dionysus and the infernal deities (time of the awakening of nature).
- *Elaphebolion* (March/April): Festival of deer hunting, in honor of the Goddess Artemis.

Spring

- *Mounichion* (April/May), named after the Festival in honor of Artemis Mounichia.
- *Thargelion* (May/June), named after the festivals in honor of Apollo and Artemis held on their birthdays on the 6th and 7th of Thargelion.
- *Skirophorion* (June/July), named after the festival in honor of Athena.

Delphic Calendar

As important reference for people working on oracles, we want to mention also the Delphic months:
- *Bucatios* (Approximately September – Month of harvesting grapes)

- *Heraios* (App. October – Month of falling leaves)
- *Apellaios* (App. November – Cold month)
- *Diosthyos* (App. December – Snowy month)
- *Dadaphorios* (App. January – Month of burning trunks)
- *Poitropios* (App. February – Month of dreadful ice)
- *Bysios* (App. March – Month of budding)
- *Artemisios* (App. April – Month of grass)
- *Heracleios* (App. May – Month of mowing)
- *Boathoos* (App. June – Month of grain)
- *Ilaios* (App. July – Golden month)
- *Theoxenios* (App. August – Month of harvesting)

Start of the Calendar

As mentioned, this calendar begins with the first New Moon after the Summer Solstice, with the month called Hekatombaion.

It is always challenging to find a continuity in the numbering of the years, as a starting point is necessary. In this case, the common method is to use the "Olympiad Calendar."

During the 3rd century BCE, Eratosthenes of Cyrene established a sequence of four years corresponding to the time when the Olympic Games were celebrated in Olympia.

According the sophist Hippias of Elis (5th Century BCE), the first Olympiad took place during the summer of 776 BCE. Consequently, as the years go from Summer to Summer, the sequence of the first years can be established as follows:

Olympiad 1 (1st year) (Ol. 1.1) = 776/5 BCE.
Olympiad 1 (2nd year) (Ol. 1.2) = 775/4 BCE
Olympiad 1 (3rd year) (Ol. 1.3) = 774/3 BCE
Olympiad 1 (4th year) (Ol. 1.4) = 773/2 BCE
Olympiad 2 (1st year) (Ol. 2.1) = 772/1 BCE
And so on.

As for the current year, we obtain:

January 2019 CE (1st part of the year) = Olympiad 699, 2nd year (Ol. 699.2)

Summer 2019 CE (2nd part of the year) = Olympiad 699, 3rd year (Ol. 699.3)

Days of the Month

According to the Athenian custom, days ran from sunrise to sunrise. Eight days per month were associated with the birthdays of deities and celebrated as such. They are listed below:
- Day 1: New Moon (Noumenia)
- Day 2: Agathos Daimon
- Day 3: Athena's Birthday
- Day 4: Heracles, Hermes, Aphrodite and Eros
- Day 6: Artemis' Birthday
- Day 7: Apollo's Birthday
- Day 8: Poseidon and Theseus

Other days had special names as you can see below:
- 1st day: *Noumenia* (Day of the new moon)
- 10th day: The tenth day of the month (waxing moon)
- 20th day: The earlier tenth (waning moon)
- 21st day: The later tenth (waning moon)
- The last day: *Henē kai nea* (The old and the new)

Festivals

The Attic calendar was mainly a festival calendar of 12 months based on the cycle of the moon. Numerous festivals, most of them local, were celebrated throughout the year. The Hellenistic religion, named such by the Emperor Julian, as well as initiatic orders such as the Aurum Solis in some of its aspects, continue to honor the Gods and Goddesses at the traditional time. You will find the indications in the calendar.

Egyptian Calendar

Egyptian civilization brings us to the origins of Western Tradition. Before the existence of any real culture in the north part of the Mediterranean Sea, Egyptians already had an amazing architecture, complex religious rituals, and a well-organized priesthood. For hundreds of years, until the Ptolemaic period, this civilization enlightened this land. Famous figures such as Pythagoras and Plato spent numerous years of study in Egypt. Afterwards, Pythagoras founded his school in Greece and created the word "philosopher," "friend of wisdom." There, this virtue was associated with Thoth and Maat. We tend to forget that Plato studied for 13 years at Heliopolis before creating his own school in Greece, the "Academy."

Structure of the Year

The first lunar calendar was in use for a very long time, ultimately replaced around 5,000 BCE with a new calendar based on the seasons starting with the flooding of the Nile. The calendar had 12 months of 30 days organized in 3 seasons of four months. Each season corresponded to a period of culture: 1-Flooding; 2- Sowing; 3- Harvest.

At first, the months were not named but numbered. After a few centuries, divinities were associated with each of them and they became known by these names (attested from what is called the "New Kingdom").

The transcription of the months' names, coming from the transliteration of hieroglyphs, can be confusing. For clarification, we provide below the earliest numbering of months for the seasons, followed by the original transliteration of the name of the month from the New Kingdom, its Greek name, and its common English transcript (if needed).

Season Akhet (*ꜣḥt*) (Flooding)

1st of Akhet, *Ḏḥwtyt*, Θωθ, Thoth (Sometimes "Djehuti").

2nd of Akhet, *P-n-ip.t*, Θωθ, Phaophi.

3rd of Akhet, *Ḥwt-ḥwr*, Αθυρ (Athur), Athyr.

4th of Akhet, *Kꜣ-ḥr-Kꜣ*, Χοιακ (Khoiak), Choiak.

Season Peret (*prt*) (Going forth)

1st of Peret, *Tꜣ-ꜥb*, Τυβι (Tubi), Tybi.

2nd of Peret, *Mḫyr*, Μεχιρ (Mekhir), Mechir.

3rd of Peret, *P-n-imn-ḥtp-w*, Φαμενωθ, Phamenoth.

4th of Peret, *P-n-rnn.t*, Φαρμουθι (Pharmouthi), Pharmuthi.

Season Shemu (*šmw*) (Harvest)

1st of Shemu, *P-n-ḫns.w*, Παχων (Pakhon), Pachon.

2nd of Shemu, *P-n-in.t*, Παυνι (Pauni), Payni.

3rd of Shemu, *Ipip*, Επιφι, Epiphi.

4th of Shemu, *Mswt Rꜥ*, Μεσορη, Mesore.

We don't want to delve into the details of the three different calendars that existed in Ancient Egypt. Our purpose is to give you the essential keys allowing you to read the following calendar, which focus on the religious part of this amazing civilization.

You should keep in mind that, as was common in antiquity, the calendar was rooted on the moon cycles (religious calendar) while integrating seasons (civil calendar) and deities (names of the months).

The beginning of the flooding corresponded at this time to the heliacal rising of the brightest star in the sky, Sirius (α of the constellation Canis Major); consequently, this celestial event was chosen as a marker for the start of the year. The heliacal rising of a star is its appearance on the eastern horizon in the early dawn. This implies that the star has a certain height above the horizon, and the Sun a certain height below the horizon (the *arcus visionis*). As you might expect, the observation is not easy and depends upon many factors such as: The Arcus Visionis, which varies each day; the observer's location; the brightness of the star; the proximity of the sun and the star; the weather, etc. Today we have a more accurate way to calculate this rising, thanks to a formula developed by Pierre Bretagnon (IMCCE), but the location remains crucial.

For this calendar we have chosen the location of Heliopolis in Egypt and an Arcus Visionis of 8°, within a minimum of 6° and a maximum of 12°. Then we have applied the usual rules developed by the Egyptologist Richard A. Parker.

The necessity to keep the lunar calendar as a reference resulted in the final determination of the first day of the first month (Thoth) of the season Akhet. It became the sunrise of the first day following the new moon that follows the heliacal rising of Sirius.

In years that would contain a 13th new Moon, an additional month was intercalated at the end. When the rising of Sirius occurred in the last eleven days of the twelfth month of the year, an extra month called Djehuty was added. The start of the year was then modified accordingly, but always associated with a new moon.

Interestingly, the heliacal rising of Sothis returned to the same point in the calendar every 1460 years, a period called the "Sothic cycle."

Before going further, we should mention three interesting facts:

- As the civil (12 months of 30 days) and religious calendars do not match, Egyptians added five days called "epagomenal days," each one being associated with the birth of a deity: Osiris, Horus, Seth, Isis, and Nephthys. To keep these important birthdays, the calendar here places them on the days that follow the 360th day of the year.

- The Egyptian calendar did not have a starting time we can identify. The counting of the years started from the beginning of each reign of a pharaoh. Consequently, dates are written as: Year(s) of reign + month of the season + number of the day of the month.

- The year was divided into 36 decans lasting 10 days each. As explained previously, we added their hermetic names in the calendar.

Structure of the month

The lunar month began at sunrise. Each day was divided into night (darkness) called "gereh" and day (clarity) called "heriou." Both were divided into 12 equal periods of time. Consequently, the length of these periods varies over the seasons. We can see here the origin of the planetary hours used in theurgy.

There is much debate regarding the determination of the first day. We will not enter into these very specialized arguments: instead, we'll provide a simple explanation of this system. Generally speaking, the month starts when we observe the new moon (when the moon is totally invisible). Obviously, this "non" vision is not easy to do. but an elegant solution can be seen in a temple in Egypt, called Dendera. On the ceiling of the hypostyle hall, the waxing of the moon is represented as a staircase of 15 stairs. A deity stands on each one. On the 15th stands a large mirror blessed by Thoth. At the center of the representation of the full moon is placed the "eye of Horus" called Oudjat. Each stair represents a day of ascension toward the full moon, and each one has a specific name (provided below). Since observing the full moon is easy, the first day of the month can be chosen by counting back. Most of the time, this method will reveal the exact day of the astronomic new moon, although sometimes it shifts slightly, which is not important. The essential aspect is to follow the indication of this rising moon to the full moon fifteen days later. This is the determination we have applied to this calendar.

In the Egyptian religion, the important part of the month was the waxing moon. This is why we will limit our naming of the days to the first fifteen.

Day 1: *Psḏtyw*, Pesedjtiou, "Day of the new moon" (or the fifteen day before full moon).

Day 2: *Tp ȝbd*, Tep abed, "Beginning of the moon."

Day 3: *Mspr*, Meseper, "Arrival."

Day 4: *Prt Sm*, Peret sem, "The going forth of the Sem."

Day 5: *ʾIḫt Ḥr Ḫȝwt*, Iret rer raout, "Offerings upon the altar."

Day 6: *Snt*, Senet, "The sixth."

Day 7: *Dnit,* Denit, "Crescent."

Day 8: *Tp*, Tep, *Meaning unknown.*

Day 9: *Kȝp*, Kap, *Meaning unknown.*

Day 10: *Sif*, Sif, *Meaning unknown.*

Day 11: *Stt*, Setet, *Meaning unknown.*

Day 12: *Translation unknown.*

Day 13: *Mȝȝ Sṯy*, Maa setji, *Meaning unknown.*

Day 14: *Siȝw*, Siaou, *Meaning unknown.*

Day 15: *Tp Smdt*, Tep semedet, "Full moon."

Festivals

Traditional festivals are indicated at the correct date following the determination previously explained of the 1st day of the year and the 1st day of each moon cycle.

In this way, you will be able to follow the calendar and make the most of it.

CALENDAR

2019

NORTHERN HEMISPHERE
EDITIONS NORTH AMERICA

Lustre 4
MMDCCLXXII a.U.c.
2446 A.P.
Olympiad 699, 3rd year

JANUARY

6: ● **14:** ☽ **21:** ○

27 (Europe, Balkans) **28** (Central & East Europe): ☾

1   Tuesday

Real Planetary Day: Mercury
Moon: Waning Crescent
Zodiac: Capricorn (♑-▽)
Decan: 2nd Decan: Srô (Epitek) | Ruler: Mars
Pletho's Calendar: Apiontos 5 | 12th Month
Attic Calendar & Festivals: 25 of Poseideon, **2nd year of the 699 Olympiad.**
Roman Calendar & Festivals: A.D. XIV KAL. IAN. MMDCCLXXI (2771) | Saturnalia: 3rd day.
Opalia: Festival honoring Ops (fertility deity and earth goddess).
Gaulish Calendar and Festivals: Lustre 4: MID DUMANIOS 4 ANMATU MDVMAN ANM | Dumanios II of Atenoux - MD - SAMONI – IVOS
Egyptian Calendar: Season Peret (Month 1 - Tybi) Day 26

2   Wednesday

Real Planetary Day: Jupiter
Moon: Waning Crescent
Zodiac: Capricorn (♑-▽)
Decan: 2nd Decan: Srô (Epitek) | Ruler: Mars
Pletho's Calendar: Apiontos 4 | 12th Month
Attic Calendar & Festivals: 26 of Poseideon | Haloa: Festival in honor of Demeter, Dionysus, and Poseidon Phytalmios, god of seashore vegetation.

Roman Calendar & Festivals: A.D. XIII KAL. IAN. | Saturnalia: 4th day.

Gaulish Calendar and Festivals: Dumanios III of Atenoux - D - AMB - IVOS | Offerings to Moccus (boar/pig/swine God, Moccus is the protector of boar hunters, and warriors).

Egyptian Calendar: Season Peret (Month 1 - Tybi) Day 27

---

3   Thursday

Real Planetary Day: Venus
Moon: Waning Crescent
Zodiac: Capricorn (♑-▽)
Decan: 2nd Decan: Srô (Epitek) | Ruler: Mars
Pletho's Calendar: Apiontos 3 | 12th Month
Attic Calendar & Festivals: 27 of Poseideon
Roman Calendar & Festivals: A.D. XII KAL. IAN. | Saturnalia: 5th day.

Divalia: Festival honoring Angerona (Goddess who relieved men from pain and sorrow).

Offerings to Hercules and Ceres (Goddess of agriculture, grain, and mother love).

Gaulish Calendar and Festivals: Dumanios IIII of Atenoux - D

Egyptian Calendar: Season Peret (Month 1 - Tybi) Day 28

---

4   Friday

Real Planetary Day: Saturn
Moon: Waning Crescent
Zodiac: Capricorn (♑-▽)
Decan: 2nd Decan: Srô (Epitek) | Ruler: Mars
Pletho's Calendar: Apiontos 2 | 12th Month
Attic Calendar & Festivals: 28 of Poseideon.

Roman Calendar & Festivals: A.D. XI KAL. IAN. | Saturnalia: 6th day.

Dies natalis (founding day) of the Temple of the Lares Permarini.

Gaulish Calendar and Festivals: Dumanios V of Atenoux - D - AMB - IVOS

Egyptian Calendar: Season Peret (Month 1 - Tybi) Day 29 Sailing of Bast; Festival of Raising the Willow.

---

5   *Saturday*

Real Planetary Day: Aether
Moon: Waning Crescent
Zodiac: Capricorn (♑-▽)
Decan: 2nd Decan: Srô (Epitek) | Ruler: Mars
Astral Event: Partial Solar Eclipse (East Asia and Pacific)
Celebration: Sacred day of the God Pluto, chief-god of the underworld.
Pletho's Calendar: Hene
Attic Calendar & Festivals: Gamelion 1.
Roman Calendar & Festivals: A.D. X KAL. IAN. | Saturnalia (Sigillaria): 7th and last day were pottery or wax figurines are given as traditional gifts.
Larentalia: Festival honoring Diana, Juno Regina, and Tempestates (Goddess of storms or sudden change of weather).
Gaulish Calendar and Festivals: Dumanios VI of Atenoux - D
Egyptian Calendar: Season Peret (Month 1 - Tybi) Day 30 Sailing of Shesmet.

---

6   *Sunday*

Real Planetary Day: Saturn
Moon: New Moon (●)
Zodiac: Capricorn (♑-▽)

Decan: 2nd Decan: Srô (Epitek) | **Ruler:** Mars
Astral Event: Partial Solar Eclipse (East Asia and Pacific)
Celebration and Remembrance: 1st day of the Platonic Year 2446
Pletho's Calendar: Hene Kai Nea ("the old and the new"); It is a day of self-examination and analysis.
Attic Calendar & Festivals: Gamelion 2
Roman Calendar & Festivals: 2772 a.U.c. - A.D. IX KAL. IAN.
Gaulish Calendar (G.F.): Lustre 4: MID DUMANIOS 4 ANMATU; M DVMAN ANm - VII of Atenoux - d - amb riuri.
Gaulish Calendar and Festivals: Dumanios VII of Atenoux - D - AMB RIURI
Egyptian Calendar: Season Peret (Month 2 - Mechir) Day 1 Sailing of Anubis.

---

7   Monday (New Platonic Year 2446)

Real Planetary Day: Sun
Moon: Waxing Crescent
Zodiac: Capricorn ($\frak{Z}$-$\triangledown$)
Decan: 2nd Decan: Srô (Epitek) | **Ruler:** Mars
Celebration and Remembrance: 1st day of the Platonic Year 2446.
Pletho's Calendar: Noumenia (Histamenou 1) | 1st Month
Attic Calendar & Festivals: Gamelion 3
Roman Calendar & Festivals: A.D. VIII KAL. IAN. | Dies Natalis Solis Invicti (Birthday of the Unconquered Sun) linked the Mithraic Mysteries.
Brumalia: Winter (solstice) festival honoring Saturn, Ceres, and Bacchus.
Gaulish Calendar and Festivals: Dumanios VIII of Atenoux - D - PETI UX RIURI ANAG
Egyptian Calendar: Season Peret (Month 2 - Mechir) Day 2

---

8   Tuesday

Real Planetary Day: Moon
Moon: Waxing Crescent
Zodiac: Capricorn (♑-▽)
Decan: 2nd Decan: Srô (Epitek) | Ruler: Mars
Celebration and Remembrance: Day dedicated to Agathos Daimon.
Pletho's Calendar: Histamenou 2 | 1st Month
Attic Calendar & Festivals: Gamelion 4
Roman Calendar & Festivals: A.D. VII KAL. IAN.
Gaulish Calendar and Festivals: Dumanios VIIII of Atenoux - D - AMB RIURI | Offerings to Ogmios, God of eloquence, also known as Ogmius or Ogimius.
Egyptian Calendar: Season Peret (Month 2 - Mechir) Day 3

---

9   Wednesday

Real Planetary Day: Mars
Moon: Waxing Crescent
Zodiac: Capricorn (♑-▽)
Decan: 2nd Decan: Srô (Epitek) | Ruler: Mars
Pletho's Calendar: Histamenou 4 | 1st Month
Attic Calendar & Festivals: Gamelion 5
Roman Calendar & Festivals: A.D. VI KAL. IAN.
Gaulish Calendar and Festivals: Dumanios X of Atenoux - D
Egyptian Calendar: Season Peret (Month 2 - Mechir) Day 4

---

10   Thursday

Real Planetary Day: Mercury
Moon: Waxing Crescent
Zodiac: Capricorn (♑-▽)
Decan: 2nd Decan: Srô (Epitek) | Ruler: Mars

Pletho's Calendar: Histamenou 5 | 1ˢᵗ Month
Attic Calendar & Festivals: Gamelion 6
Roman Calendar & Festivals: A.D. V KAL. IAN.
Gaulish Calendar and Festivals: Dumanios XI of Atenoux - D - AMB - IVOS
Egyptian Calendar: Season Peret (Month 2 - Mechir) Day 5

11 Friday

Real Planetary Day: Jupiter
Moon: Waxing Crescent
Zodiac: Capricorn (♑-▽)
Decan: 3ʳᵈ Decan: Isrô (Epikhnaus) | Ruler: Sun
Pletho's Calendar: Histamenou 6 | 1ˢᵗ Month
Attic Calendar & Festivals: Gamelion 7
Roman Calendar & Festivals: A.D. IV KAL. IAN.
Gaulish Calendar and Festivals: Dumanios XII of Atenoux - N - INIS R – IVOS| Offerings to the hunting God Veteris (also spelled Vitiris, Vheteris, Huetiris, or Hueteris).
Egyptian Calendar: Season Peret (Month 2 - Mechir) Day 6

12 Saturday

Real Planetary Day: Venus
Moon: Waxing Crescent
Zodiac: Capricorn (♑-▽)
Decan: 3ʳᵈ Decan: Isrô (Epikhnaus) | Ruler: Sun
Pletho's Calendar: Histamenou 7 | 1ˢᵗ Month
Attic Calendar & Festivals: Gamelion 8
Roman Calendar & Festivals: A.D. III KAL. IAN.
Gaulish Calendar and Festivals: Dumanios XIII of Atenoux - D - AMB - IVOS
Egyptian Calendar: Season Peret (Month 2 - Mechir) Day 7

13 Sunday

Real Planetary Day: Saturn
Moon: Waxing Crescent
Zodiac: Capricorn (♑-▽)
Decan: 3rd Decan: Isrô (Epikhnaus) | Ruler: Sun
Celebration: Day dedicated to Poseidon, son of Zeus.
Pletho's Calendar: Histamenou 8 | 1st Month
Attic Calendar & Festivals: Gamelion 9
Roman Calendar & Festivals: PRID. ID. IAN.
Gaulish Calendar and Festivals: Dumanios XIIII of Atenoux - NSDS - IVOS
Egyptian Calendar: Season Peret (Month 2 - Mechir) Day 8

14 Monday

Real Planetary Day: Sun
Moon: First Quarter
Zodiac: Capricorn (♑-▽)
Decan: 3rd Decan: Isrô (Epikhnaus) | Ruler: Sun
Pletho's Calendar: Mesountos 7 | 1st Month
Attic Calendar & Festivals: Gamelion 10
Roman Calendar & Festivals: **IANVARIVS - MMDCCLXXII a.U.c. (2772)** - KAL. IAN. (A.F.) | Festivals of Aesculapius and the God Vediovis. Offerings to Jupiter, Juno, Minerva, Salus, and Janus (Ianus).
Gaulish Calendar and Festivals: **Lustre 4: MID RIUROS 4 MATU M RIUROS MAT** | Riuros I - D - ANAGANTIO – IVOS.
Egyptian Calendar: Season Peret (Month 2 - Mechir) Day 9

15   Tuesday

Real Planetary Day: Moon
Moon: Waxing Gibbous
Zodiac: Capricorn (♑-▽)
Decan: 3rd Decan: Isrô (Epikhnaus) | Ruler: Sun
Pletho's Calendar: Mesountos 6 | 1st Month
Attic Calendar & Festivals: Gamelion 11
Roman Calendar & Festivals: A.D. IV NON. IAN. (B.F.)
Gaulish Calendar and Festivals: Riuros II - PRINNI LOUD –
IVOS | Offering to Lugus, God of creation and learning.
Egyptian Calendar: Season Peret (Month 2 - Mechir) Day 10
Going Forth of Wadjet singing in Heliopolis.

16   Wednesday

Real Planetary Day: Mars
Moon: Waxing Gibbous
Zodiac: Capricorn (♑-▽)
Decan: 3rd Decan: Isrô (Epikhnaus) | Ruler: Sun
Pletho's Calendar: Mesountos 5 | 1st Month
Attic Calendar & Festivals: Gamelion 12 | Lenaia: First day of
the four-day Festival in honor of Lenaeus Bacchus Dionysus hold
in the theater of Dionysus in Athens. The Lênaia is most likely
named for the Lênai, who are Maenads.
Roman Calendar & Festivals: A.D. III NON. IAN. (C.C.)
Gaulish Calendar and Festivals: Riuros III - MD - IVOS
Egyptian Calendar: Season Peret (Month 2 - Mechir) Day 11

17   Thursday

Real Planetary Day: Mercury
Moon: Waxing Gibbous
Zodiac: Capricorn (♑-▽)

Decan: 3rd Decan: Isrô (Epikhnaus) | Ruler: Sun
Pletho's Calendar: Mesountos 4 | 1st Month
Attic Calendar & Festivals: Gamelion 13 | Lenaia: Second day of the four-day Festival.
Roman Calendar & Festivals: PRID. NON. IAN. (D.C.)
Gaulish Calendar and Festivals: Riuros IIII - MD - BRIG RIVRI
Egyptian Calendar: Season Peret (Month 2 - Mechir) Day 12

---

18   Friday

Real Planetary Day: Jupiter
Moon: Waxing Gibbous
Zodiac: Capricorn (♑-▽)
Decan: 3rd Decan: Isrô (Epikhnaus) | Ruler: Sun
Pletho's Calendar: Mesountos 3 | 1st Month
Attic Calendar & Festivals: Gamelion 14 | Lenaia: Third day of the four-day Festival.
Roman Calendar & Festivals: NON. IAN. (E.F.) | Compitalia (Latin: Ludi Compitalicii) festival in honor of the Lares Compitales, household deities of the crossroads.
Dies natalis (founding day) of the shrine of Vica Pota
Gaulish Calendar and Festivals: Riuros V - N - INIS R
Egyptian Calendar: Season Peret (Month 2 - Mechir) Day 13

---

19   Saturday

Real Planetary Day: Venus
Moon: Waxing Gibbous
Zodiac: Capricorn (♑-▽)
Decan: 3rd Decan: Isrô (Epikhnaus) | Ruler: Sun
Pletho's Calendar: Mesountos 2 | 1st Month

Attic Calendar & Festivals: Gamelion 15 | Lenaia: Fourth and last day of the four-day Festival.
Roman Calendar & Festivals: A.D. VIII ID. IAN. (F.F.)
Gaulish Calendar and Festivals: Riuros VI - MD
Egyptian Calendar: Season Peret (Month 2 - Mechir) Day 14
Two-day festival known as "dragging Sokar."

20 Sunday

Real Planetary Day: Saturn
Moon: Waxing Gibbous
Zodiac: Capricorn (♑-▽)
Decan: 3rd Decan: Isrô (Epikhnaus) | Ruler: Sun
Astral Event: Total Lunar Eclipse (Europe, Asia, Africa, North and South America, Pacific, Atlantic, Indian Ocean, Arctic)
Celebration: Day sacred to Athena.
Pletho's Calendar: Dichomenia | 1st Month
Attic Calendar & Festivals: Gamelion 16.
Roman Calendar & Festivals: A.D. VII ID. IAN. (G.C.)
Gaulish Calendar and Festivals: Riuros VII - D - ANAGANTIOS
Egyptian Calendar: Season Peret (Month 2 - Mechir) Day 15

21 Monday

Real Planetary Day: Sun
Moon: Full Moon (◯)
Zodiac: Aquarius (♒-△)
Decan: 1st Decan: Ptiaou (Isu or Thrô) | Ruler: Venus
Astral Event: Total Lunar Eclipse (Europe, Asia, Africa, North and South America, Pacific, Atlantic, Indian Ocean, Arctic)
Pletho's Calendar: Phthiontos 2 | 1st Month
Attic Calendar & Festivals: Gamelion 17.

Roman Calendar & Festivals: A.D. VI ID. IAN. (H.C.)
Gaulish Calendar and Festivals: Riuros VIII - D – ANAG |
Offerings to Oleandossus, God of eloquence.
Egyptian Calendar: Season Peret (Month 2 - Mechir) Day 16

22   Tuesday

Real Planetary Day: Moon
Moon: Waning Gibbous
Zodiac: Aquarius (♒-♒)
Decan: 1st Decan: Ptiaou (Isu or Thrô) | Ruler: Venus
Celebration and Remembrance: Birth of Francis Bacon (1561)
Pletho's Calendar: Phthiontos 3 | 1st Month
Attic Calendar & Festivals: Gamelion 18.
Roman Calendar & Festivals: A.D. V ID. IAN. (A.NP.) |
Agonalia in honor of Janus.
Gaulish Calendar and Festivals: Riuros VIIII - D - ANAG
Egyptian Calendar: Season Peret (Month 2 - Mechir) Day 17

23   Wednesday

Real Planetary Day: Mars
Moon: Waning Gibbous
Zodiac: Aquarius (♒-♒)
Decan: 1st Decan: Ptiaou (Isu or Thrô) | Ruler: Venus
Pletho's Calendar: Phthiontos 4 | 1st Month
Attic Calendar & Festivals: Gamelion 19.
Roman Calendar & Festivals: A.D. IV ID. IAN. (B.C.)
Gaulish Calendar and Festivals: Riuros X – MD | Offerings to
Grannus (sometimes also called Granus, Mogounus, and
Amarcolitanus), God associated with spas, healing mineral
springs, and the sun.
Egyptian Calendar: Season Peret (Month 2 - Mechir) Day 18

24   Thursday

Real Planetary Day: Mercury
Moon: Waning Gibbous
Zodiac: Aquarius (♒-♒)
Decan: 1ˢᵗ Decan: Ptiaou (Isu or Thrô) | Ruler: Venus
Pletho's Calendar: Phthiontos 5 | 1ˢᵗ Month
Attic Calendar & Festivals: Gamelion 20.
Roman Calendar & Festivals: A.D. III ID. IAN. (C.NP.) |
Carmentalia: Two-day festival in honor of Carmentis (Goddess of
childbirth and Prophecy).
Festival of Iuturna (Goddess of fountains and prophetic waters).
Gaulish Calendar and Festivals: Riuros XI - N - INIS R |
Offerings to Alaunus (Alaunius), God of healing and prophecy.
Egyptian Calendar: Season Peret (Month 2 - Mechir) Day 19

25   Friday

Real Planetary Day: Jupiter
Moon: Waning Gibbous
Zodiac: Aquarius (♒-♒)
Decan: 1ˢᵗ Decan: Ptiaou (Isu or Thrô) | Ruler: Venus
Celebration and Remembrance: Dies Ater (Mourning Day,
also called "day of the Great Disaster"): Birth of Christianity by
the conversion of "Saint" Paul (Saul) on the way to Damas.
Pletho's Calendar: Phthiontos 6 | 1ˢᵗ Month
Attic Calendar & Festivals: Gamelion 21.
Roman Calendar & Festivals: PRID. ID. IAN. (D.C.)
Gaulish Calendar and Festivals: Riuros XII - MD
Egyptian Calendar: Season Peret (Month 2 - Mechir) Day 20

26   Saturday

Real Planetary Day: Venus
Moon: Waning Gibbous
Zodiac: Aquarius (♒-♒)

Decan: 1st Decan: Ptiaou (Isu or Thrô) | Ruler: Venus
Pletho's Calendar: Phthiontos 7 | 1st Month
Attic Calendar & Festivals: Gamelion 22.
Roman Calendar & Festivals: ID. IAN. (E.NP.)
Gaulish Calendar and Festivals: Riuros XIII - DEUOR IVG RIVRI | Offerings to Cacus, Fire God.
Egyptian Calendar: Season Peret (Month 2 - Mechir) Day 21

27   *Sunday*

Real Planetary Day: Saturn
Moon: Third (last) Quarter (Europe, Balkans)
Zodiac: Aquarius (♒-♒)
Decan: 1st Decan: Ptiaou (Isu or Thrô) | Ruler: Venus
Pletho's Calendar: Phthiontos 8 | 1st Month
Attic Calendar & Festivals: Gamelion 23.
Roman Calendar & Festivals: A.D. XIX KAL. FEB.
Gaulish Calendar and Festivals: Riuros XIIII - DSNS MAT
Egyptian Calendar: Season Peret (Month 2 - Mechir) Day 22

28   *Monday*

Real Planetary Day: Sun
Moon: Third (last) Quarter (East Europe)
Zodiac: Aquarius (♒-♒)
Decan: 1st Decan: Ptiaou (Isu or Thrô) | Ruler: Venus
Pletho's Calendar: Apiontos 7 | 1st Month
Attic Calendar & Festivals: Gamelion 24.
Roman Calendar & Festivals: A.D. XVIII KAL. FEB. | Second day of the Carmentalia festival.
Gaulish Calendar and Festivals: Riuros XV - DS MAT NS
Egyptian Calendar: Season Peret (Month 2 - Mechir) Day 23

29   Tuesday

Real Planetary Day: Moon
Moon: Waning Crescent
Zodiac: Aquarius (♒-♌)
Decan: 1st Decan: Ptiaou (Isu or Thrô) | Ruler: Venus
Pletho's Calendar: Apiontos 6 | 1st Month
Attic Calendar & Festivals: Gamelion 25.
Roman Calendar & Festivals: A.D. XVII KAL. FEB. | Dies natalis (founding day) of the re-dedication of the Temple of Concordia.
Gaulish Calendar and Festivals: Riuros I of Atenoux - MD
Egyptian Calendar: Season Peret (Month 2 - Mechir) Day 24

30   Wednesday

Real Planetary Day: Mars
Moon: Waning Crescent
Zodiac: Aquarius (♒-♌)
Decan: 1st Decan: Ptiaou (Isu or Thrô) | Ruler: Venus
Pletho's Calendar: Apiontos 5 | 1st Month
Attic Calendar & Festivals: Gamelion 26.
Roman Calendar & Festivals: A.D. XVI KAL. FEB.
Gaulish Calendar and Festivals: Riuros II of Atenoux - MD
Egyptian Calendar: Season Peret (Month 2 - Mechir) Day 25

31   Thursday

Real Planetary Day: Mercury
Moon: Waning Crescent
Zodiac: Aquarius (♒-♌)
Decan: 2nd Decan: Aeu (Sosomnô) | Ruler: Mercury
Pletho's Calendar: Apiontos 4 | 1st Month

Attic Calendar & Festivals: Gamelion 27 | Theogomia: Wedding between Zeus Teleios and Hera Teleia.
Roman Calendar & Festivals: A.D. XV KAL. FEB.
Gaulish Calendar and Festivals: Riuros III of Atenoux - D - AMB
Egyptian Calendar: Season Peret (Month 2 - Mechir) Day 26

FEBRUARY

4 (Europe, Balkans) **5** (East Europe): ● **12** (West Europe) **13** (Balkans, Central & East Europe): ☽ **19:** ○ **26:** ☾

1 Friday

Real Planetary Day: Jupiter
Moon: Waning Crescent
Zodiac: Aquarius (♒-♒)
Decan: 2nd Decan: Aeu (Sosomnô) | Ruler: Mercury
Pletho's Calendar: Apiontos 3 | 1st Month
Attic Calendar & Festivals: Gamelion 28.
Roman Calendar & Festivals: A.D. XIV KAL. FEB.
Gaulish Calendar and Festivals: Riuros IIII of Atenoux - MD
Egyptian Calendar: Season Peret (Month 2 - Mechir) Day 27

2 Saturday

Real Planetary Day: Venus
Moon: Waning Crescent
Zodiac: Aquarius (♒-♒)
Decan: 2nd Decan: Aeu (Sosomnô) | Ruler: Mercury
Pletho's Calendar: Apiontos 2 | 1st Month
Attic Calendar & Festivals: Gamelion 29.
Roman Calendar & Festivals: A.D. XIII KAL. FEB.
Gaulish Calendar and Festivals: Riuros V of Atenoux - D - AMB
Egyptian Calendar: Season Peret (Month 2 - Mechir) Day 28

3   Sunday

Real Planetary Day: Saturn
Moon: Waning Crescent
Zodiac: Aquarius (♒-♒)
Decan: 2nd Decan: Aeu (Sosomnô) | Ruler: Mercury
Celebration: Sacred day of the God Pluto, chief-god of the underworld.
Pletho's Calendar: Hene
Attic Calendar & Festivals: Gamelion 30.
Roman Calendar & Festivals: A.D. XII KAL. FEB.
Gaulish Calendar and Festivals: Riuros VI of Atenoux - MD
Egyptian Calendar: Season Peret (Month 2 - Mechir) Day 29

---

4   Monday (Imbolc)

Real Planetary Day (Europe, Balkans): Saturn
Real Planetary Day (East Europe): Aether
Moon: New Moon (●) (Europe, Balkans)
Zodiac: Aquarius (♒-♒)
Decan: 2nd Decan: Aeu (Sosomnô) | Ruler: Mercury
Astral Event: Imbolc.
Celebration and Remembrance: An imperial edict in 364 order the confiscation of all properties of pagans.
Pletho's Calendar *(Europe, Balkans)*: Hene Kai Nea ("the old and the new"); It is a day of self-examination and analysis.
Pletho's Calendar *(East Europe)*: Hene. Sacred day of the God Pluto, chief-god of the underworld.
Attic Calendar & Festivals: Anthesterion 1.
Roman Calendar & Festivals: A.D. XI KAL. FEB.
Gaulish Calendar and Festivals: Riuros VII of Atenoux - N - ANAG INIS R
Egyptian Calendar: Season Peret (Month 2 - Mechir) Day 30 Culmination of the festival known as "Amun in the festival of raising heaven".

5   Tuesday

Real Planetary Day (Europe, Balkans): Sun
Real Planetary Day (East Europe): Saturn
Moon: New Moon (●) (East Europe)
Zodiac: Aquarius (♒-♒)
Decan: 2nd Decan: Aeu (Sosomnô) | Ruler: Mercury
Pletho's Calendar *(Europe, Balkans)*: Noumenia (Histamenou 1) | 2nd Month
Pletho's Calendar *(East Europe)*: Hene Kai Nea ("the old and the new"); It is a day of self-examination and analysis.
Attic Calendar & Festivals: Anthesterion 2.
Roman Calendar & Festivals: A.D. X KAL. FEB.
Gaulish Calendar and Festivals: Riuros VIII of Atenoux - D - ANAG
Egyptian Calendar: Season Peret (Month 3 - Phamenoth) Day 1 Festival of Ptah.

6   Wednesday

Real Planetary Day (Europe, Balkans): Moon
Real Planetary Day (East Europe): Sun
Moon: Waxing Crescent
Zodiac: Aquarius (♒-♒)
Decan: 2nd Decan: Aeu (Sosomnô) | Ruler: Mercury
Celebration and Remembrance: Day dedicated to Agathos Daimon.
Pletho's Calendar *(Europe, Balkans)*: Histamenou 2 | 2nd Month
Pletho's Calendar *(East Europe)*: Noumenia (Histamenou 1) | 2nd Month
Attic Calendar & Festivals: Anthesterion 3.
Roman Calendar & Festivals: A.D. IX KAL. FEB. | Sementivae: 1st day of the Festival of sowing.

Gaulish Calendar and Festivals: Riuros VIIII of Atenoux - N - ANAG INIS R
Egyptian Calendar: Season Peret (Month 3 - Phamenoth) Day 2

---

7   *Thursday*

Real Planetary Day (Europe, Balkans): Mars
Real Planetary Day (East Europe): Moon
Moon: Waxing Crescent
Zodiac: Aquarius (♒-♒)
Decan: 2nd Decan: Aeu (Sosomnô) | Ruler: Mercury
Pletho's Calendar *(Europe, Balkans)*: Histamenou 3 | 2nd Month
Pletho's Calendar *(East Europe)*: Histamenou 2 | 2nd Month
Attic Calendar & Festivals: Anthesterion 4.
Roman Calendar & Festivals: A.D. VIII KAL. FEB. | Sementivae: 2nd day of the Festival of sowing.
Gaulish Calendar and Festivals: Riuros X of Atenoux - MD - PETI UX RIURI
Egyptian Calendar: Season Peret (Month 3 - Phamenoth) Day 3

---

8   *Friday*

Real Planetary Day (Europe, Balkans): Mercury
Real Planetary Day (East Europe): Mars
Moon: Waxing Crescent
Zodiac: Aquarius (♒-♒)
Decan: 2nd Decan: Aeu (Sosomnô) | Ruler: Mercury
Celebration and Remembrance: Birth of the Master Proclus (412-485 AD)
Pletho's Calendar *(Europe, Balkans)*: Histamenou 4 | 2nd Month
Pletho's Calendar *(East Europe)*: Histamenou 3 | 2nd Month
Attic Calendar & Festivals: Anthesterion 5.

Roman Calendar & Festivals: A.D. VII KAL. FEB. | Sementivae: 3rd day of the Festival of sowing.
Gaulish Calendar and Festivals: Riuros XI of Atenoux - D - AMB
Egyptian Calendar: Season Peret (Month 3 - Phamenoth) Day 4

---

9 Saturday

Real Planetary Day (Europe, Balkans): Jupiter
Real Planetary Day (East Europe): Mercury
Moon: Waxing Crescent
Zodiac: Aquarius (♒-♒)
Decan: 2nd Decan: Aeu (Sosomnô) | Ruler: Mercury
Pletho's Calendar *(Europe, Balkans)*: Histamenou 5 | 2nd Month
Pletho's Calendar *(East Europe)*: Histamenou 4 | 2nd Month
Attic Calendar & Festivals: Anthesterion 6.
Roman Calendar & Festivals: A.D. VI KAL. FEB. | Dies natalis (founding day) of the Temple of Castor and Pollux.
Gaulish Calendar and Festivals: Riuros XII of Atenoux - MD
Egyptian Calendar: Season Peret (Month 3 - Phamenoth) Day 5

---

10 Sunday

Real Planetary Day (Europe, Balkans): Venus
Real Planetary Day (East Europe): Jupiter
Moon: Waxing Crescent
Zodiac: Aquarius (♒-♒)
Decan: 3rd Decan: Ptêbuou (Khonoumous) | Ruler: Moon
Pletho's Calendar (Europe, Balkans): Histamenou 6 | 2nd Month
Pletho's Calendar *(East Europe)*: Histamenou 5 | 2nd Month
Attic Calendar & Festivals: Anthesterion 7.
Roman Calendar & Festivals: A.D. V KAL. FEB.

Gaulish Calendar and Festivals: Riuros XIII of Atenoux - D - AMB
Egyptian Calendar: Season Peret (Month 3 - Phamenoth) Day 6

---

11   *Monday*

Real Planetary Day (Europe, Balkans): Saturn
Real Planetary Day (East Europe): Venus
Moon: Waxing Crescent
Zodiac: Aquarius (♒-♎)
Decan: 3rd Decan: Ptêbuou (Khonoumous) | Ruler: Moon
Pletho's Calendar (Europe, Balkans): Histamenou 7 | 2nd Month
Pletho's Calendar *(East Europe)*: Histamenou 6 | 2nd Month
Attic Calendar & Festivals: Anthesterion 8 |Anthesphoria: Festival in honor of Demeter and her daughter, Persephone. This is a reminder of the flowers collected by Persephone before her abduction by Hades.
Roman Calendar & Festivals: A.D. IV KAL. FEB.
Gaulish Calendar and Festivals: Riuros XIIII of Atenoux - MD
Egyptian Calendar: Season Peret (Month 3 - Phamenoth) Day 7

---

12   *Tuesday*

Real Planetary Day (Europe, Balkans): Sun
Real Planetary Day (East Europe): Saturn
Moon: First Quarter (West Europe)
Zodiac: Aquarius (♒-♎)
Decan: 3rd Decan: Ptêbuou (Khonoumous) | Ruler: Moon
Celebration: Day dedicated to Poseidon, son of Zeus.
Pletho's Calendar (Europe, Balkans): Histamenou 8 | 2nd Month
Pletho's Calendar *(East Europe)*: Histamenou 7 | 2nd Month

Attic Calendar & Festivals: Anthesterion 9.
Roman Calendar & Festivals: A.D. III KAL. FEB. | Offerings on the Ara Pacis (Altar of Peace) erected by Emperor Augustus.
Gaulish Calendar and Festivals: Riuros XV of Atenoux - D - AMB
Egyptian Calendar: Season Peret (Month 3 - Phamenoth) Day 8

13   Wednesday

Real Planetary Day (Europe, Balkans): Moon
Real Planetary Day (East Europe): Sun
Moon: First Quarter (Balkans, East Europe)
Zodiac: Aquarius (♒-♒)
Decan: 3rd Decan: Ptêbuou (Khonoumous) | Ruler: Moon
Pletho's Calendar (Europe, Balkans): Mesountos 7 | 2nd Month
Pletho's Calendar *(East Europe)***:** Histamenou 8 | 2nd Month
Attic Calendar & Festivals: Anthesterion 10.
Roman Calendar & Festivals: PRID. KAL. FEB.
Gaulish Calendar and Festivals: Lustre 4: **MID ANAGANTIOS 4 ANMATU M ANAGANT ANM** | Anagantios I - MD - RIVRI
Egyptian Calendar: Season Peret (Month 3 - Phamenoth) Day 9

14   Thursday

Real Planetary Day (Europe, Balkans): Mars
Real Planetary Day (East Europe): Moon
Moon: Waxing Gibbous
Zodiac: Aquarius (♒-♒)
Decan: 3rd Decan: Ptêbuou (Khonoumous) | Ruler: Moon
Pletho's Calendar (Europe, Balkans): Mesountos 6 | 2nd Month

Pletho's Calendar *(East Europe)*: Mesountos 7 | 2nd Month
Attic Calendar & Festivals: Anthesterion 11 | Anthesteria[1]:
First day of the three-day "festival of Flowers," named "Pithoigia"
(Jar-opening). It is hold approximately when the first shoots of
blossom appear. Procession symbolizing the coming of Dionysos.
This is one of the oldest Greek festivals.
Roman Calendar & Festivals: FEBRVARIS - KAL. FEB.
(F.N.) | Dies natalis (founding day) for the Temple of Juno
Sospita, Mother and Queen.
Offerings at the Grove of Alernus (chthonic god), near the Tiber.
Gaulish Calendar and Festivals: Anagantios II - D
Egyptian Calendar: Season Peret (Month 3 - Phamenoth) Day
10

---

15   Friday

Real Planetary Day (Europe, Balkans): Mercury
Real Planetary Day (East Europe): Mars
Moon: Waxing Gibbous
Zodiac: Aquarius (♒-♒)
Decan: 3rd Decan: Ptêbuou (Khonoumous) | Ruler: Moon
Pletho's Calendar (Europe, Balkans): Mesountos 5 | 2nd
Month
Pletho's Calendar *(East Europe)*: Mesountos 6 | 2nd Month
Attic Calendar & Festivals: Anthesterion 12 | Anthesteria:
Second day of the three-day festival, named "Khoes" (Pitcher
Feast). Everyone drinks old wine while sharing food.
Roman Calendar & Festivals: A.D. IV NON. FEB. (G.N.) |
Sacred to Juno Februra (mother of Mars and goddess of the
passion of love) and Sacred to Ceres (goddess of grain).
Gaulish Calendar and Festivals: Anagantios III - D
Egyptian Calendar: Season Peret (Month 3 - Phamenoth)
Day 11

---

[1] More information about these celebrations can be found on the Aurum Solis
website at: www.aurumsolis.org

16   Saturday

Real Planetary Day (Europe, Balkans): Jupiter
Real Planetary Day (East Europe): Mercury
Moon: Waxing Gibbous
Zodiac: Aquarius (♒-♒)
Decan: 3rd Decan: Ptêbuou (Khonoumous) | Ruler: Moon
Pletho's Calendar (Europe, Balkans): Mesountos 4 | 2nd Month
Pletho's Calendar *(East Europe)*: Mesountos 5 | 2nd Month
Attic Calendar & Festivals: Anthesterion 13 | Anthesteria: Third and last day of the three-day festival, named "Khutroi" (Pot Feasts). This day was honoring Hermes Chthonios. People boiled food for the dead in the pots and offered it to their deceased. Celebration of the Hydrophoria.
Roman Calendar & Festivals: A.D. III NON. FEB. (H.N.)
Gaulish Calendar and Festivals: Anagantios IIII - MD - OCIOMV RIVRI | Offerings to Luxovios, God of waters.
Egyptian Calendar: Season Peret (Month 3 - Phamenoth) Day 12

17   Sunday

Real Planetary Day (Europe, Balkans): Venus
Real Planetary Day (East Europe): Jupiter
Moon: Waxing Gibbous
Zodiac: Aquarius (♒-♒)
Decan: 3rd Decan: Ptêbuou (Khonoumous) | Ruler: Moon
Celebration and Remembrance: Death of Giordano Bruno (1548-1600).
Pletho's Calendar (Europe, Balkans): Mesountos 3 | 2nd Month

Pletho's Calendar *(East Europe)*: Mesountos 4 | 2nd Month
Attic Calendar & Festivals: Anthesterion 14 | Lesser Eleusinian Mysteries: First of the two-days celebration in honor of Demeter and her daughter, Persephone. It is a prerequisite to the Great Mysteries.
Roman Calendar & Festivals: PRID. NON. FEB. (A.N.)
Gaulish Calendar and Festivals: Anagantios V - N - INIS R
Egyptian Calendar: Season Peret (Month 3 - Phamenoth) Day 13

---

18   Monday

Real Planetary Day (Europe, Balkans): Saturn
Real Planetary Day (East Europe): Venus
Moon: Waxing Gibbous
Zodiac: Aquarius (♒-△)
Decan: 3rd Decan: Ptêbuou (Khonoumous) | Ruler: Moon
Pletho's Calendar (Europe, Balkans): Mesountos 2 | 2nd Month
Pletho's Calendar *(East Europe)*: Mesountos 3 | 2nd Month
Attic Calendar & Festivals: Anthesterion 15 | Lesser Eleusinian Mysteries: Second and last of the two-days celebration.
Roman Calendar & Festivals: NON. FEB. (B.N.)
Gaulish Calendar and Festivals: Anagantios VI - PRINNI IAG
Egyptian Calendar: Season Peret (Month 3 - Phamenoth) Day 14

---

19   Tuesday

Real Planetary Day (Europe, Balkans): Sun
Real Planetary Day (East Europe): Saturn
Moon: Full Moon (◯)
Zodiac: Pisces (♓-▽)

Decan: 1st Decan: Biou (Tetimô) | Ruler: Saturn
Celebration and Remembrance: Julian is declared Emperor in Lutece (ancient name of Paris, France) in 360.
Day sacred to Athena.
Pletho's Calendar (Europe, Balkans): Dichomenia
Pletho's Calendar *(East Europe)*: Mesountos 2 | 2nd Month
Attic Calendar & Festivals: Anthesterion 16.
Roman Calendar & Festivals: A.D. VIII ID. FEB. (C.N.)
| Amburbium: Festival for purifying the city with lustration (lustratio urbis). This festival can be applied to purify one's property.
Gaulish Calendar and Festivals: Anagantios VII - MD - OGRONI | Offerings to Acionna, Goddess of waters.
Egyptian Calendar: Season Peret (Month 3 - Phamenoth) Day 15

---

20   *Wednesday*

Real Planetary Day (Europe, Balkans): Moon
Real Planetary Day (East Europe): Sun
Moon: Waning Gibbous
Zodiac: Pisces   (♓·▽)
Decan: 1st Decan: Biou (Tetimô) | Ruler: Saturn
Pletho's Calendar (Europe, Balkans): Phthiontos 2 | 2nd Month
Pletho's Calendar *(East Europe)*: Dichomenia
Attic Calendar & Festivals: Anthesterion 17.
Roman Calendar & Festivals: A.D. VII ID. FEB. (D.N.)
Gaulish Calendar and Festivals: Anagantios VIII - MD - OGRONI
Egyptian Calendar: Season Peret (Month 3 - Phamenoth) Day 16

21   Thursday

Real Planetary Day (Europe, Balkans): Mars
Real Planetary Day (East Europe): Moon
Moon: Waning Gibbous
Zodiac: Pisces (♓-▽)
Decan: 1ˢᵗ Decan: Biou (Tetimô) | Ruler: Saturn
Pletho's Calendar (Europe, Balkans): Phthiontos 3 | 2ⁿᵈ Month
Pletho's Calendar *(East Europe)*: Phthiontos 2 | 2ⁿᵈ Month
Attic Calendar & Festivals: Anthesterion 18.
Roman Calendar & Festivals: A.D. VI ID. FEB. (E.N.)
Gaulish Calendar and Festivals: Anagantios VIIII - MD - OGRONI
Egyptian Calendar: Season Peret (Month 3 - Phamenoth) Day 17

22   Friday

Real Planetary Day (Europe, Balkans): Mercury
Real Planetary Day (East Europe): Mars
Moon: Waning Gibbous
Zodiac: Pisces (♓-▽)
Decan: 1ˢᵗ Decan: Biou (Tetimô) | Ruler: Saturn
Pletho's Calendar (Europe, Balkans): Phthiontos 4 | 2ⁿᵈ Month
Pletho's Calendar *(East Europe)*: Phthiontos 3 | 2ⁿᵈ Month
Attic Calendar & Festivals: Anthesterion 19.
Roman Calendar & Festivals: A.D. V ID. FEB. (F.N.) | Sacred to Apollo (god of the sun).
Gaulish Calendar and Festivals: Anagantios X – D | Offerings to Cernunnos (Jupiter Cernenus), horned God or God of fertility, life, animals, wealth, and the underworld.
Egyptian Calendar: Season Peret (Month 3 - Phamenoth) Day 18

23 Saturday

Real Planetary Day (Europe, Balkans): Jupiter
Real Planetary Day (East Europe): Mercury
Moon: Waning Gibbous
Zodiac: Pisces (♓-▽)
Decan: 1ˢᵗ Decan: Biou (Tetimô) | Ruler: Saturn
Pletho's Calendar (Europe, Balkans): Phthiontos 5 | 2ⁿᵈ Month
Pletho's Calendar *(East Europe)*: Phthiontos 4 | 2ⁿᵈ Month
Attic Calendar & Festivals: Anthesterion 20.
Roman Calendar & Festivals: A.D. IV ID. FEB. (G.N.)
Gaulish Calendar and Festivals: Anagantios XI - D – AMB | Offerings to Vintius, God of winds.
Egyptian Calendar: Season Peret (Month 3 - Phamenoth) D. 19

24 Sunday

Real Planetary Day (Europe, Balkans): Venus
Real Planetary Day (East Europe): Jupiter
Moon: Waning Gibbous
Zodiac: Pisces (♓-▽)
Decan: 1ˢᵗ Decan: Biou (Tetimô) | Ruler: Saturn
Celebration and Remembrance: Birth of Giovanni Pico della Mirandola (1463-1494). An edict of Theodosius (391) prohibits to visit pagan Temples and to look at vandalized statues.
Pletho's Calendar (Europe, Balkans): Phthiontos 6 | 2ⁿᵈ Month
Pletho's Calendar *(East Europe)*: Phthiontos 5 | 2ⁿᵈ Month
Attic Calendar & Festivals: Anthesterion 21.
Roman Calendar & Festivals: A.D. III ID. FEB. (H.N.)
Gaulish Calendar and Festivals: Anagantios XII - D
Egyptian Calendar: Season Peret (Month 3 - Phamenoth) D. 20

25   Monday

Real Planetary Day (Europe, Balkans): Saturn
Real Planetary Day (East Europe): Venus
Moon: Waning Gibbous
Zodiac: Pisces (♓-▽)
Decan: 1ˢᵗ Decan: Biou (Tetimô) | Ruler: Saturn
Pletho's Calendar (Europe, Balkans): Phthiontos 7 | 2ⁿᵈ Month
Pletho's Calendar *(East Europe)*: Phthiontos 6 | 2ⁿᵈ Month
Attic Calendar & Festivals: Anthesterion 22.
Roman Calendar & Festivals: PRID. ID. FEB. (A.N.) | Sacred to Diana (goddess of the moon and the hunt).
Gaulish Calendar and Festivals: Anagantios XIII - D
Egyptian Calendar: Season Peret (Month 3 - Phamenoth) Day 21

---

26   Tuesday

Real Planetary Day (Europe, Balkans): Sun
Real Planetary Day (East Europe): Saturn
Moon: Third (last) Quarter
Zodiac: Pisces (♓-▽)
Decan: 1ˢᵗ Decan: Biou (Tetimô) | Ruler: Saturn
Pletho's Calendar (Europe, Balkans): Phthiontos 8 | 2ⁿᵈ Month
Pletho's Calendar *(East Europe)*: Phthiontos 7 | 2ⁿᵈ Month
Attic Calendar & Festivals: Anthesterion 23 | Diasia: Principal festival for Zeus Meilikhios (The Kindly), who is Zeus in chthonic aspect, manifesting as a giant snake. (bloodless Spring offerings).
Roman Calendar & Festivals: ID. FEB. (B.NP.) | Parentalia: Festival commemorating the Manes, spirits of the ancestors. Offerings are made to the dead, ancestors of one's own family. Fires are not allowed on altars.
Faunalia: Offerings to Faunus (horned God of the forest, plains and fields).

Gaulish Calendar and Festivals: Anagantios XIIII - D
Egyptian Calendar: Season Peret (Month 3 - Phamenoth)
Day 22

---

27 Wednesday

Real Planetary Day (Europe, Balkans): Moon
Real Planetary Day (East Europe): Sun
Moon: Waning Crescent
Zodiac: Pisces (♓-▽)
Decan: 1st Decan: Biou (Tetimô) | Ruler: Saturn
Celebration and Remembrance: An edict of the Emperor Flavius Theodosius (380) institutes Christianity as the exclusive Religion of the Roman Empire.
Pletho's Calendar (Europe, Balkans): Apiontos 7 | 2nd Month
Pletho's Calendar *(East Europe)*: Phthiontos 8 | 2nd Month
Attic Calendar & Festivals: Anthesterion 24.
Roman Calendar & Festivals: A.D. XVI KAL. MART. (C.N.) | 2nd day of Parentalia.
Gaulish Calendar and Festivals: Anagantios XV - D
Egyptian Calendar: Season Peret (Month 3 - Phamenoth) Day 23

---

28 Thursday

Real Planetary Day (Europe, Balkans): Mars
Real Planetary Day (East Europe): Moon
Moon: Waning Crescent
Zodiac: Pisces (♓-▽)
Decan: 1st Decan: Biou (Tetimô) | Ruler: Saturn
Pletho's Calendar (Europe, Balkans): Apiontos 6 | 2nd Month
Pletho's Calendar *(East Europe)*: Apiontos 7 | 2nd Month
Attic Calendar & Festivals: Anthesterion 25.

Roman Calendar & Festivals: A.D. XV KAL. MART. (D.NP.) | 3rd day of Parentalia.

Lupercalia: Festival of Faunus (Avert evil spirits and purify the city; health and fertility.)

Gaulish Calendar and Festivals: Anagantios I of Atenoux - D

Egyptian Calendar: Season Peret (Month 3 - Phamenoth) Day 24

MARCH

6: ● 14: ☽ 21: ○ 28: ☾

1 Friday

Real Planetary Day (Europe, Balkans): Mercury
Real Planetary Day (East Europe): Mars
Moon: Waning Crescent
Zodiac: Pisces (♓-▽)
Decan: 2nd Decan: Kontare (Sopfi) | Ruler: Jupiter
Celebration and Remembrance: Hypatia (370 CE – 415 CE), Neoplatonist philosopher, theurgist, astronomer, and mathematician, savagely murdered a Christian mob in Alexandria).
Pletho's Calendar (Europe, Balkans): Apiontos 5 | 2nd Month
Pletho's Calendar *(East Europe)*: Apiontos 6 | 2nd Month
Attic Calendar & Festivals: Anthesterion 26.
Roman Calendar & Festivals: A.D. XIV KAL. MART. (E.EN.) | 4th day of Parentalia.
Gaulish Calendar and Festivals: Anagantios II of Atenoux – D | Offerings to the God Hu associated with the sun.
Egyptian Calendar: Season Peret (Month 3 - Phamenoth) Day 25

2 Saturday

Real Planetary Day (Europe, Balkans): Jupiter
Real Planetary Day (East Europe): Mercury
Moon: Waning Crescent
Zodiac: Pisces (♓-▽)
Decan: 2nd Decan: Kontare (Sopfi) | Ruler: Jupiter
Pletho's Calendar (Europe, Balkans): Apiontos 4 | 2nd Month

Pletho's Calendar *(East Europe)*: Apiontos 5 | 2nd Month
Attic Calendar & Festivals: Anthesterion 27.
Roman Calendar & Festivals: A.D. XIII KAL. MART. (F.NP.) | 5th day of Parentalia.
Fornacalia: Baking festival celebrated in honor of the goddess Fornax, a divine personification of the oven (fornax), and to the proper baking of bread.
Sacred to Quirinus, one of the Capitoline Triad of gods (Jupiter, Mars, and Quirinus).
Gaulish Calendar and Festivals: Anagantios III of Atenoux - D - AMB
Egyptian Calendar: Season Peret (Month 3 - Phamenoth) Day 26

---

3   Sunday

Real Planetary Day (Europe, Balkans): Venus
Real Planetary Day (East Europe): Jupiter
Moon: Waning Crescent
Zodiac: Pisces (♓-▽)
Decan: 2nd Decan: Kontare (Sopfi) | Ruler: Jupiter
Celebration and Remembrance: Dies Ater (Mourning Day): "Saint" Patrick, Romano-British Christian missionary, known as the "Apostle of Ireland." (5th century)
Pletho's Calendar (Europe, Balkans): Apiontos 3 | 2nd Month
Pletho's Calendar *(East Europe)*: Apiontos 4 | 2nd Month
Attic Calendar & Festivals: Anthesterion 28.
Roman Calendar & Festivals: A.D. XII KAL. MART. (G.C.) | 6th day of Parentalia.
Sacred to Tacita (goddess of silence, the halting of unfriendly speech, and hostile tongues).
Gaulish Calendar and Festivals: Anagantios IIII of Atenoux – D | Offerings to Meduio, God of drunkenness.
Egyptian Calendar: Season Peret (Month 3 - Phamenoth) Day 27

---

4   Monday

Real Planetary Day (Europe, Balkans): Saturn
Real Planetary Day (East Europe): Venus
Moon: Waning Crescent
Zodiac: Pisces (♓-▽)
Decan: 2nd Decan: Kontare (Sopfi) | Ruler: Jupiter
Pletho's Calendar (Europe, Balkans): Apiontos 2 | 2nd Month
Pletho's Calendar *(East Europe)*: Apiontos 3 | 2nd Month
Attic Calendar & Festivals: Anthesterion 29.
Roman Calendar & Festivals: A.D. XI KAL. MART. (H.C.) | 7th day of Parentalia.
Gaulish Calendar and Festivals: Anagantios V of Atenoux - D - AMB
Egyptian Calendar: Season Peret (Month 3 - Phamenoth) Day 28

5   Tuesday

Real Planetary Day (Europe, Balkans): Aether
Real Planetary Day (East Europe): Saturn
Moon: Waning Crescent
Zodiac: Pisces (♓-▽)
Decan: 2nd Decan: Kontare (Sopfi) | Ruler: Jupiter
Pletho's Calendar (Europe, Balkans): Hene (Sacred day of the God Pluto, chief-god of the underworld.)
Pletho's Calendar *(East Europe)*: Apiontos 2 | 2nd Month
Attic Calendar & Festivals: Anthesterion 30.
Roman Calendar & Festivals: X KAL. MART. (A.C.) | 8th day of Parentalia.
Gaulish Calendar and Festivals: Anagantios VI of Atenoux - N - INIS R | Offerings to Ailinn, Tree Goddess of love and magic and Bergusia, Goddess of the crafts.
Egyptian Calendar: Season Peret (Month 3 - Phamenoth) Day 29

6   Wednesday

Real Planetary Day: Saturn
Moon: New Moon (●)
Zodiac: Pisces (♓-▽)
Decan: 2ⁿᵈ Decan: Kontare (Sopfi) | Ruler: Jupiter
Pletho's Calendar: Hene Kai Nea ("the old and the new"); It is a day of self-examination and analysis.
Attic Calendar & Festivals: Elaphebolion 1.
Roman Calendar & Festivals: IX KAL. MART. (B.F.) | Last day of Parentalia.
Public honoring of the Manes. Unique public observation of the Parentalia.
Gaulish Calendar and Festivals: Anagantios VII of Atenoux - I+I - D - AMB OGRON
Egyptian Calendar: Season Peret (Month 4 - Pharmuthi) Day 1

7   Thursday

Real Planetary Day: Sun
Moon: Waxing Crescent
Zodiac: Pisces (♓-▽)
Decan: 2ⁿᵈ Decan: Kontare (Sopfi) | Ruler: Jupiter
Pletho's Calendar: Noumenia (Histamenou 1) | 3ʳᵈ Month
Attic Calendar & Festivals: Elaphebolion 2.
Roman Calendar & Festivals: A.D. VIII KAL. MART. (C.C.) | Caristia (or Cara cognatio): Day of Reconciliation; Families gathered to dine together in a spirit of love and forgiveness, offering food and incense to the Lares as their household gods.
Gaulish Calendar and Festivals: Anagantios VIII of Atenoux - I+I - MD - QVTI OGRON
Egyptian Calendar: Season Peret (Month 4 - Pharmuthi) Day 2

8 Friday

Real Planetary Day: Moon
Moon: Waxing Crescent
Zodiac: Pisces (♓-▽)
Decan: 2nd Decan: Kontare (Sopfi) | Ruler: Jupiter
Celebration and Remembrance: Day dedicated to Agathos Daimon.
Pletho's Calendar: Histamenou 2 | 3rd Month
Attic Calendar & Festivals: Elaphebolion 3.
Roman Calendar & Festivals: A.D. VII KAL. MART. (D.NP.) | Terminalia: Sacred to Terminus, the god of boundary stones and markers.
Gaulish Calendar and Festivals: Anagantios VIIII of Atenoux - D - OGRON AMB
Egyptian Calendar: Season Peret (Month 4 - Pharmuthi) Day 3

9 Saturday

Real Planetary Day: Mars
Moon: Waxing Crescent
Zodiac: Pisces (♓-▽)
Decan: 2nd Decan: Kontare (Sopfi) | Ruler: Jupiter
Pletho's Calendar: Histamenou 3 | 3rd Month
Attic Calendar & Festivals: Elaphebolion 4.
Roman Calendar & Festivals: A.D. VI KAL. MART. (E.N.) | Regifugium: Celebration of the founding of the Republic and the expulsion of the last King of Rome.
Gaulish Calendar and Festivals: Anagantios X of Atenoux - NSDS
Egyptian Calendar: Season Peret (Month 4 - Pharmuthi) Day 4 Festival of Bastet (Day of chewing onions for Bast)

10 Sunday

Real Planetary Day: Mercury
Moon: Waxing Crescent
Zodiac: Pisces (♓-▽)
Decan: 2nd Decan: Kontare (Sopfi) | Ruler: Jupiter
Pletho's Calendar: Histamenou 4 | 3rd Month
Attic Calendar & Festivals: Elaphebolion 5.
Roman Calendar & Festivals: V KAL. MART. (F.C.)
Gaulish Calendar and Festivals: Anagantios XI of Atenoux - D - AMB
Egyptian Calendar: Season Peret (Month 4 - Pharmuthi) Day 5
Appearance of Bastet on her boat.

11 Monday

Real Planetary Day: Jupiter
Moon: Waxing Crescent
Zodiac: Pisces (♓-▽)
Decan: 3rd Decan: Ptibiou (Surô) | Ruler: Mars
Pletho's Calendar: Histamenou 5 | 3rd Month
Attic Calendar & Festivals: Elaphebolion 6.
Roman Calendar & Festivals: A.D. IV KAL. MART. (G.EN.)
Gaulish Calendar and Festivals: Anagantios XII of Atenoux - D
Egyptian Calendar: Season Peret (Month 4 - Pharmuthi) Day 6

12 Tuesday

Real Planetary Day: Venus
Moon: Waxing Crescent
Zodiac: Pisces (♓-▽)
Decan: 3rd Decan: Ptibiou (Surô) | Ruler: Mars

Pletho's Calendar: Histamenou 6 | 3rd Month
Attic Calendar & Festivals: Elaphebolion 7 | Elaphebolia: Festival honoring Artemis Elaphêbolos (Deer-shooting), huntress-Goddess.
Roman Calendar & Festivals: III KAL. MART. (H.NP.) | Equirria, first of two horse-racing festivals to Mars (god of war and agriculture).
Gaulish Calendar and Festivals: Anagantios XIII of Atenoux - D – AMB | Offerings to Camulus (Camulos), God of war and the sky and to Aufaniae, mother Goddess.
Egyptian Calendar: Season Peret (Month 4 - Pharmuthi) Day 7

13   *Wednesday*

Real Planetary Day: Saturn
Moon: Waxing Crescent
Zodiac: Pisces (♓-▽)
Decan: 3rd Decan: Ptibiou (Surô) | Ruler: Mars
Pletho's Calendar: Histamenou 7 | 3rd Month
Attic Calendar & Festivals: Elaphebolion 8 | Galaxia: Festival in honor of Cybele, the Mother of gods.
Asklepia (Honoring Asklepios)
Roman Calendar & Festivals: PRID. KAL. MART. (A.C.)
Gaulish Calendar and Festivals: Anagantios XIIII of Atenoux – D | **DIVERTOMV** | Offerings to Ankou, personification of death.
Egyptian Calendar: Season Peret (Month 4 - Pharmuthi) Day 8

14   *Thursday*

Real Planetary Day: Sun
Moon: First Quarter
Zodiac: Pisces (♓-▽)

Decan: 3rd Decan: Ptibiou (Surô) | Ruler: Mars
Celebration: Day dedicated to Poseidon, son of Zeus.
Pletho's Calendar: Histamenou 8 | 3rd Month
Attic Calendar & Festivals: Elaphebolion 9 | The Great Dyonisia: First of the five-day festival hold in the city of Athens in honor of Dionysus Eleuthereus.
Roman Calendar & Festivals: MARTIUS - KAL. MART. (B.NP.) | Original New Year's Day when the sacred fire of Rome was renewed.
The Salii celebrated the Feriae Marti (holiday for Mars), which was also the dies natalis ("birthday") of Mars.
Matronalia, in honor of Juno Lucina, Mars' mother (presides over women and childbirth in particular).
Gaulish Calendar and Festivals: Lustre 4: MID OGRONNIOS 4 MATU M OGRONN MAT | Ogronnios I - MD
Egyptian Calendar: Season Peret (Month 4 - Pharmuthi) Day 9

---

15   Friday

Real Planetary Day: Moon
Moon: Waxing Gibbous
Zodiac: Pisces (♓-▽)
Decan: 3rd Decan: Ptibiou (Surô) | Ruler: Mars
Pletho's Calendar: Mesountos 7 | 3rd Month
Attic Calendar & Festivals: Elaphebolion 10 | The Great Dyonisia: Second of the five-day festival.
Roman Calendar & Festivals: A.D. VI NON. MART. (C.F.)
Gaulish Calendar and Festivals: Ogronnios II - MD
Egyptian Calendar: Season Peret (Month 4 - Pharmuthi) Day 10

---

16   Saturday

Real Planetary Day: Mars
Moon: Waxing Gibbous
Zodiac: Pisces (♓-▽)
Decan: 3ʳᵈ Decan: Ptibiou (Surô) | Ruler: Mars
Pletho's Calendar: Mesountos 6 | 3ʳᵈ Month
Attic Calendar & Festivals: Elaphebolion 11 | The Great Dyonisia: Third of the five-day festival.
Roman Calendar & Festivals: A.D. V NON. MART. (D.C.)
Gaulish Calendar and Festivals: Ogronnios III - PRINNI LOUDIN
Egyptian Calendar: Season Peret (Month 4 - Pharmuthi) Day 11

17   Sunday

Real Planetary Day: Mercury
Moon: Waxing Gibbous
Zodiac: Pisces (♓-▽)
Decan: 3ʳᵈ Decan: Ptibiou (Surô) | Ruler: Mars
Pletho's Calendar: Mesountos 5 | 3ʳᵈ Month
Attic Calendar & Festivals: Elaphebolion 12 | The Great Dyonisia: Fourth of the five-day festival.
Roman Calendar & Festivals: A.D. IV NON. MART. (E.C.)
Gaulish Calendar and Festivals: Ogronnios IIII - MD
Egyptian Calendar: Season Peret (Month 4 - Pharmuthi) Day 12

18   Monday

Real Planetary Day: Jupiter
Moon: Waxing Gibbous
Zodiac: Pisces (♓-▽)
Decan: 3ʳᵈ Decan: Ptibiou (Surô) | Ruler: Mars

Pletho's Calendar: Mesountos 4 | 3rd Month
Attic Calendar & Festivals: Elaphebolion 13 | The Great Dyonisia: Fifth and last day of the five-day festival.
Roman Calendar & Festivals: A.D. III NON. MART. (F.C.)
Gaulish Calendar and Festivals: Ogronnios V - N - INIS R
Egyptian Calendar: Season Peret (Month 4 - Pharmuthi) Day 13

19 Tuesday

Real Planetary Day: Venus
Moon: Waxing Gibbous
Zodiac: Pisces (♓-▽)
Decan: 3rd Decan: Ptibiou (Surô) | Ruler: Mars
Pletho's Calendar: Mesountos 3 | 3rd Month
Attic Calendar & Festivals: Elaphebolion 14 | Festivals in honor of Zeus.
Roman Calendar & Festivals: PRID. MART. (G.C.)
Gaulish Calendar and Festivals: Ogronnios VI - MD
Egyptian Calendar: Season Peret (Month 4 - Pharmuthi) Day 14

20 Wednesday (Equinox)

Real Planetary Day: Saturn
Moon: Waxing Gibbous
Zodiac: Pisces (♓-▽)
Decan: 3rd Decan: Ptibiou (Surô) | Ruler: Mars
Astral Event: Equinox (2:58 pm PDT) Aurum Solis: Beginning of *Tempus Sementis* (Northern Hemisphere) or *Tempus Consilii* (Southern Hemisphere)
Celebration and Remembrance:
Pletho's Calendar: Mesountos 2 | 3rd Month
Attic Calendar & Festivals: Elaphebolion 15.

Roman Calendar & Festivals: NON. MART. (H.F.) | Agonalia: Second festival of the God Vediovis.
Gaulish Calendar and Festivals: Ogronnios VII - MD - QVTIO
Egyptian Calendar: Season Peret (Month 4 - Pharmuthi) Day 15

21   Thursday

Real Planetary Day: Sun
Moon: Full Moon (◯)
Zodiac: Aries (♈-△)
Decan: 1ˢᵗ Decan: Khontare (Khenlakhôri) | Ruler: Mars
Celebration: Day sacred to Athena.
Pletho's Calendar: Dichomenia
Attic Calendar & Festivals: Elaphebolion 16.
Roman Calendar & Festivals: A.D. VIII ID. MART. (A.F.)
Gaulish Calendar and Festivals: Ogronnios VIII - MD QVTIO
Egyptian Calendar: Season Peret (Month 4 - Pharmuthi) Day 16

22   Friday

Real Planetary Day: Moon
Moon: Waning Gibbous
Zodiac: Aries (♈-△)
Decan: 1ˢᵗ Decan: Khontare (Khenlakhôri) | Ruler: Mars
Pletho's Calendar: Phthiontos 2 | 3ʳᵈ Month
Attic Calendar & Festivals: Elaphebolion 17.
Roman Calendar & Festivals: A.D. VII ID. MART. (B.C.) | Dies religiosus when the Salii carried the sacred shields (ancilia) around the city.
Gaulish Calendar and Festivals: Ogronnios VIIII - N - QVTIO INIS R
Egyptian Calendar: Season Peret (Month 4 - Pharmuthi) Day 17

23   Saturday

Real Planetary Day: Mars
Moon: Waning Gibbous
Zodiac: Aries (♈-△)
Decan: 1ˢᵗ Decan: Khontare (Khenlakhôri) | Ruler: Mars
Celebration and Remembrance: Death of the Past Grand Master Vivian Godfrey (1921-1997)
Pletho's Calendar: Phthiontos 3 | 3ʳᵈ Month
Attic Calendar & Festivals: Elaphebolion 18.
Roman Calendar & Festivals: A.D. VI ID. MART. (C.C.)
Gaulish Calendar and Festivals: Ogronnios X - MD
Egyptian Calendar: Season Peret (Month 4 - Pharmuthi) Day 18

---

24   Sunday

Real Planetary Day: Mercury
Moon: Waning Gibbous
Zodiac: Aries (♈-△)
Decan: 1ˢᵗ Decan: Khontare (Khenlakhôri) | Ruler: Mars
Pletho's Calendar: Phthiontos 4 | 3ʳᵈ Month
Attic Calendar & Festivals: Elaphebolion 19.
Roman Calendar & Festivals: A.D. V ID. MART. (D.C.)
Gaulish Calendar and Festivals: Ogronnios XI - D - AMB
Egyptian Calendar: Season Peret (Month 4 - Pharmuthi) Day 19

---

25   Monday

Real Planetary Day: Jupiter
Moon: Waning Gibbous
Zodiac: Aries (♈-△)
Decan: 1ˢᵗ Decan: Khontare (Khenlakhôri) | Ruler: Mars
Pletho's Calendar: Phthiontos 5 | 3ʳᵈ Month

Attic Calendar & Festivals: Elaphebolion 20.
Roman Calendar & Festivals: A.D. IV ID. MART. (E.C.)
Gaulish Calendar and Festivals: Ogronnios XII - MD
Egyptian Calendar: Season Peret (Month 4 - Pharmuthi) Day 20

---

26 Tuesday

Real Planetary Day: Venus
Moon: Waning Gibbous
Zodiac: Aries (♈-△)
Decan: 1st Decan: Khontare (Khenlakhôri) | Ruler: Mars
Pletho's Calendar: Phthiontos 6 | 3rd Month
Attic Calendar & Festivals: Elaphebolion 21.
Roman Calendar & Festivals: A.D. III ID. MART. (F.EN.)
Gaulish Calendar and Festivals: Ogronnios XIII – MD |
Offerigns to Urien (Uryen), - sun God.
Egyptian Calendar: Season Peret (Month 4 - Pharmuthi) Day 21

---

27 Wednesday

Real Planetary Day: Saturn
Moon: Waning Gibbous
Zodiac: Aries (♈-△)
Decan: 1st Decan: Khontare (Khenlakhôri) | Ruler: Mars
Pletho's Calendar: Phthiontos 7 | 3rd Month
Attic Calendar & Festivals: Elaphebolion 22.
Roman Calendar & Festivals: PRID. ID. MART. (G.NP.) |
Equirria: second Equirria, a Feriae Marti also called the Mamuralia
or sacrum Mamurio.
Gaulish Calendar and Festivals: Ogronnios XIIII - MD
Egyptian Calendar: Season Peret (Month 4 - Pharmuthi) Day 22

28   Thursday

Real Planetary Day: Sun
Moon: Third (last) Quarter
Zodiac: Aries (♈-♎)
Decan: 1ˢᵗ Decan: Khontare (Khenlakhôri) | Ruler: Mars
Pletho's Calendar: Phthiontos 8 | 3ʳᵈ Month
Attic Calendar & Festivals: Elaphebolion 23.
Roman Calendar & Festivals: ID. MART. (H.NP.) | Feriae Iovi: Festival to Jove and the goddess Anna Perenna (personification of the succession of the years).
Gaulish Calendar and Festivals: Ogronnios XV - MD
Egyptian Calendar: Season Peret (Month 4 - Pharmuthi) Day 23

29   Friday

Real Planetary Day: Moon
Moon: Waning Crescent
Zodiac: Aries (♈-♎)
Decan: 1ˢᵗ Decan: Khontare (Khenlakhôri) | Ruler: Mars
Pletho's Calendar: Apiontos 7 | 3ʳᵈ Month
Attic Calendar & Festivals: Elaphebolion 24.
Roman Calendar & Festivals: A.D. XVII KAL. APR. (A.F.) | 1ˢᵗ day of the procession of the Argei (human-shaped bundles of rushes).
Gaulish Calendar and Festivals: Ogronnios I of Atenoux - I++ - MD - QVTIO
Egyptian Calendar: Season Peret (Month 4 - Pharmuthi) Day 24

30   Saturday

Real Planetary Day: Mars
Moon: Waning Crescent
Zodiac: Aries (♈-△)
Decan: 1ˢᵗ Decan: Khontare (Khenlakhôri) | Ruler: Mars
Pletho's Calendar: Apiontos 6 | 3ʳᵈ Month
Attic Calendar & Festivals: Elaphebolion 25.
Roman Calendar & Festivals: A.D. XA.D. VI KAL. APR.
(B.NP.) | 2ⁿᵈ day of the procession of the Argei.
Liberalia: Festival in honor of Liber (Liber Pater) God of
viticulture, wine, fertility, and freedom. This God can be seen as
parent of Dionysus.
Agonalia for Mars.
Gaulish Calendar and Festivals: Ogronnios II of Atenoux - I+I
- MD - QVTIO
Egyptian Calendar: Season Peret (Month 4 - Pharmuthi) Day 25
Harvest offering to Renenutet.

31   Sunday

Real Planetary Day: Mercury
Moon: Waning Crescent
Zodiac: Aries (♈-△)
Decan: 2ⁿᵈ Decan: Khontakhre (Khontaret) | Ruler: Sun
Pletho's Calendar: Apiontos 5 | 3ʳᵈ Month
Attic Calendar & Festivals: Elaphebolion 26.
Roman Calendar & Festivals: A.D. XV KAL. APR. (C.C.)
Gaulish Calendar and Festivals: Ogronnios III of Atenoux -
++I - D - AMB QVTIO | Offerings to Sucellus (Sucellos), God
associated with agriculture and wine.
Egyptian Calendar: Season Peret (Month 4 - Pharmuthi) Day 26

APRIL

5: ●   12: ☽   19: ○   27: ☾

1 Monday

Real Planetary Day: Jupiter
Moon: Waning Crescent
Zodiac: Aries (♈-△)
Decan: 2nd Decan: Khontakhre (Khontaret) | Ruler: Sun
Pletho's Calendar: Apiontos 4 | 3rd Month
Attic Calendar & Festivals: Elaphebolion 27.
Roman Calendar & Festivals: A.D. XIV KAL. APR. (D.NP.) |
Quinquatrus: (1st day of Quinquatria) Celebration of the God
Mars.
Sacred day of Minerva (goddess of handicrafts, doctors, teachers,
and artists).
Gaulish Calendar and Festivals: Ogronnios IIII of Atenoux –
MD | Dahud-Ahes, Goddess of earthly pleasure.
Egyptian Calendar: Season Peret (Month 4 - Pharmuthi) Day 27
Granary offering to Renenutet.

2 Tuesday

Real Planetary Day: Venus
Moon: Waning Crescent
Zodiac: Aries (♈-△)
Decan: 2nd Decan: Khontakhre (Khontaret) | Ruler: Sun
Pletho's Calendar: Apiontos 3 | 3rd Month
Attic Calendar & Festivals: Elaphebolion 28.
Roman Calendar & Festivals: A.D. XIII KAL. APR. (E.C.) |
2nd day of Quinquatria.

Gaulish Calendar and Festivals: Ogronnios V of Atenoux - D – AMB| Offerings to Medurinis, God of drunkenness.
Egyptian Calendar: Season Peret (Month 4 - Pharmuthi) Day 28

---

3 Wednesday

Real Planetary Day: Saturn
Moon: Waning Crescent
Zodiac: Aries (♈-△)
Decan: 2nd Decan: Khontakhre (Khontaret) | Ruler: Sun
Pletho's Calendar: Apiontos 2 | 3rd Month
Attic Calendar & Festivals: Elaphebolion 29.
Roman Calendar & Festivals: A.D. XII KAL. APR. (F.C.) | 3rd day of Quinquatria.
Gaulish Calendar and Festivals: Ogronnios VI of Atenoux - MD | Offerings to Borrum, God of the winds.
Egyptian Calendar: Season Peret (Month 4 - Pharmuthi) Day 29

---

4 Thursday

Real Planetary Day: Aether
Moon: Waning Crescent
Zodiac: Aries (♈-△)
Decan: 2nd Decan: Khontakhre (Khontaret) | Ruler: Sun
Celebration: Sacred day of the God Pluto, chief-god of the underworld.
Pletho's Calendar: Hene
Attic Calendar & Festivals: Elaphebolion 30.
Roman Calendar & Festivals: A.D. XI KAL. APR. (G.N.) | 4th day of Quinquatria.
Gaulish Calendar and Festivals: Ogronnios VII of Atenoux - +I+ - D - AMB QVTIO
Egyptian Calendar: Season Peret (Month 4 - Pharmuthi) Day 30

---

5   Friday

Real Planetary Day: Saturn
Moon: New Moon (●)
Zodiac: Aries (♈-△)
Decan: 2nd Decan: Khontakhre (Khontaret) | Ruler: Sun
Pletho's Calendar: Hene Kai Nea ("the old and the new"); It is a day of self-examination and analysis.
Attic Calendar & Festivals: Mounichion 1.
Roman Calendar & Festivals: A.D. X KAL. APR. (H.NP.) | 5th day of Quinquatria.
Tubilustrium: Purification of the trumpets.
Gaulish Calendar and Festivals: Ogronnios VIII of Atenoux - ++I - MD - OGRO QVTIO
Egyptian Calendar: Season Shemu (Month 1 - Pachons) Day 1 Festival of Renenutet also known as the birthday of Nepri[2].

6   Saturday

Real Planetary Day: Sun
Moon: Waxing Crescent
Zodiac: Aries (♈-△)
Decan: 2nd Decan: Khontakhre (Khontaret) | Ruler: Sun
Pletho's Calendar: Noumenia (Histamenou 1) | 4th Month
Attic Calendar & Festivals: Mounichion 2.
Roman Calendar & Festivals: A.D. IX KAL. APR. (A.F.)
Gaulish Calendar and Festivals: Ogronnios VIIII of Atenoux - ++I - D - AMB QVTIO | Offerings to Iovantucarus, God protector of youth.
Egyptian Calendar: Season Shemu (Month 1 - Pachons) Day 2

---

[2] Personification of grain.

7 Sunday

Real Planetary Day: Moon
Moon: Waxing Crescent
Zodiac: Aries (♈-△)
Decan: 2nd Decan: Khontakhre (Khontaret) | Ruler: Sun
Celebration and Remembrance: Day dedicated to Agathos Daimon.
Pletho's Calendar: Histamenou 2 | 4th Month
Attic Calendar & Festivals: Mounichion 3.
Roman Calendar & Festivals: A.D. VIII KAL. APR. (B.C.)
Gaulish Calendar and Festivals: Ogronnios X of Atenoux - MD
Egyptian Calendar: Season Shemu (Month 1 - Pachons) Day 3

8 Monday

Real Planetary Day: Mars
Moon: Waxing Crescent
Zodiac: Aries (♈-△)
Decan: 2nd Decan: Khontakhre (Khontaret) | Ruler: Sun
Pletho's Calendar: Histamenou 3 | 4th Month
Attic Calendar & Festivals: Mounichion 4.
Roman Calendar & Festivals: A.D. VII KAL. APR. (C.C.)
Gaulish Calendar and Festivals: Ogronnios XI of Atenoux - D – AMB | Offerings to Veraudinus, a sun god.
Egyptian Calendar: Season Shemu (Month 1 - Pachons) Day 4

9 Tuesday

Real Planetary Day: Mercury
Moon: Waxing Crescent
Zodiac: Aries (♈-△)

Decan: 2ⁿᵈ Decan: Khontakhre (Khontaret) | Ruler: Sun
Celebration and Remembrance: Death of Francis Bacon (1626)
Pletho's Calendar: Histamenou 4 | 4ᵗʰ Month
Attic Calendar & Festivals: Mounichion 5.
Roman Calendar & Festivals: A.D. VI KAL. APR. (D.C.)
Gaulish Calendar and Festivals: Ogronnios XII of Atenoux - N - INIS R
Egyptian Calendar: Season Shemu (Month 1 - Pachons) Day 5

10   Wednesday

Real Planetary Day: Jupiter
Moon: Waxing Crescent
Zodiac: Aries (♈-△)
Decan: 3ʳᵈ Decan: Siket (Khiket) | Ruler: Venus
Pletho's Calendar: Histamenou 5 | 4ᵗʰ Month
Attic Calendar & Festivals: Mounichion 6 | Delphinia: Festival in honor of Delphinius Apollo, the protector of the navigation. Procession of Athenian girls to the Delphinion.
Roman Calendar & Festivals: A.D. V KAL. APR. (E.C.)
Gaulish Calendar and Festivals: Ogronnios XIII of Atenoux - D - AMB
Egyptian Calendar: Season Shemu (Month 1 - Pachons) Day 6

11   Thursday

Real Planetary Day: Venus
Moon: Waxing Crescent
Zodiac: Aries (♈-△)
Decan: 3ʳᵈ Decan: Siket (Khiket) | Ruler: Venus
Pletho's Calendar: Histamenou 6 | 4ᵗʰ Month
Attic Calendar & Festivals: Mounichion 7.

Roman Calendar & Festivals: A.D. IV KAL. APR. (F.C.)
Gaulish Calendar and Festivals: Ogronnios XIIII of Atenoux - MD
Egyptian Calendar: Season Shemu (Month 1 - Pachons) Day 7

---

12   Friday

Real Planetary Day: Saturn
Moon: First Quarter
Zodiac: Aries (♈-△)
Decan: 3rd Decan: Siket (Khiket) | Ruler: Venus
Pletho's Calendar: Histamenou 7 | 4th Month
Attic Calendar & Festivals: Mounichion 8.
Roman Calendar & Festivals: A.D. III KAL. APR. (G.C.)
Gaulish Calendar and Festivals: Ogronnios XV of Atenoux - D – AMB | Offerings to Glanis and Glanicae, God and Goddess associated with a healing springs.
Egyptian Calendar: Season Shemu (Month 1 - Pachons) Day 8

---

13   Saturday

Real Planetary Day: Sun
Moon: Waxing Gibbous
Zodiac: Aries (♈-△)
Decan: 3rd Decan: Siket (Khiket) | Ruler: Venus
Celebration: Day dedicated to Poseidon, son of Zeus.
Pletho's Calendar: Histamenou 8 | 4th Month
Attic Calendar & Festivals: Mounichion 9.
Roman Calendar & Festivals: PRID. KAL. APR. (H.C.) | Sacred day of Luna.
Gaulish Calendar and Festivals: Lustre 4: **MID CUTIOS 4 MATU M CUTIOS MAT** | Cutios I - MD
Egyptian Calendar: Season Shemu (Month 1 - Pachons) Day 9

---

14   Sunday

Real Planetary Day: Moon
Moon: Waxing Gibbous
Zodiac: Aries (♈-△)
Decan: 3rd Decan: Siket (Khiket) | Ruler: Venus
Pletho's Calendar: Mesountos 7 | 4th Month
Attic Calendar & Festivals: Mounichion 10.
Roman Calendar & Festivals: APRILIS - KAL. APR. (A.F.) |
Veneralia: Festival of Venus.
Sacred day to Fortuna Virilis and Ceres.
Gaulish Calendar and Festivals: Cutios II - MD
Egyptian Calendar: Season Shemu (Month 1 - Pachons) Day 10
Adoration of Anubis.

15   Monday

Real Planetary Day: Mars
Moon: Waxing Gibbous
Zodiac: Aries (♈-△)
Decan: 3rd Decan: Siket (Khiket) | Ruler: Venus
Pletho's Calendar: Mesountos 6 | 4th Month
Attic Calendar & Festivals: Mounichion 11.
Roman Calendar & Festivals: A.D. IV NON. APR. (B.F.)
Gaulish Calendar and Festivals: Cutios III - MD
Egyptian Calendar: Season Shemu (Month 1 - Pachons) Day 11
First day of the festival of Min.

16   Tuesday

Real Planetary Day: Mercury
Moon: Waxing Gibbous
Zodiac: Aries (♈-△)
Decan: 3rd Decan: Siket (Khiket) | Ruler: Venus

Pletho's Calendar: Mesountos 5 | 4th Month
Attic Calendar & Festivals: Mounichion 12.
Roman Calendar & Festivals: A.D. III NON. APR. (C.C.)
Gaulish Calendar and Festivals: Cutios IIII - PRINNI LOUDIN
Egyptian Calendar: Season Shemu (Month 1 - Pachons) Day 12
Second day of the festival of Min.

17   Wednesday

Real Planetary Day: Jupiter
Moon: Waxing Gibbous
Zodiac: Aries (♈-△)
Decan: 3rd Decan: Siket (Khiket) | Ruler: Venus
Celebration and Remembrance: Death of the Master Proclus (412-485 AD)
Pletho's Calendar: Mesountos 4 | 4th Month
Attic Calendar & Festivals: Mounichion 13.
Roman Calendar & Festivals: PRID. NON. APR. (D.C.) | Megalesia: 1st day of the seven-days festival of the Magna Mater (Cybel).
Gaulish Calendar and Festivals: Cutios V - N - INIS R
Egyptian Calendar: Season Shemu (Month 1 - Pachons) Day 13
Third day of the festival of Min.

18   Thursday

Real Planetary Day: Venus
Moon: Waxing Gibbous
Zodiac: Aries (♈-△)
Decan: 3rd Decan: Siket (Khiket) | Ruler: Venus
Pletho's Calendar: Mesountos 3 | 4th Month
Attic Calendar & Festivals: Mounichion 14.

Roman Calendar & Festivals: NON. APR. (E.N.) |
Megalesia: 2ⁿᵈ day.
Day sacred to Fortuna Publica (Luck of the People).
Gaulish Calendar and Festivals: Cutios VI - MD
Egyptian Calendar: Season Shemu (Month 1 - Pachons) Day 14
Fourth day of the festival of Min.

---

19   Friday

Real Planetary Day: Saturn
Moon: Full Moon (◯)
Zodiac: Aries (♈-△)
Decan: 3ʳᵈ Decan: Siket (Khiket) | Ruler: Venus
Pletho's Calendar: Mesountos 2 | 4ᵗʰ Month
Attic Calendar & Festivals: Mounichion 15.
Roman Calendar & Festivals: A.D. VIII ID. APR. (F.N.) |
Megalesia: 3ʳᵈ day.
Gaulish Calendar and Festivals: Cutios VII - MD - QVTIO
Egyptian Calendar: Season Shemu (Month 1 - Pachons) Day 15

---

20   Saturday

Real Planetary Day: Sun
Moon: Waning Gibbous
Zodiac: Aries (♈-△)
Decan: 3ʳᵈ Decan: Siket (Khiket) | Ruler: Venus
Celebration: Day sacred to Athena.
Pletho's Calendar: Dichomenia
Attic Calendar & Festivals: Mounichion 16 | Mounichia[3]:
Festival of Artemis of Mounykhia.

---

[3] Cheese cakes adorned with two burning candles, representing the moonrise
and moonset, called amphiphontes, were offered to the goddess. Young girls
were dressed up as bears, as for the Brauronia.

Brauronia: Festival held at Brauron of Attica in honor of Artemis of Brauron.
Roman Calendar & Festivals: A.D. VII ID. APR. (G.N.) | Megalesia: 4th day.
Gaulish Calendar and Festivals: Cutios VIII - MD QVTIO
Egyptian Calendar: Season Shemu (Month 1 - Pachons) Day 16

21   Sunday

Real Planetary Day: Moon
Moon: Waning Gibbous
Zodiac: Taurus (♉♉)
Decan: 1st Decan: Khôou (Sôou) | Ruler: Mercury
Pletho's Calendar: Phthiontos 2 | 4th Month
Attic Calendar & Festivals: Mounichion 17.
Roman Calendar & Festivals: A.D. VI ID. APR. (H.N.) | Megalesia: 5th day.
Gaulish Calendar and Festivals: Cutios VIIII - N - QVTIO INIS R | Offerings to Nabia Coronae, protective virgin and Nymph.
Egyptian Calendar: Season Shemu (Month 1 - Pachons) Day 17

22   Monday

Real Planetary Day: Mars
Moon: Waning Gibbous
Zodiac: Taurus (♉♉)
Decan: 1st Decan: Khôou (Sôou) | Ruler: Mercury
Pletho's Calendar: Phthiontos 3 | 4th Month
Attic Calendar & Festivals: Mounichion 18.
Roman Calendar & Festivals: A.D. V ID. APR. (A.N.) | Megalesia: 6th day.
Gaulish Calendar and Festivals: Cutios X - MD

MAY

5: ● **12:** ☽ **18** (West Europe) **19** (Balkans, East Europe): ○
26: ☾

1 Wednesday

Real Planetary Day: Jupiter
Moon: Waning Crescent
Zodiac: Taurus (♉▽)
Decan: 2nd Decan: Erô (Arôn) | Ruler: Moon
Pletho's Calendar: Apiontos 4 | 4th Month
Attic Calendar & Festivals: Mounichion 27.
Roman Calendar & Festivals: A.D. XIV KAL. MAI. | Cerialia: 7th day.
Gaulish Calendar and Festivals: Cutios IIII of Atenoux - N - INIS R
Egyptian Calendar: Season Shemu (Month 1 - Pachons) Day 27

2 Thursday

Real Planetary Day: Venus
Moon: Waning Crescent
Zodiac: Taurus (♉▽)
Decan: 2nd Decan: Erô (Arôn) | Ruler: Moon
Celebration and Remembrance: In 381 the Emperor Theodosius deprives of all their rights the Christians that return back to the pagan Religion.
Pletho's Calendar: Apiontos 3 | 4th Month
Attic Calendar & Festivals: Mounichion 28.
Roman Calendar & Festivals: A.D. XIII KAL. MAI. | Cerialia: 8th day (culmination of the celebration).

Gaulish Calendar and Festivals: Cutios V of Atenoux - D - AMB
Egyptian Calendar: Season Shemu (Month 1 - Pachons) Day 28

---

3   *Friday*

Real Planetary Day: Saturn
Moon: Waning Crescent
Zodiac: Taurus (♉▽)
Decan: 2nd Decan: Erô (Arôn) | Ruler: Moon
Pletho's Calendar: Apiontos 2 | 4th Month
Attic Calendar & Festivals: Mounichion 29.
Roman Calendar & Festivals: A.D. XII KAL. MAI.
Gaulish Calendar and Festivals: Cutios VI of Atenoux - N - INIS R
Egyptian Calendar: Season Shemu (Month 1 - Pachons) Day 29

---

4   *Saturday*

Real Planetary Day: Aether
Moon: Waning Crescent
Zodiac: Taurus (♉▽)
Decan: 2nd Decan: Erô (Arôn) | Ruler: Moon
Celebration: Sacred day of the God Pluto, chief-god of the underworld.
Pletho's Calendar: Hene.
Attic Calendar & Festivals: Thargelion 1.
Roman Calendar & Festivals: A.D. XI KAL. MAI. | Parilia: rustic festival in honor of Pales. Dies natalis (foundation) of Rome.
Gaulish Calendar and Festivals: Cutios VII of Atenoux - D - QVTIO AMB

Egyptian Calendar: Season Shemu (Month 2 - Payni) Day 1 (West Europe)
Festival of the Valley. Festival in honor of Ptolemy III Eurgetes and his wife Berenice.

---

5   Sunday (Beltane)

Real Planetary Day: Saturn
Moon: New Moon (●)
Zodiac: Taurus (♉)
Decan: 2nd Decan: Erô (Arôn) | Ruler: Moon
Pletho's Calendar: Hene Kai Nea ("the old and the new"); It is a day of self-examination and analysis.
Attic Calendar & Festivals: Thargelion 2.
Roman Calendar & Festivals: A.D. X KAL. MAI.
Gaulish Calendar and Festivals: Cutios VIII of Atenoux - MD - OGRONI QVTIO
Egyptian Calendar: Season Shemu (Month 2 - Payni) Day 2 (West Europe) | Day 1 (Balkans, Central & East Europe)

---

6   Monday

Real Planetary Day: Sun
Moon: Waxing Crescent
Zodiac: Taurus (♉)
Decan: 2nd Decan: Erô (Arôn) | Ruler: Moon
Pletho's Calendar: Noumenia (Histamenou 1) | 5th Month
Attic Calendar & Festivals: Thargelion 3.
Roman Calendar & Festivals: A.D. IX KAL. MAI. | Vinalia Prioria: Festival for the previous year's wine, held originally for Jupiter and later Venus.
Gaulish Calendar and Festivals: Cutios VIIII of Atenoux - D - QVTIO AMB

Egyptian Calendar: Season Shemu (Month 2 - Payni) Day 3 (West Europe) | Day 2 (Balkans, Central & East Europe)

---

7 Tuesday

Real Planetary Day: Moon
Moon: Waxing Crescent
Zodiac: Taurus (♉🜄)
Decan: 2nd Decan: Erô (Arôn) | Ruler: Moon
Celebration and Remembrance: Day dedicated to Agathos Daimon.
Pletho's Calendar: Histamenou 2 | 5th Month
Attic Calendar & Festivals: Thargelion 4.
Roman Calendar & Festivals: A.D. VIII KAL. MAI.
Gaulish Calendar and Festivals: Cutios X of Atenoux - MD
Egyptian Calendar: Season Shemu (Month 2 - Payni) Day 4 (West Europe) | Day 3 (Balkans, Central & East Europe)

---

8 Wednesday

Real Planetary Day: Mars
Moon: Waxing Crescent
Zodiac: Taurus (♉🜄)
Decan: 2nd Decan: Erô (Arôn) | Ruler: Moon
Pletho's Calendar: Histamenou 3 | 5th Month
Attic Calendar & Festivals: Thargelion 5 | Celebration of the birthday of Artemis.
Roman Calendar & Festivals: A.D. VII KAL. MAI. | Robigalia: Festival celebrated to appease the God Robigus (or Goddess Robigo).
Gaulish Calendar and Festivals: Cutios XI of Atenoux - D - AMB

Egyptian Calendar: Season Shemu (Month 2 - Payni) Day 5 (West Europe) | Day 4 (Balkans, Central & East Europe)

---

9 Thursday

Real Planetary Day: Mercury
Moon: Waxing Crescent
Zodiac: Taurus (♉▽)
Decan: 2nd Decan: Erô (Arôn) | Ruler: Moon
Pletho's Calendar: Histamenou 4 | 5th Month
Attic Calendar & Festivals: Thargelion 6 |Thargelia: First day of a two-day festival hold in honor of Apollo, God of the sunny warmth. This is the birthday of Apollo in Delos.
Roman Calendar & Festivals: A.D. VI KAL. MAI.
Gaulish Calendar and Festivals: Cutios XII of Atenoux - MD
Egyptian Calendar: Season Shemu (Month 2 - Payni) Day 6 (West Europe) | Day 5 (Balkans, Central & East Europe)

---

10 Friday

Real Planetary Day: Jupiter
Moon: Waxing Crescent
Zodiac: Taurus (♉▽)
Decan: 2nd Decan: Erô (Arôn) | Ruler: Moon
Pletho's Calendar: Histamenou 5| 5th Month
Attic Calendar & Festivals: Thargelion 7 | Thargelia: Second and last day of a two-day festival hold in honor of Apollo.
Roman Calendar & Festivals: A.D. V KAL. MAI. | Floralia (Ludi Florales): 1st day of the six-days festival honoring Flora (goddess of flowers and spring).
Gaulish Calendar and Festivals: Cutios XIII of Atenoux - D - AMB IVOS QVTIO
Egyptian Calendar: Season Shemu (Month 2 - Payni) Day 7

Festival of Wadjet. (West Europe) | Day 6 (Balkans, Central & East Europe)

---

11   Saturday

Real Planetary Day: Venus
Moon: Waxing Crescent
Zodiac: Taurus (♉▽)
Decan: 3rd Decan: Rombromare (Rômenôs) | Ruler: Saturn
Pletho's Calendar: Histamenou 6 | 5th Month
Attic Calendar & Festivals: Thargelion 8.
Roman Calendar & Festivals: A.D. IV KAL. MAI. | Floralia (Ludi Florales): 2nd day.
Gaulish Calendar and Festivals: Cutios XIIII of Atenoux - MD - IVOS QVTIO
Egyptian Calendar: Season Shemu (Month 2 - Payni) Day 8 (West Europe) | Day 7 (Balkans, Central & East Europe) Festival of Wadjet.

---

12   Sunday

Real Planetary Day: Saturn
Moon: First Quarter
Zodiac: Taurus (♉▽)
Decan: 3rd Decan: Rombromare (Rômenôs) | Ruler: Saturn
Celebration: Day dedicated to Poseidon, son of Zeus.
Pletho's Calendar: Histamenou 7 | 5th Month
Attic Calendar & Festivals: Thargelion 9.
Roman Calendar & Festivals: A.D. III KAL. MAI. | Floralia (Ludi Florales): 3rd day.
Gaulish Calendar and Festivals: Cutios XV of Atenoux - D - AMB

Egyptian Calendar: Season Shemu (Month 2 - Payni) Day 9 (West Europe) | Day 8 (Balkans, Central & East Europe)

13   *Monday*

Real Planetary Day: Sun
Moon: Waxing Gibbous
Zodiac: Taurus (♉▽)
Decan: 3rd Decan: Rombromare (Rômenôs) | Ruler: Saturn
Pletho's Calendar: Histamenou 8 | 5th Month
Attic Calendar & Festivals: Thargelion 10.
Roman Calendar & Festivals: PRID. KAL. MAI. | Floralia (Ludi Florales): 4th day.
Gaulish Calendar and Festivals: Lustre 4: **MID GIAMONIOS 4 ANMATU M GIAMON ANM** | Giamonios I - N - SIMIVIS EXO – IVOS | Offerings to Vindonnus, a sun God.
Egyptian Calendar: Season Shemu (Month 2 - Payni) Day 10 (West Europe) | Day 9 (Balkans, Central & East Europe)

14   *Tuesday*

Real Planetary Day: Moon
Moon: Waxing Gibbous
Zodiac: Taurus (♉▽)
Decan: 3rd Decan: Rombromare (Rômenôs) | Ruler: Saturn
Pletho's Calendar: Mesountos 7 | 5th Month
Attic Calendar & Festivals: Thargelion 11.
Roman Calendar & Festivals: **MAIVS** - KAL. MAI. (F.F.) | Floralia (Ludi Florales): 5th day.
Gaulish Calendar and Festivals: Giamonios II - D - IVOS
Egyptian Calendar: Season Shemu (Month 2 - Payni) Day 11 (West Europe) | Day 10 (Balkans, Central & East Europe)

15   Wednesday

Real Planetary Day: Mars
Moon: Waxing Gibbous
Zodiac: Taurus (♉▽)
Decan: 3rd Decan: Rombromare (Rômenôs) | Ruler: Saturn
Pletho's Calendar: Mesountos 6 | 5th Month
Attic Calendar & Festivals: Thargelion 12.
Roman Calendar & Festivals: A.D. VI NON. MAI. (G.F.) |
Floralia (Ludi Florales): 6th day (culmination of the celebration).
Veneralia: Festival in honor of Venus.
Day sacred to Maia (Earth-Goddess Terra), to Bona Dea (Good
Goddess), restricted to women.
Celebration of the Lares Praestites (Lares Publici) s who look after
the State.
Gaulish Calendar and Festivals: Giamonios III - D – IVOS |
Offerings to Jupiter Arubianus and Bedaius.
Egyptian Calendar: Season Shemu (Month 2 - Payni) Day 12
(West Europe) | Day 11 (Balkans, Central & East Europe)

16   Thursday

Real Planetary Day: Mercury
Moon: Waxing Gibbous
Zodiac: Taurus (♉▽)
Decan: 3rd Decan: Rombromare (Rômenôs) | Ruler: Saturn
Pletho's Calendar: Mesountos 5 | 5th Month
Attic Calendar & Festivals: Thargelion 13.
Roman Calendar & Festivals: A.D. V NON. MAI. (H.C.)
Gaulish Calendar and Festivals: Giamonios IIII- D
Egyptian Calendar: Season Shemu (Month 2 - Payni) Day 13
(West Europe) | Day 12 (Balkans, Central & East Europe)

17   Friday

Real Planetary Day: Jupiter
Moon: Waxing Gibbous
Zodiac: Taurus (♉︎▽)
Decan: 3rd Decan: Rombromare (Rômenôs) | **Ruler:** Saturn
Pletho's Calendar: Mesountos 4 | 5th Month
Attic Calendar & Festivals: Thargelion 14.
Roman Calendar & Festivals: A.D. IV NON. MAI. (A.C.)
Gaulish Calendar and Festivals: Giamonios V - D - AMB
Egyptian Calendar: Season Shemu (Month 2 - Payni) Day 14
(West Europe) | Day 13 (Balkans, Central & East Europe)

18   Saturday

Real Planetary Day: Venus
Moon: Full Moon (◯) (West Europe)
Zodiac: Taurus (♉︎▽)
Decan: 3rd Decan: Rombromare (Rômenôs) | **Ruler:** Saturn
Pletho's Calendar: Mesountos 3 | 5th Month
Attic Calendar & Festivals: Thargelion 15.
Roman Calendar & Festivals: A.D. III NON. MAI. (B.C.)
Gaulish Calendar and Festivals: Giamonios VI - D
Egyptian Calendar: Season Shemu (Month 2 - Payni) Day 15
(West Europe) | Day 14 (Balkans, Central & East Europe)

19   Sunday

Real Planetary Day: Saturn
Moon: Full Moon (◯) (Balkans, Central & East Europe)
Zodiac: Taurus (♉︎▽)
Decan: 3rd Decan: Rombromare (Rômenôs) | **Ruler:** Saturn
Celebration: Day sacred to Athena.

Pletho's Calendar: Mesountos 2
Attic Calendar & Festivals: Thargelion 16.
Roman Calendar & Festivals: PRID. MAI. (C.C.)
Gaulish Calendar and Festivals: Giamonios VII - PRINNI LAGET
Egyptian Calendar: Season Shemu (Month 2 - Payni) Day 16 (West Europe) | Day 15 (Balkans, Central & East Europe)

20 Monday

Real Planetary Day: Sun
Moon: Waning Gibbous
Zodiac: Taurus (♉▽)
Decan: 3rd Decan: Rombromare (Rômenôs) | Ruler: Saturn
Pletho's Calendar: Dichomenia | 5th Month
Attic Calendar & Festivals: Thargelion 17.
Roman Calendar & Festivals: NON. MAI. (D.F.)
Gaulish Calendar and Festivals: Giamonios VIII - D
Egyptian Calendar: Season Shemu (Month 2 - Payni) Day 17 (West Europe) | Day 16 (Balkans, Central & East Europe)

21 Tuesday

Real Planetary Day: Moon
Moon: Waning Gibbous
Zodiac: Taurus (♉▽)
Decan: 3rd Decan: Rombromare (Rômenôs) | Ruler: Saturn
Pletho's Calendar: Phthiontos 2 | 5th Month
Attic Calendar & Festivals: Thargelion 18.
Roman Calendar & Festivals: A.D. VIII ID. MAI. (E.F.)
Gaulish Calendar and Festivals: Giamonios VIIII - N - INIS R
Egyptian Calendar: Season Shemu (Month 2 - Payni) Day 18 (West Europe) | Day 17 (Balkans, Central & East Europe)

22 Wednesday

Real Planetary Day: Mars
Moon: Waning Gibbous
Zodiac: Gemini (Ⅱ♊)
Decan: 1ˢᵗ Decan: Thosolk (Kokha) | Ruler: Jupiter
Pletho's Calendar: Phthiontos 3 | 5ᵗʰ Month
Attic Calendar & Festivals: Thargelion 19 | Kallynteria: Festival for the beautification of the temple of Arhena.
Artemis Vendis: First day of the two-day festival in honor of Vendis, Threacean Goddess the Moon, close to Artemis, Hecate, and Persephone.
Roman Calendar & Festivals: A.D. VII ID. MAI. (F.N.) | Lemuria: 1ˢᵗ day of the three-day festival to exorcise the malevolent and fearful ghosts of the dead from the homes.
Gaulish Calendar and Festivals: Giamonios X - D
Egyptian Calendar: Season Shemu (Month 2 - Payni) Day 19 (West Europe) Hb HqA anx wDA snb; Festival of the ruler. "May he live, be healthy and well." | Day 18 (Balkans, Central & East Europe)

23 Thursday

Real Planetary Day: Mercury
Moon: Waning Gibbous
Zodiac: Gemini (Ⅱ♊)
Decan: 1ˢᵗ Decan: Thosolk (Kokha) | Ruler: Jupiter
Pletho's Calendar: Phthiontos 4 | 5ᵗʰ Month
Attic Calendar & Festivals: Thargelion 20 | Artemis Vendis: Second day of the two-day festival in honor of Vendis, Threacean Goddess the Moon.
Roman Calendar & Festivals: A.D. VI ID. MAI. (G.C.)
Gaulish Calendar and Festivals: Giamonios XI – D | Offerings to Ancamna, water Goddess, consort of Lenus Mars.
Egyptian Calendar: Season Shemu (Month 2 - Payni) Day 20 (West Europe) | Day 19 (Balkans, Central & East Europe)

24   Friday

Real Planetary Day: Jupiter
Moon: Waning Gibbous
Zodiac: Gemini (♊♎)
Decan: 1st Decan: Thosolk (Kokha) | Ruler: Jupiter
Pletho's Calendar: Phthiontos 5 | 5th Month
Attic Calendar & Festivals: Thargelion 21 | Lesser Panathenaea (According Proclus).
Roman Calendar & Festivals: A.D. V ID. MAI. (H.N.) | Lemuria: 2nd day of the festival.
Day of honoring Mania (Manea) Goddess of the dead mother of ghosts, the undead, Lares, Manes, and other spirits of the night.
Gaulish Calendar and Festivals: Giamonios XII – D | Offerings to the Goddess Vercanua.
Egyptian Calendar: Season Shemu (Month 2 - Payni) Day 21 (West Europe) | Day 20 (Balkans, Central & East Europe)

25   Saturday

Real Planetary Day: Venus
Moon: Waning Gibbous
Zodiac: Gemini (♊♎)
Decan: 1st Decan: Thosolk (Kokha) | Ruler: Jupiter
Pletho's Calendar: Phthiontos 6 | 5th Month
Attic Calendar & Festivals: Thargelion 22.
Roman Calendar & Festivals: A.D. IV ID. MAI. (A.C.)
Gaulish Calendar and Festivals: Giamonios XIII – D | Offerings to Dia Greine, a sun goddess.
Egyptian Calendar: Season Shemu (Month 2 - Payni) Day 22 (West Europe) | Day 21 (Balkans, Central & East Europe)

26   Sunday

Real Planetary Day: Saturn
Moon: Third (last) Quarter
Zodiac: Gemini (♊♎)
Decan: 1st Decan: Thosolk (Kokha) | Ruler: Jupiter
Pletho's Calendar: Phthiontos 7 | 5th Month
Attic Calendar & Festivals: Thargelion 23.
Roman Calendar & Festivals: A.D. III ID. MAI. (B.N.) | Lemuria: 3rd day of the festival.
Gaulish Calendar and Festivals: Giamonios XIIII – D | Offerings to Dinomogetimarus, a powerful protector God.
Egyptian Calendar: Season Shemu (Month 2 - Payni) Day 23 (West Europe) | Day 22 (Balkans, Central & East Europe)

27   Monday

Real Planetary Day: Sun
Moon: Waning Crescent
Zodiac: Gemini (♊♎)
Decan: 1st Decan: Thosolk (Kokha) | Ruler: Jupiter
Pletho's Calendar: Phthiontos 8 | 5th Month
Attic Calendar & Festivals: Thargelion 24.
Roman Calendar & Festivals: PRID. ID. MAI. (C.C.) | Dies natalis (founding day) of the Temple of Mars Invictus (Mars the Unconquered).
Gaulish Calendar and Festivals: Giamonios XV – D | Offerings to the healing God Lenus, always identified with the Roman god Mars.
Egyptian Calendar: Season Shemu (Month 2 - Payni) Day 24 (West Europe) | Day 23 (Balkans, Central & East Europe)

28   *Tuesday*

Real Planetary Day: Moon
Moon: Waning Crescent
Zodiac: Gemini (♊♍)
Decan: 1st Decan: Thosolk (Kokha) | Ruler: Jupiter
Pletho's Calendar: Apiontos 7 | 5th Month
Attic Calendar & Festivals: Thargelion 25 | Plyntheria: Cleaning of the veils of the archaic xoanon (wooden statue) of Polias Athena in Phaleron.
Roman Calendar & Festivals: ID. MAI. (D.NP.) | Mercuralia: Festival honoring Mercury;
Feriae of Jove: Traditional birthday of the Patron of Merchants. Day also sacred to Maia (mother of Mercury).
Gaulish Calendar and Festivals: Giamonios I of Atenoux - D
Egyptian Calendar: Season Shemu (Month 2 - Payni) Day 25 (West Europe) | Day 24 (Balkans, Central & East Europe)

29   *Wednesday*

Real Planetary Day: Mars
Moon: Waning Crescent
Zodiac: Gemini (♊♍)
Decan: 1st Decan: Thosolk (Kokha) | Ruler: Jupiter
Pletho's Calendar: Apiontos 6 | 5th Month
Attic Calendar & Festivals: Thargelion 26.
Roman Calendar & Festivals: A.D. XVII KAL. IVN. (E.F.) | Agonalia: Second festival of the God Vediovis.
Gaulish Calendar and Festivals: Giamonios II of Atenoux - D - NSDS
Egyptian Calendar: Season Shemu (Month 2 - Payni) Day 26 (West Europe) | Day 25 (Balkans, Central & East Europe)

30   *Thursday*

Real Planetary Day: Mercury
Moon: Waning Crescent
Zodiac: Gemini (♊♎)
Decan: 1ˢᵗ Decan: Thosolk (Kokha) | Ruler: Jupiter
Pletho's Calendar: Apiontos 5 | 5ᵗʰ Month
Attic Calendar & Festivals: Thargelion 27.
Roman Calendar & Festivals: A.D. XVI KAL. IVN. (F.C.)
Gaulish Calendar and Festivals: Giamonios III of Atenoux - D – AMB | Offerings to the mother Goddess Dea Aveta, also associated with the fresh-water spring.
Egyptian Calendar: Season Shemu (Month 2 - Payni) Day 27 (West Europe) | Day 26 (Balkans, Central & East Europe)

31   *Friday*

Real Planetary Day: Jupiter
Moon: Waning Crescent
Zodiac: Gemini (♊♎)
Decan: 1ˢᵗ Decan: Thosolk (Kokha) | Ruler: Jupiter
Pletho's Calendar: Apiontos 4 | 5ᵗʰ Month
Attic Calendar & Festivals: Thargelion 28.
Roman Calendar & Festivals: A.D. XV KAL. IVN. (G.C.) | Ambarvalia: Ritual of purification of the fields, invoking the agricultural deities Ceres, Bacchus, and Mars.
Gaulish Calendar and Festivals: Giamonios IIII of Atenoux - D
Egyptian Calendar: Season Shemu (Month 2 - Payni) Day 28 (West Europe) | Day 27 (Balkans, Central & East Europe)

JUNE

3: ●   10: ☽   17: ○   25: ☾

1   *Saturday*

Real Planetary Day: Venus
Moon: Waning Crescent
Zodiac: Gemini (Ⅱ♌)
Decan: 2nd Decan: Ouare (Ouari) | Ruler: Mars
Pletho's Calendar: Apiontos 3 | 5th Month
Attic Calendar & Festivals: Thargelion 29.
Roman Calendar & Festivals: A.D. XIV KAL. IVN. (H.C.)
Gaulish Calendar and Festivals: Giamonios V of Atenoux - D - AMB
Egyptian Calendar: Season Shemu (Month 2 - Payni) Day 29 (West Europe) | Day 28 (Balkans, Central & East Europe)

2   *Sunday*

Real Planetary Day: Saturn
Moon: Waning Crescent
Zodiac: Gemini (Ⅱ♌)
Decan: 2nd Decan: Ouare (Ouari) | Ruler: Mars
Celebration: Sacred day of the God Pluto, chief-god of the underworld.
Pletho's Calendar: Apiontos 2 | 5th Month
Attic Calendar & Festivals: Thargelion 30.
Roman Calendar & Festivals: A.D. XIII KAL. IVN. (A.C.)
Gaulish Calendar and Festivals: Giamonios VI of Atenoux - D
Egyptian Calendar: Season Shemu (Month 2 - Payni) Day 30 (West Europe) | Day 29 (Balkans, Central & East Europe)

3   Monday

Real Planetary Day: Saturn
Moon: New Moon (●)
Zodiac: Gemini (ΙΙΔ)
Decan: 2nd Decan: Ouare (Ouari) | Ruler: Mars
Pletho's Calendar: Hene Kai Nea ("the old and the new"); It is a day of self-examination and analysis.
Attic Calendar & Festivals: Skirophorion 1.
Roman Calendar & Festivals: A.D. XII KAL. IVN. (B.NP.)
Gaulish Calendar and Festivals: Giamonios VII of Atenoux - N - INIS R
Egyptian Calendar: Season Shemu (Month 3 - Epiphi) Day 1

4   Tuesday

Real Planetary Day: Sun
Moon: Waxing Crescent
Zodiac: Gemini (ΙΙΔ)
Decan: 2nd Decan: Ouare (Ouari) | Ruler: Mars
Pletho's Calendar: Noumenia (Histamenou 1) | 6th Month
Attic Calendar & Festivals: Skirophorion 2.
Roman Calendar & Festivals: A.D. XI KAL. IVN. (C.N.)
Gaulish Calendar and Festivals: Giamonios VIII of Atenoux - N - INIS R
Egyptian Calendar: Season Shemu (Month 3 - Epiphi) Day 2

5   Wednesday

Real Planetary Day: Moon
Moon: Waxing Crescent
Zodiac: Gemini (ΙΙΔ)
Decan: 2nd Decan: Ouare (Ouari) | Ruler: Mars

Celebration and Remembrance: Day dedicated to Agathos Daimon.

Pletho's Calendar: Histamenou 2 | 6th Month

Attic Calendar & Festivals: Skirophorion 3 | Arrhetophoria: Festival also known as "The Thesmophoria of the unmarried girls." Its name means: "the carrying of which is forbidden." This festival is honoring Athena as well as Demeter in the underground megara of her temple.

Roman Calendar & Festivals: A.D. X KAL. IVN. (D.NP.) | Second Festival of Volcanus (Vulcan).

Tubilustrium: Day of purification of the trumpets.

Gaulish Calendar and Festivals: Giamonios VIIII of Atenoux - D - AMB

Egyptian Calendar: Season Shemu (Month 3 - Epiphi) Day 3

---

6   Thursday

Real Planetary Day: Mars
Moon: Waxing Crescent
Zodiac: Gemini (♊♌)
Decan: 2nd Decan: Ouare (Ouari) | Ruler: Mars
Pletho's Calendar: Histamenou 3 | 6th Month
Attic Calendar & Festivals: Skirophorion 4.
Roman Calendar & Festivals: A.D. IX KAL. IVN. (E.F.)
Gaulish Calendar and Festivals: Giamonios X of Atenoux - D
Egyptian Calendar: Season Shemu (Month 3 - Epiphi) Day 4

---

7   Friday

Real Planetary Day: Mercury
Moon: Waxing Crescent
Zodiac: Gemini (♊♌)
Decan: 2nd Decan: Ouare (Ouari) | Ruler: Mars

Pletho's Calendar: Histamenou 4 | 6th Month
Attic Calendar & Festivals: Skirophorion 5.
Roman Calendar & Festivals: A.D. VIII KAL. IVN. (F.C.) |
Sacred day to Fortuna (Goddess of fate, chance, luck, and
fortune).
Gaulish Calendar and Festivals: Giamonios XI of Atenoux - N
- INI R
Egyptian Calendar: Season Shemu (Month 3 - Epiphi) Day 5

---

8   Saturday

Real Planetary Day: Jupiter
Moon: Waxing Crescent
Zodiac: Gemini (ⅡА)
Decan: 2nd Decan: Ouare (Ouari) | Ruler: Mars
Pletho's Calendar: Histamenou 5 | 6th Month
Attic Calendar & Festivals: Skirophorion 6.
Roman Calendar & Festivals: A.D. VII KAL. IVN. (G.C.)
Gaulish Calendar and Festivals: Giamonios XII of Atenoux -
MD
Egyptian Calendar: Season Shemu (Month 3 - Epiphi) Day 6

---

9   Sunday

Real Planetary Day: Venus
Moon: Waxing Crescent
Zodiac: Gemini (ⅡА)
Decan: 2nd Decan: Ouare (Ouari) | Ruler: Mars
Pletho's Calendar: Histamenou 6 | 6th Month
Attic Calendar & Festivals: Skirophorion 7.
Roman Calendar & Festivals: A.D. VI KAL. IVN. (H.C.)
Gaulish Calendar and Festivals: Giamonios XIII of Atenoux -
D - AMB

Egyptian Calendar: Season Shemu (Month 3 - Epiphi) Day 7

---

10 Monday

Real Planetary Day: Saturn
Moon: First Quarter
Zodiac: Gemini (♊♎)
Decan: 2nd Decan: Ouare (Ouari) | Ruler: Mars
Pletho's Calendar: Histamenou 7 | 6th Month
Attic Calendar & Festivals: Skirophorion 8 | Arrephoria: Festival in honor to Athena and the "unspoken things".
Roman Calendar & Festivals: A.D. V KAL. IVN. (A.C.)
Gaulish Calendar and Festivals: Giamonios XIIII of Atenoux – D | DIVERTOMV
Egyptian Calendar: Season Shemu (Month 3 - Epiphi) Day 8

---

11 Tuesday

Real Planetary Day: Sun
Moon: Waxing Gibbous
Zodiac: Gemini (♊♎)
Decan: 2nd Decan: Ouare (Ouari) | Ruler: Mars
Celebration: Day dedicated to Poseidon, son of Zeus.
Pletho's Calendar: Histamenou 8 | 6th Month
Attic Calendar & Festivals: Skirophorion 9.
Roman Calendar & Festivals: A.D. IV KAL. IVN. (B.C.)
Gaulish Calendar and Festivals: Lustre 4: MID SIMIUISONNA 4 MATU M SIMIVIS MAT | Simiuisonna I - GIAMO PRINI LAG
Egyptian Calendar: Season Shemu (Month 3 - Epiphi) Day 9

12 Wednesday

Real Planetary Day: Moon
Moon: Waxing Gibbous
Zodiac: Gemini (♊︎♎︎)
Decan: 3rd Decan: Fouori (Pepisôth) | Ruler: Sun
Pletho's Calendar: Mesountos 7 | 6th Month
Attic Calendar & Festivals: Skirophorion 10.
Roman Calendar & Festivals: III KAL. IVN. (C.C.)
Gaulish Calendar and Festivals: Simiuisonna II - N
Egyptian Calendar: Season Shemu (Month 3 - Epiphi) Day 10

13 Thursday

Real Planetary Day: Mars
Moon: Waxing Gibbous
Zodiac: Gemini (♊︎♎︎)
Decan: 3rd Decan: Fouori (Pepisôth) | Ruler: Sun
Pletho's Calendar: Mesountos 6 | 6th Month
Attic Calendar & Festivals: Skirophorion 11.
Roman Calendar & Festivals: PRID. KAL. IVN (D.C.)
Gaulish Calendar and Festivals: Simiuisonna III - +I+ - D - EQVI
Egyptian Calendar: Season Shemu (Month 3 - Epiphi) Day 11

14 Friday

Real Planetary Day: Mercury
Moon: Waxing Gibbous
Zodiac: Gemini (♊︎♎︎)
Decan: 3rd Decan: Fouori (Pepisôth) | Ruler: Sun
Pletho's Calendar: Mesountos 5 | 6th Month

Attic Calendar & Festivals: Skirophorion 12 | Skirophoria (or Skira): Festival of dissolution; During this festival a great procession followed the great white umbrella (skiron) of Athena.
Roman Calendar & Festivals: IVNIVS - KAL. IVN. (E.N.) | Dies natalis (founding day) of the Temple of Juno Moneta (warns of impending disasters and harmful events); of the Temple of Mars on the clivus (slope, street).
Celebration of the Tempestates (Goddesses of storms and weather).
Festival of the goddess Cardea/Carna: (Goddess of door hinges as well as bodily health).
Gaulish Calendar and Festivals: Simiuisonna IIII – MD | Offerings to Loucetios, God of thunder (identified with the Roman Mars) and the Goddess Nemetona.
Egyptian Calendar: Season Shemu (Month 3 - Epiphi) Day 12

---

15   Saturday

Real Planetary Day: Jupiter
Moon: Waxing Gibbous
Zodiac: Gemini (♊)
Decan: 3rd Decan: Fouori (Pepisôth) | Ruler: Sun
Pletho's Calendar: Mesountos 4 | 6th Month
Attic Calendar & Festivals: Skirophorion 13
Roman Calendar & Festivals: IV NON. IVN. (F.F.)
Gaulish Calendar and Festivals: Simiuisonna V - N - INIS R
Egyptian Calendar: Season Shemu (Month 3 - Epiphi) Day 13

---

16   Sunday

Real Planetary Day: Venus
Moon: Waxing Gibbous
Zodiac: Gemini (♊)

Decan: 3rd Decan: Fouori (Pepisôth) | **Ruler:** Sun
Celebration and Remembrance: Emperor Theodosius outlaws (386) the care of the vandalized pagan Temples.
Pletho's Calendar: Mesountos 3 | 6th Month
Attic Calendar & Festivals: Skirophorion 14 | Buphonia: Festival hold in honor of Zeus Soterios (Savior) and Athena Soteira (Savior) in Piraeus.
Roman Calendar & Festivals: A.D. III NON. IVN. (G.C.) | Dies natalis (founding day) of the Temple of Bellona (Goddess of war).
Gaulish Calendar and Festivals: Simiuisonna VI - D – EQVI | Offerings to Caturix, Warrior God.
Egyptian Calendar: Season Shemu (Month 3 - Epiphi) Day 14

---

17   Monday

Real Planetary Day: Saturn
Moon: Full Moon (◯)
Zodiac: Gemini (♊︎♎)
Decan: 3rd Decan: Fouori (Pepisôth) | **Ruler:** Sun
Celebration and Remembrance: Apuleius de Madaura (124–170 CE)
Pletho's Calendar: Mesountos 2 | 6th Month
Attic Calendar & Festivals: Skirophorion 15.
Roman Calendar & Festivals: PRID. NON. IVN. (H.C.) | Dies natalis (founding day) of the restoration of the Temple of Hercules Custos (Great Custodian).
Gaulish Calendar and Festivals: Simiuisonna VII - MD - TIOCOBREX
Egyptian Calendar: Season Shemu (Month 3 - Epiphi) Day 15 Offerings to Hapy and Amun (to secure a good flood).

---

18 Tuesday

Real Planetary Day: Sun
Moon: Waning Gibbous
Zodiac: Gemini (♊♌)
Decan: 3rd Decan: Fouori (Pepisôth) | Ruler: Sun
Celebration: Day sacred to Athena.
Pletho's Calendar: Dichomenia
Attic Calendar & Festivals: Skirophorion 16.
Roman Calendar & Festivals: NON. IVN. (A.N.) | Dies natalis (founding day) of the Temple of Dius Fidius, "Divine Faith."
Gaulish Calendar and Festivals: Simiuisonna VIII - MD
Egyptian Calendar: Season Shemu (Month 3 - Epiphi) Day 16

19 Wednesday

Real Planetary Day: Moon
Moon: Waning Gibbous
Zodiac: Gemini (♊♌)
Decan: 3rd Decan: Fouori (Pepisôth) | Ruler: Sun
Pletho's Calendar: Phthiontos 2 | 6th Month
Attic Calendar & Festivals: Skirophorion 17.
Roman Calendar & Festivals: A.D. VIII ID. IVN. (B.N.)
Gaulish Calendar and Festivals: Simiuisonna VIIII - MD - SINDIV - IVOS
Egyptian Calendar: Season Shemu (Month 3 - Epiphi) Day 17

20 Thursday

Real Planetary Day: Mars
Moon: Waning Gibbous
Zodiac: Gemini (♊♌)
Decan: 3rd Decan: Fouori (Pepisôth) | Ruler: Sun
Pletho's Calendar: Phthiontos 3 | 6th Month

Attic Calendar & Festivals: Skirophorion 18.
Roman Calendar & Festivals: A.D. VII ID. IVN. (C.N.)
| Vestalia: First of the Nine-days religious festival in honor of
Vesta, the goddess of the hearth and the burning continuation of
the sacred fire of Rome.
Sacred to Tiberinus, God of the river Tiber
Gaulish Calendar and Festivals: Simiuisonna X - MD
Egyptian Calendar: Season Shemu (Month 3 - Epiphi) Day 18

---

21   Friday (Solstice)

Real Planetary Day: Mercury
Moon: Waning Gibbous
Zodiac: Gemini (♊♌)
Decan: 3rd Decan: Fouori (Pepisôth) | **Ruler:** Sun
Astral Event: Solstice (8:54 am PDT)
Celebration and Remembrance: Aurum Solis: Beginning of
Tempus Messis (Northern Hemisphere) or *Tempus Eversionis*
(Southern Hemisphere). No initiations are allowed in the
Southern Hemisphere during this period of the year.
Pletho's Calendar: Phthiontos 4 | 6th Month
Attic Calendar & Festivals: Skirophorion 19.
Roman Calendar & Festivals: A.D. VI ID. IVN. (D.N.) |
Vestalia: 2nd day of the festival in honor to Vesta.
Dies natalis (founding day) of the Temple of Mens (Goddess of
right thinking).
Gaulish Calendar and Festivals: Simiuisonna XI - N
Egyptian Calendar: Season Shemu (Month 3 - Epiphi) Day 19

---

22   Saturday

Real Planetary Day: Jupiter
Moon: Waning Gibbous
Zodiac: Cancer (♋▽)
Decan: 1ˢᵗ Decan: Sôthis (Sôtheir) | Ruler: Venus
Pletho's Calendar: Phthiontos 5 | 6ᵗʰ Month
Attic Calendar & Festivals: Skirophorion 20.
Roman Calendar & Festivals: A.D. V ID. IVN. (E.N.) |
Vestalia: 3ʳᵈ day of the festival in honor to Vesta.
Gaulish Calendar and Festivals: Simiuisonna XII - MD
Egyptian Calendar: Season Shemu (Month 3 - Epiphi) Day 20

23   Sunday

Real Planetary Day: Venus
Moon: Waning Gibbous
Zodiac: Cancer (♋▽)
Decan: 1ˢᵗ Decan: Sôthis (Sôtheir) | Ruler: Venus
Pletho's Calendar: Phthiontos 6 | 6ᵗʰ Month
Attic Calendar & Festivals: Skirophorion 21.
Roman Calendar & Festivals: A.D. IV ID. IVN. (F.N.)
| Vestalia: 4ᵗʰ day of the festival in honor to Vesta.
Gaulish Calendar and Festivals: Simiuisonna XIII - D - EQVI
Egyptian Calendar: Season Shemu (Month 3 - Epiphi) Day 21

24   Monday

Real Planetary Day: Saturn
Moon: Waning Gibbous
Zodiac: Cancer (♋▽)
Decan: 1ˢᵗ Decan: Sôthis (Sôtheir) | Ruler: Venus
Pletho's Calendar: Phthiontos 7 | 6ᵗʰ Month
Attic Calendar & Festivals: Skirophorion 22.

Roman Calendar & Festivals: A.D. III ID. IVN. (G.N.) |
Vestalia: 5th day of the festival in honor to Vesta.
Matralia: Festival of the Mater Matuta (Goddess of growth,
childbirth, motherhood, and the raising of children.)
Dies natalis (founding day) of the Temple of Fortuna (Goddess
of fate, chance, luck, and fortune).
Gaulish Calendar and Festivals: Simiuisonna XIIII - NSDS
EQVI | Offerings to the Gods upiter Optimus Maximus
Karnuntinus and Jupiter Optimus Maximus Teutanus.
Egyptian Calendar: Season Shemu (Month 3 - Epiphi) Day 22

25   Tuesday

Real Planetary Day: Sun
Moon: Third (last) Quarter
Zodiac: Cancer (♋)
Decan: 1st Decan: Sôthis (Sôtheir) | Ruler: Venus
Pletho's Calendar: Phthiontos 8 | 6th Month
Attic Calendar & Festivals: Skirophorion 23.
Roman Calendar & Festivals: PRID. ID. IVN. (H.N.) |
Vestalia: 6th day of the festival in honor to Vesta.
Gaulish Calendar and Festivals: Simiuisonna XV - NSDS
EQVI
Egyptian Calendar: Season Shemu (Month 3 - Epiphi) Day 23

26   Wednesday

Real Planetary Day: Moon
Moon: Waning Crescent
Zodiac: Cancer (♋)
Decan: 1st Decan: Sôthis (Sôtheir) | Ruler: Venus
Celebration and Remembrance: Death of the Master Gemistus
Pletho (1355-1452), Death of the Emperor Julian (330-363 AD)

Pletho's Calendar: Apiontos 7 | 6th Month
Attic Calendar & Festivals: Skirophorion 24.
Roman Calendar & Festivals: ID. IVN. (A. NP.) | Vestalia: 7th day of the festival in honor to Vesta and Jove.
Quinquatrus minusculae: First day of the three-days lesser celebrated by tibicines (religious flute-players).
Gaulish Calendar and Festivals: Simiuisonna I of Atenoux - D - EQVI
Egyptian Calendar: Season Shemu (Month 3 - Epiphi) Day 24

27   Thursday

Real Planetary Day: Mars
Moon: Waning Crescent
Zodiac: Cancer (♋︎▽)
Decan: 1st Decan: Sôthis (Sôtheir) | Ruler: Venus
Pletho's Calendar: Apiontos 6 | 6th Month
Attic Calendar & Festivals: Skirophorion 25.
Roman Calendar & Festivals: A.D. XVIII KAL. IVL. | Vestalia: 8th day of the festival in honor to Vesta.
Quinquatrus minusculae: 2nd day.
Gaulish Calendar and Festivals: Simiuisonna II of Atenoux - D - EQVI
Egyptian Calendar: Season Shemu (Month 3 - Epiphi) Day 25

28   Friday

Real Planetary Day: Mercury
Moon: Waning Crescent
Zodiac: Cancer (♋︎▽)
Decan: 1st Decan: Sôthis (Sôtheir) | Ruler: Venus
Pletho's Calendar: Apiontos 5 | 6th Month
Attic Calendar & Festivals: Skirophorion 26.

Roman Calendar & Festivals: A.D. XVII KAL. IVL. | Vestalia: 9th and last day (culmination) of the festival in honor to Vesta. Quinquatrus minusculae: 3rd day.
Gaulish Calendar and Festivals: Simiuisonna III of Atenoux - D - EQVI AMB
Egyptian Calendar: Season Shemu (Month 3 - Epiphi) Day 26

---

29   Saturday

Real Planetary Day: Jupiter
Moon: Waning Crescent
Zodiac: Cancer (♋)
Decan: 1st Decan: Sôthis (Sôtheir) | Ruler: Venus
Pletho's Calendar: Apiontos 4 | 6th Month
Attic Calendar & Festivals: Skirophorion 27.
Roman Calendar & Festivals: A.D. XVI KAL. IVL.
Gaulish Calendar and Festivals: Simiuisonna IIII of Atenoux - MD
Egyptian Calendar: Season Shemu (Month 3 - Epiphi) Day 27

---

30   Sunday

Real Planetary Day: Venus
Moon: Waning Crescent
Zodiac: Cancer (♋)
Decan: 1st Decan: Sôthis (Sôtheir) | Ruler: Venus
Pletho's Calendar: Apiontos 3 | 6th Month
Attic Calendar & Festivals: Skirophorion 28.
Roman Calendar & Festivals: A.D. XV KAL. IVL.
Gaulish Calendar and Festivals: Simiuisonna V of Atenoux - D - AMB
Egyptian Calendar: Season Shemu (Month 3 - Epiphi) Day 28

JULY

2: ●   9: ☽   16 (West Europe) 17 (Balkans, Central & East Europe): ○   25: ☾

1   *Monday*

Real Planetary Day: Saturn
Moon: Waning Crescent
Zodiac: Cancer (♋▽)
Decan: 1st Decan: Sôthis (Sôtheir) | Ruler: Venus
Pletho's Calendar: Apiontos 2 | 6th Month
Attic Calendar & Festivals: Skirophorion 29.
Roman Calendar & Festivals: A.D. XIV KAL. IVL.
Gaulish Calendar and Festivals: Simiuisonna VI of Atenoux - D - EQVI
Egyptian Calendar: Season Shemu (Month 3 - Epiphi) Day 29 Eve of the Hathor festival (Thebes).

---

2   *Tuesday*

Real Planetary Day: Saturn
Moon: New Moon (●)
Zodiac: Cancer (♋▽)
Decan: 1st Decan: Sôthis (Sôtheir) | Ruler: Venus
Astral Event: Total Solar Eclipse (South America, Pacific)
Pletho's Calendar: Hene Kai Nea ("the old and the new"); It is a day of self-examination and analysis.
Attic Calendar & Festivals: Hekatombaion 1.
Roman Calendar & Festivals: A.D. XIII KAL. IVL. | Sacred day to Minerva (Goddess of crafts and trade guilds).

Gaulish Calendar and Festivals: Simiuisonna VII of Atenoux - D - AMB
Egyptian Calendar: Season Shemu (Month 4 - Mesore) Day 1 (West Europe) Hathor festival (Thebes).

---

3 Wednesday

Real Planetary Day: Sun
Moon: Waxing Crescent
Zodiac: Cancer (♋︎▽)
Decan: 2nd Decan: Sit (Oufisit) | Ruler: Mercury
Pletho's Calendar: Noumenia (Histamenou 1) | 7th Month
Attic Calendar & Festivals: Hekatombaion 2.
Roman Calendar & Festivals: A.D. XII KAL. IVL. | Dies natalis (founding day) of the Temple of Summanus (God of nocturnal thunder).
Gaulish Calendar and Festivals: Simiuisonna VIII of Atenoux – MD | Offerings to Taranis, God of thunder.
Egyptian Calendar: Season Shemu (Month 4 - Mesore) Day 2 (West Europe) Ipip festival. Isis festival (Late period). | Day 1 (Balkans, Central & East Europe) Hathor festival (Thebes).

---

4 Thursday

Real Planetary Day: Moon
Moon: Waxing Crescent
Zodiac: Cancer (♋︎▽)
Decan: 2nd Decan: Sit (Oufisit) | Ruler: Mercury
Celebration and Remembrance: Day dedicated to Agathos Daimon.
Pletho's Calendar: Histamenou 2 | 7th Month
Attic Calendar & Festivals: Hekatombaion 3.
Roman Calendar & Festivals: A.D. XI KAL. IVL.

Gaulish Calendar and Festivals: Simiuisonna VIIII of Atenoux - D – AMB | Offerings to the God protector Toutatis.
Egyptian Calendar: Season Shemu (Month 4 - Mesore) Day 3 (West Europe) | Day 2 (Balkans, Central & East Europe) Ipip festival. Isis festival (Late period).

5   Friday

Real Planetary Day: Mars
Moon: Waxing Crescent
Zodiac: Cancer (♋▽)
Decan: 2nd Decan: Sit (Oufisit) | Ruler: Mercury
Pletho's Calendar: Histamenou 3 | 7th Month
Attic Calendar & Festivals: Hekatombaion 4 | Aphrodisia: Festival hold in honor of Pandemos Aphrodite, the goddess of the sensual pleasures.
Roman Calendar & Festivals: A.D. X KAL. IVL.
Gaulish Calendar and Festivals: Simiuisonna X of Atenoux - MD
Egyptian Calendar: Season Shemu (Month 4 - Mesore) Day 4 (West Europe) | Day 3 (Balkans, Central & East Europe)

6   Saturday

Real Planetary Day: Mercury
Moon: Waxing Crescent
Zodiac: Cancer (♋▽)
Decan: 2nd Decan: Sit (Oufisit) | Ruler: Mercury
Pletho's Calendar: Histamenou 4 | 7th Month
Attic Calendar & Festivals: Hekatombaion 5.
Roman Calendar & Festivals: A.D. IX KAL. IVL.
Gaulish Calendar and Festivals: Simiuisonna XI of Atenoux - D - AMB

Egyptian Calendar: Season Shemu (Month 4 - Mesore) Day 5 (West Europe) | Day 4 (Balkans, Central & East Europe)

7   Sunday

Real Planetary Day: Jupiter
Moon: Waxing Crescent
Zodiac: Cancer (♋▽)
Decan: 2nd Decan: Sit (Oufisit) | Ruler: Mercury
Pletho's Calendar: Histamenou 5 | 7th Month
Attic Calendar & Festivals: Hekatombaion 6.
Roman Calendar & Festivals: A.D. VIII KAL. IVL. | Festival to Fors Fortuna (Goddess of good fortune).
Gaulish Calendar and Festivals: Simiuisonna XII of Atenoux - MD
Egyptian Calendar: Season Shemu (Month 4 - Mesore) Day 6 (West Europe) | Day 5 (Balkans, Central & East Europe)

8   Monday

Real Planetary Day: Venus
Moon: Waxing Crescent
Zodiac: Cancer (♋▽)
Decan: 2nd Decan: Sit (Oufisit) | Ruler: Mercury
Pletho's Calendar: Histamenou 6 | 7th Month
Attic Calendar & Festivals: Hekatombaion 7.
Roman Calendar & Festivals: A.D. VII KAL. IVL.
Gaulish Calendar and Festivals: Simiuisonna XIII of Atenoux - D - AMB
Egyptian Calendar: Season Shemu (Month 4 - Mesore) Day 7 (West Europe) | Day 6 (Balkans, Central & East Europe)

9   Tuesday

Real Planetary Day: Saturn
Moon: First Quarter
Zodiac: Cancer (♋▽)
Decan: 2nd Decan: Sit (Oufisit) | Ruler: Mercury
Pletho's Calendar: Histamenou 7 | 7th Month
Attic Calendar & Festivals: Hekatombaion 8.
Roman Calendar & Festivals: A.D. VI KAL. IVL.
Gaulish Calendar and Festivals: Simiuisonna XIIII of Atenoux - MD
Egyptian Calendar: Season Shemu (Month 4 - Mesore) Day 8 (West Europe) Ceremony of Wadjet. | Day 7 (Balkans, Central & East Europe)

10   Wednesday

Real Planetary Day: Sun
Moon: Waxing Gibbous
Zodiac: Cancer (♋▽)
Decan: 2nd Decan: Sit (Oufisit) | Ruler: Mercury
Celebration: Day dedicated to Poseidon, son of Zeus.
Pletho's Calendar: Histamenou 8 | 7th Month
Attic Calendar & Festivals: Hekatombaion 9.
Roman Calendar & Festivals: A.D. V KAL. IVL. | Dies natalis (founding day) of the Temple of Jupiter Stator.
Gaulish Calendar and Festivals: Simiuisonna XV of Atenoux - D - AMB
Egyptian Calendar: Season Shemu (Month 4 - Mesore) Day 9 (West Europe) | Day 8 (Balkans, Central & East Europe) Ceremony of Wadjet.

11   Thursday

Real Planetary Day: Moon
Moon: Waxing Gibbous
Zodiac: Cancer (♋▽)
Decan: 2nd Decan: Sit (Oufisit) | Ruler: Mercury
Pletho's Calendar: Mesountos 7 | 7th Month
Attic Calendar & Festivals: Hekatombaion 10.
Roman Calendar & Festivals: A.D. IV KAL. IVL.
Gaulish Calendar and Festivals: Lustre 4: MID EQUOS 4 ANMATU M EQVOS ANM | Equos I - D
Egyptian Calendar: Season Shemu (Month 4 - Mesore) Day 10 (West Europe) | Day 9 (Balkans, Central & East Europe)

---

12   Friday

Real Planetary Day: Mars
Moon: Waxing Gibbous
Zodiac: Cancer (♋▽)
Decan: 2nd Decan: Sit (Oufisit) | Ruler: Mercury
Pletho's Calendar: Mesountos 6 | 7th Month
Attic Calendar & Festivals: Hekatombaion 11.
Roman Calendar & Festivals: A.D. III KAL. IVL. |
Dies natalis (founding day) of the Temple of Hercules Musarum (Hercules of the Muses).
Gaulish Calendar and Festivals: Equos II - PRINI LAG
Egyptian Calendar: Season Shemu (Month 4 - Mesore) Day 11 (West Europe) | Day 10 (Balkans, Central & East Europe)

---

13   Saturday

Real Planetary Day: Mercury
Moon: Waxing Gibbous
Zodiac: Cancer (♋▽)

Decan: 3rd Decan: Knoumis (Khnoufos) | **Ruler:** Moon
Celebration and Remembrance: Emperor Flavius Arcadius orders (399) all the still standing pagan Temples to be immediately demolished.
Pletho's Calendar: Mesountos 5 | 7th Month
Attic Calendar & Festivals: Hekatombaion 12 | Kronia: Festival in honor of Kronos, father of Zeus.
Roman Calendar & Festivals: PRID. KAL. IVL.
Gaulish Calendar and Festivals: Equos III - N - SEMIVI
Egyptian Calendar: Season Shemu (Month 4 - Mesore) Day 12 (West Europe) | Day 11 (Balkans, Central & East Europe)

---

14   Sunday

Real Planetary Day: Jupiter
Moon: Waxing Gibbous
Zodiac: Cancer (♋▽)
Decan: 3rd Decan: Knoumis (Khnoufos) | **Ruler:** Moon
Pletho's Calendar: Mesountos 4 | 7th Month
Attic Calendar & Festivals: Hekatombaion 13.
Roman Calendar & Festivals: IVLIVS - KAL. IVL. (B.N.) | Dies natalis (founding day) of the temple to Juno Felicitas (Goddess of good luck and fortune).
Gaulish Calendar and Festivals: Equos IIII - ++I - D
Egyptian Calendar: Season Shemu (Month 4 - Mesore) Day 13 (West Europe) | Day 12 (Balkans, Central & East Europe)

---

15   Monday

Real Planetary Day: Venus
Moon: Waxing Gibbous
Zodiac: Cancer (♋▽)
Decan: 3rd Decan: Knoumis (Khnoufos) | **Ruler:** Moon

Pletho's Calendar: Mesountos 3 | 7th Month
Attic Calendar & Festivals: Hekatombaion 14.
Roman Calendar & Festivals: A.D. VI NON. IVL. (C.N.)
Gaulish Calendar and Festivals: Equos V - D - AMB
Egyptian Calendar: Season Shemu (Month 4 - Mesore) Day 14
(West Europe) | Day 13 (Balkans, Central & East Europe)

16   Tuesday

Real Planetary Day: Saturn
Moon: Full Moon (◯) (West Europe)
Zodiac: Cancer (♋▽)
Decan: 3rd Decan: Knoumis (Khnoufos) | Ruler: Moon
Astral Event: Partial Lunar Eclipse (Europe, Asia, Australia, Africa, South/East North America, South America, Pacific, Atlantic, Indian Ocean, Antarctica)
Pletho's Calendar: Mesountos 2 | 7th Month
Attic Calendar & Festivals: Hekatombaion 15.
Roman Calendar & Festivals: A.D. V NON. IVL. (D.N.)
Gaulish Calendar and Festivals: Equos VI - MD – SIM | Offerings to the mother Goddess Matronae Aufaniae (also called Matres Aufaniae or Deae Aufaniae).
Egyptian Calendar: Season Shemu (Month 4 - Mesore) Day 15
(West Europe) | Day 14 (Balkans, Central & East Europe)

17   Wednesday

Real Planetary Day: Sun
Moon: Full Moon (◯) (Balkans, Central & East Europe)
Zodiac: Cancer (♋▽)
Decan: 3rd Decan: Knoumis (Khnoufos) | Ruler: Moon

Astral Event: Partial Lunar Eclipse (Europe, Asia, Australia, Africa, South/East North America, South America, Pacific, Atlantic, Indian Ocean, Antarctica)
Celebration: Day sacred to Athena.
Pletho's Calendar: Dichomenia
Attic Calendar & Festivals: Hekatombaion 16 | Synoikia: Oldest yearly celebrations in honor of Athena.
Panathenaea (Other possible date) See the date of the "Lesser Panathenaea" according to Proclus on May 25th.
Roman Calendar & Festivals: A.D. IV NON. IVL. (E.N.)
Gaulish Calendar and Festivals: Equos VII - D
Egyptian Calendar: Season Shemu (Month 4 - Mesore) Day 16 (West Europe) | Day 15 (Balkans, Central & East Europe)

18   Thursday

Real Planetary Day: Moon
Moon: Waning Gibbous
Zodiac: Cancer (♋▽)
Decan: 3rd Decan: Knoumis (Khnoufos) | Ruler: Moon
Pletho's Calendar: Phthiontos 2 | 7th Month
Attic Calendar & Festivals: Hekatombaion 17.
Roman Calendar & Festivals: A.D. III NON. IVL. (F.NP.) | Poplifugia: The Flight of the People (festival of ancient rome).
Gaulish Calendar and Festivals: Equos VIII - PRINI LAG
Egyptian Calendar: Season Shemu (Month 4 - Mesore) Day 17 (West Europe) | Day 16 (Balkans, Central & East Europe)

19   Friday

Real Planetary Day: Mars
Moon: Waning Gibbous
Zodiac: Cancer (♋▽)
Decan: 3rd Decan: Knoumis (Khnoufos) | Ruler: Moon
Pletho's Calendar: Phthiontos 3 | 7th Month

Attic Calendar & Festivals: Hekatombaion 18.
Roman Calendar & Festivals: PRID. IVL. (G.N.) | Dies natalis (founding day) of the Temple of Fortuna Muliebris (Fortune of Women).
Gaulish Calendar and Festivals: Equos VIIII - +II - D
Egyptian Calendar: Season Shemu (Month 4 - Mesore) Day 18 (West Europe) Lychnapsia Lamp lit festival. Birthday of Isis. | Day 17 (Balkans, Central & East Europe)

---

20   Saturday

Real Planetary Day: Mercury
Moon: Waning Gibbous
Zodiac: Cancer (☽▽)
Decan: 3rd Decan: Knoumis (Khnoufos) | Ruler: Moon
Pletho's Calendar: Phthiontos 4 | 7th Month
Attic Calendar & Festivals: Hekatombaion 19.
Roman Calendar & Festivals: NON. IVL. (H.N.) |
Ancillarum Feriae: Festival of the Serving Women.
Minor festival to the two Pales (deity of shepherds, flocks and livestock. His gender varied).
Gaulish Calendar and Festivals: Equos X - +II - D
Egyptian Calendar: Season Shemu (Month 4 - Mesore) Day 19 (West Europe) | Day 18 (Balkans, Central & East Europe) Lychnapsia Lamp lit festival. Birthday of Isis.

---

21   Sunday

Real Planetary Day: Jupiter
Moon: Waning Gibbous
Zodiac: Cancer (☽▽)
Decan: 3rd Decan: Knoumis (Khnoufos) | Ruler: Moon
Pletho's Calendar: Phthiontos 5 | 7th Month

Attic Calendar & Festivals: Hekatombaion 20.
Roman Calendar & Festivals: A.D. VIII ID. IVL. (A.N.) |
Vitulatio: Annual thanksgiving in ancient Rome.
Gaulish Calendar and Festivals: Equos XI - D - AMB
Egyptian Calendar: Season Shemu (Month 4 - Mesore) Day 20
(West Europe) | Day 19 (Balkans, Central & East Europe)

---

22   Monday

Real Planetary Day: Venus
Moon: Waning Gibbous
Zodiac: Cancer (♋︎▽)
Decan: 3rd Decan: Knoumis (Khnoufos) | Ruler: Moon
Pletho's Calendar: Phthiontos 6 | 7th Month
Attic Calendar & Festivals: Hekatombaion 21 | Panathenaea:
First day of the eight-day festival in honor of the birthday of
Athena Polias (protector of the city of Athens).
Roman Calendar & Festivals: A.D. VII ID. IVL. (B.N.)
Gaulish Calendar and Festivals: Equos XII - D
Egyptian Calendar: Season Shemu (Month 4 - Mesore) Day 21
(West Europe) | Day 20 (Balkans, Central & East Europe)

---

23   Tuesday

Real Planetary Day: Saturn
Moon: Waning Gibbous
Zodiac: Cancer (♋︎▽)
Decan: 3rd Decan: Knoumis (Khnoufos) | Ruler: Moon
Pletho's Calendar: Phthiontos 7 | 7th Month
Attic Calendar & Festivals: Hekatombaion 22 | Panathenaea:
Second day of the eight-day festival in honor of Athena Polias.
Roman Calendar & Festivals: A.D. VI ID. IVL. (C.C.)
Gaulish Calendar and Festivals: Equos XIII - MD - SIMI

Egyptian Calendar: Season Shemu (Month 4 - Mesore) Day 22 (West Europe) | Day 21 (Balkans, Central & East Europe)

---

24   Wednesday

Real Planetary Day: Sun
Moon: Waning Gibbous
Zodiac: Leo (♌⟨⟩)
Decan: 1ˢᵗ Decan: Kharkhnoumis (Khnoumos) | Ruler: Saturn
Pletho's Calendar: Phthiontos 8 | 7ᵗʰ Month
Attic Calendar & Festivals: Hekatombaion 23 | Panathenaea: Third day of the eight-day festival in honor of Athena Polias.
Roman Calendar & Festivals: A.D. V ID. IVL. (D.C.)
Gaulish Calendar and Festivals: Equos XIIII - MD - SIMI
Egyptian Calendar: Season Shemu (Month 4 - Mesore) Day 23 (West Europe) | Day 22 (Balkans, Central & East Europe)

---

25   Thursday

Real Planetary Day: Moon
Moon: Third (last) Quarter
Zodiac: Leo (♌⟨⟩)
Decan: 1ˢᵗ Decan: Kharkhnoumis (Khnoumos) | Ruler: Saturn
Pletho's Calendar: Apiontos 7 | 7ᵗʰ Month
Attic Calendar & Festivals: Hekatombaion 24 | Panathenaea: Fourth day of the eight-day festival in honor of Athena Polias.
Roman Calendar & Festivals: A.D. IV ID. IVL. (E.C.)
Gaulish Calendar and Festivals: Equos XV - MD - SIMI
Egyptian Calendar: Season Shemu (Month 4 - Mesore) Day 24 (West Europe) Festival of Ptah (local). | Day 23 (Balkans, Central & East Europe)

26   Friday

Real Planetary Day: Mars
Moon: Waning Crescent
Zodiac: Leo (♌︎△)
Decan: 1st Decan: Kharkhnoumis (Khnoumos) | Ruler: Saturn
Pletho's Calendar: Apiontos 6 | 7th Month
Attic Calendar & Festivals: Hekatombaion 25 | Panathenaea:
Fifth day of the eight-day festival in honor of Athena Polias.
Roman Calendar & Festivals: A.D. III ID. IVL. (F.C.) | Ludi
Apollinares: Games in honor of Apollo.
Gaulish Calendar and Festivals: Equos I of Atenoux - MD –
SEMIV | Offerings to the Great Protector God Anextiomarus
(associated to the sun-god Apollo).
Egyptian Calendar: Season Shemu (Month 4 - Mesore) Day 25
(West Europe) | Day 24 (Balkans, Central & East Europe)
Festival of Ptah (local).

27   Saturday

Real Planetary Day: Mercury
Moon: Waning Crescent
Zodiac: Leo (♌︎△)
Decan: 1st Decan: Kharkhnoumis (Khnoumos) | Ruler: Saturn
Pletho's Calendar: Apiontos 5 | 7th Month
Attic Calendar & Festivals: Hekatombaion 26 | Panathenaea:
Sixth day of the eight-day festival in honor of Athena Polias.
Roman Calendar & Festivals: PRID. ID. IVL. (G.C.)
Gaulish Calendar and Festivals: Equos II of Atenoux - MD -
SEMIV
Egyptian Calendar: Season Shemu (Month 4 - Mesore) Day 26
(West Europe) | Day 25 (Balkans, Central & East Europe)

28   Sunday

Real Planetary Day: Jupiter
Moon: Waning Crescent
Zodiac: Leo (♌△)
Decan: 1st Decan: Kharkhnoumis (Khnoumos) | Ruler: Saturn
Pletho's Calendar: Apiontos 4 | 7th Month
Attic Calendar & Festivals: Hekatombaion 27 | Panathenaea:
Seventh day of the eight-day festival in honor of Athena Polias.
Roman Calendar & Festivals: ID. IVL. (H.NP.) | Transvectio
equitum: Procession of cavalry.
Gaulish Calendar and Festivals: Equos III of Atenoux - D -
AMB - MD SEMIV | Offerings to the Goddess Aufaniae.
Egyptian Calendar: Season Shemu (Month 4 - Mesore) Day 27
(West Europe) | Day 26 (Balkans, Central & East Europe)

29   Monday

Real Planetary Day: Venus
Moon: Waning Crescent
Zodiac: Leo (♌△)
Decan: 1st Decan: Kharkhnoumis (Khnoumos) | Ruler: Saturn
Pletho's Calendar: Apiontos 3 | 7th Month
Attic Calendar & Festivals: Hekatombaion 28 | Panathenaea:
Eight and last day of the eight-day festival in honor of Athena
Polias. Proclus mentioned this particular day as the most solemn
day of the festival on which the great procession took place.
Roman Calendar & Festivals: A.D. XVII KAL. AVG. (A.F.)
Gaulish Calendar and Festivals: Equos IIII of Atenoux - D
Egyptian Calendar: Season Shemu (Month 4 - Mesore) Day 28
(West Europe) | Day 27 (Balkans, Central & East Europe)

30 Tuesday

Real Planetary Day: Saturn
Moon: Waning Crescent
Zodiac: Leo (♌︎△)
Decan: 1st Decan: Kharkhnoumis (Khnoumos) | Ruler: Saturn
Pletho's Calendar: Apiontos 2 | 7th Month
Attic Calendar & Festivals: Hekatombaion 29.
Roman Calendar & Festivals: A.D. XVI KAL. AVG. (B.C.) | Dies natalis (founding day) of the Temple of Honos and Virtus. Offerings to Victory (Goddess of victory.).
Gaulish Calendar and Festivals: Equos V of Atenoux - D - AMB
Egyptian Calendar: Season Shemu (Month 4 - Mesore) Day 29 (West Europe) | Day 28 (Balkans, Central & East Europe)

31 Wednesday

Real Planetary Day: Aether
Moon: Waning Crescent
Zodiac: Leo (♌︎△)
Decan: 1st Decan: Kharkhnoumis (Khnoumos) | Ruler: Saturn
Celebration: Sacred day of the God Pluto, chief-god of the underworld.
Pletho's Calendar: Hene.
Attic Calendar & Festivals: Metageitnion 1.
Roman Calendar & Festivals: A.D. XV KAL. AVG. (C.C.)
Gaulish Calendar and Festivals: Equos VI of Atenoux - MD - SEMIV
Egyptian Calendar: Season Shemu (Month 4 - Mesore) Day 30 (West Europe) | Day 29 (Balkans, Central & East Europe)

AUGUST

1: ● 7: ☽ 15: ○ 23: ☾ 30: ●

1   Thursday

Real Planetary Day: Saturn
Moon: New Moon (●)
Zodiac: Leo (♌︎△)
Decan: 1ˢᵗ Decan: Kharkhnoumis (Khnoumos) | Ruler: Saturn
Astral Event: Start of the rising of Sirius in Heliopolis (Arcus visionis 6°)
Celebration and Remembrance: Death of Cosimo de' Medici (1464).
Pletho's Calendar: Hene Kai Nea ("the old and the new"); It is a day of self-examination and analysis.
Attic Calendar & Festivals: Metageitnion 2 | Heracleia (Festival honoring the divine hero Heracles.)
Roman Calendar & Festivals: A.D. XIV KAL. AVG. (D.NP.) | Lucaria: First day of the two-days festival of the grove.
Gaulish Calendar and Festivals: Equos VII of Atenoux - D - AMB
Egyptian Calendar: Thoth - Day 1

2   Friday

Real Planetary Day: Sun
Moon: Waxing Crescent
Zodiac: Leo (♌︎△)
Decan: 1ˢᵗ Decan: Kharkhnoumis (Khnoumos) | Ruler: Saturn
Celebration and Remembrance: Remembrance of Iamblichus of Chalcis (245-325 CE).
Pletho's Calendar: Noumenia (Histamenou 1) | 8ᵗʰ Month

Attic Calendar & Festivals: Metageitnion 3.
Roman Calendar & Festivals: A.D. XIII KAL. AVG. (E.C.)
Gaulish Calendar and Festivals: Equos VIII of Atenoux - D
Egyptian Calendar: Thoth - Day 2

3   Saturday

Real Planetary Day: Moon
Moon: Waxing Crescent
Zodiac: Leo (♌△)
Decan: 2nd Decan: Êpe (Ipi) | Ruler: Jupiter
Astral Event: Rising of Sirius in Heliopolis (Arcus visionis 8°)
Celebration and Remembrance: Day dedicated to Agathos Daimon.
Pletho's Calendar: Histamenou 2 | 8th Month
Attic Calendar & Festivals: Metageitnion 4.
Roman Calendar & Festivals: A.D. XII KAL. AVG. (F.NP.) | Lucaria: 2nd day of the festival of the grove.
Gaulish Calendar and Festivals: Equos VIIII of Atenoux - D - AMB
Egyptian Calendar: Thoth - Day 3

4   Sunday

Real Planetary Day: Mars
Moon: Waxing Crescent
Zodiac: Leo (♌△)
Decan: 2nd Decan: Êpe (Ipi) | Ruler: Jupiter
Pletho's Calendar: Histamenou 3 | 8th Month
Attic Calendar & Festivals: Metageitnion 5.
Roman Calendar & Festivals: A.D. XI KAL. AVG. (G.C.) | Dies natalis (founding day) of the Temple of Concordia (Goddess of agreement in marriage and society).

Gaulish Calendar and Festivals: Equos X of Atenoux - D
Egyptian Calendar: Thoth - Day 4

5   Monday

Real Planetary Day: Mercury
Moon: Waxing Crescent
Zodiac: Leo (♌︎△)
Decan: 2nd Decan: Êpe (Ipi) | Ruler: Jupiter
Pletho's Calendar: Histamenou 4 | 8th Month
Attic Calendar & Festivals: Metageitnion 6.
Roman Calendar & Festivals: A.D. X KAL. AVG. (H.NP.) | Neptunalia: Festival in honor of Neptune (God of freshwater and the sea).
Gaulish Calendar and Festivals: Equos XI of Atenoux - D - AMB – IVOS | Offerings to the war God Erudinus (also called Rudiobus, or Rudianus).
Egyptian Calendar: Thoth - Day 5

6   Tuesday

Real Planetary Day: Jupiter
Moon: Waxing Crescent
Zodiac: Leo (♌︎△)
Decan: 2nd Decan: Êpe (Ipi) | Ruler: Jupiter
Astral Event:
Pletho's Calendar: Histamenou 5 | 8th Month
Attic Calendar & Festivals: Metageitnion 7 | Metageitnia: festival marks the relocating in another neighborhood according real event that occurred in ancient Athens.
Roman Calendar & Festivals: A.D. IX KAL. AVG. (A.N.)
Gaulish Calendar and Festivals: Equos XII of Atenoux - MD - IVOS
Egyptian Calendar: Thoth - Day 6

7 Wednesday (Lughnasadh)

Real Planetary Day: Venus
Moon: First Quarter
Zodiac: Leo (♌︎△)
Decan: 2nd Decan: Êpe (Ipi) | Ruler: Jupiter
Pletho's Calendar: Histamenou 6 | 8th Month
Attic Calendar & Festivals: Metageitnion 8.
Roman Calendar & Festivals: A.D. VIII KAL. AVG. (B.NP.) | Furrinalia: Public festival honoring Furrina (Very ancient Goddess associated with water).
Gaulish Calendar and Festivals: Equos XIII of Atenoux - D - AMB – IVOS | DIVERTOMV | Offerings to Gwendolleu, God of strategy.
Egyptian Calendar: Thoth - Day 7

8 Thursday

Real Planetary Day: Saturn
Moon: Waxing Gibbous
Zodiac: Leo (♌︎△)
Decan: 2nd Decan: Êpe (Ipi) | Ruler: Jupiter
Astral Event: End of the rising of Sirius in Heliopolis (Arcus visionis 12°)
Celebration: Day dedicated to Poseidon, son of Zeus.
Pletho's Calendar: Histamenou 7 | 8th Month
Attic Calendar & Festivals: Metageitnion 9.
Roman Calendar & Festivals: A.D. VII KAL. AVG. (C.C.)
Gaulish Calendar and Festivals: Lustre 4: MID ELEMBIUOS 4 ANMATU M ELEMBIU ANM | Elembiuos I - D - IVOS
Egyptian Calendar: Thoth - Day 8 | First of the five Epagnomenal days in honor to Osiris.

9   Friday

Real Planetary Day: Sun
Moon: Waxing Gibbous
Zodiac: Leo (♌△)
Decan: 2nd Decan: Êpe (Ipi) | Ruler: Jupiter
Pletho's Calendar: Histamenou 8 | 8th Month
Attic Calendar & Festivals: Metageitnion 10.
Roman Calendar & Festivals: A.D. VI KAL. AVG. (D.C.)
Gaulish Calendar and Festivals: Elembiuos II - D - IVOS
Egyptian Calendar: Thoth - Day 9 | Second of the five Epagnomenal days in honor to Horus.

10   Saturday

Real Planetary Day: Moon
Moon: Waxing Gibbous
Zodiac: Leo (♌△)
Decan: 2nd Decan: Êpe (Ipi) | Ruler: Jupiter
Pletho's Calendar: Mesountos 7 | 8th Month
Attic Calendar & Festivals: Metageitnion 11.
Roman Calendar & Festivals: A.D. V KAL. AVG. (E.C.)
Gaulish Calendar and Festivals: Elembiuos III - PRINNI LAGET - IVOS
Egyptian Calendar: Thoth - Day 10 | Third of the five Epagnomenal days in honor to Seth.

11   Sunday

Real Planetary Day: Mars
Moon: Waxing Gibbous
Zodiac: Leo (♌△)
Decan: 2nd Decan: Êpe (Ipi) | Ruler: Jupiter
Pletho's Calendar: Mesountos 6 | 8th Month

Attic Calendar & Festivals: Metageitnion 12.
Roman Calendar & Festivals: A.D. IV KAL. AVG. (F.C.)
Gaulish Calendar and Festivals: Elembiuos IIII - N – IVOS |
Offerings to Fagus, God of babies and children.
Egyptian Calendar: Thoth - Day 11 | Fourth of the five
Epagnomenal days in honor to Isis.

12   Monday

Real Planetary Day: Mercury
Moon: Waxing Gibbous
Zodiac: Leo (♌︎)
Decan: 2ⁿᵈ Decan: Êpe (Ipi) | Ruler: Jupiter
Pletho's Calendar: Mesountos 5 | 8ᵗʰ Month
Attic Calendar & Festivals: Metageitnion 13.
Roman Calendar & Festivals: A.D. III KAL. AVG. (G.C.) |
Dies natalis (founding day) of the Temple of the "Fortune of This
Day," "Today's Fortune" (Aspect of the Goddess Fortuna).
Gaulish Calendar and Festivals: Elembiuos V - D - AMB -
IVOS
Egyptian Calendar: Thoth - Day 12 | Fifth of the five
Epagnomenal days in honor to Nephthys.

13   Tuesday

Real Planetary Day: Jupiter
Moon: Waxing Gibbous
Zodiac: Leo (♌︎)
Decan: 2ⁿᵈ Decan: Êpe (Ipi) | Ruler: Jupiter
Celebration and Remembrance: Birth of John Dee (1527).
Pletho's Calendar: Mesountos 4 | 8ᵗʰ Month
Attic Calendar & Festivals: Metageitnion 14.
Roman Calendar & Festivals: PRID. KAL. AVG. (H.C.)

Gaulish Calendar and Festivals: Elembiuos VI - D
Egyptian Calendar: Thoth - Day 13

---

14   *Wednesday*

Real Planetary Day: Venus
Moon: Waxing Gibbous
Zodiac: Leo (♌△)
Decan: 3rd Decan: Foupe (Fatiti) | Ruler: Mars
Pletho's Calendar: Mesountos 3 | 8th Month
Attic Calendar & Festivals: Metageitnion 15 | Eleusinia (Festival honoring Demeter).
Roman Calendar & Festivals: AVGVSTVS - KAL. AVG. (A.F.) | Dies natalis (founding day) of the Temple of Spes (Goddess of Hope).
Gaulish Calendar and Festivals: Elembiuos VII - D
Egyptian Calendar: Thoth - Day 14

---

15   *Thursday*

Real Planetary Day: Saturn
Moon: Full Moon (○)
Zodiac: Leo (♌△)
Decan: 3rd Decan: Foupe (Fatiti) | Ruler: Mars
Celebration: Day sacred to Athena.
Pletho's Calendar: Mesountos 3 | 8th Month
Attic Calendar & Festivals: Metageitnion 16 | Eleusinia (Festival honoring Demeter).
Roman Calendar & Festivals: A.D. IV NON. AVG. (B.F.)
Gaulish Calendar and Festivals: Elembiuos VIII - D
Egyptian Calendar: Thoth - Day 15

16   Friday

Real Planetary Day: Sun
Moon: Waning Gibbous
Zodiac: Leo (♌︎△)
Decan: 3rd Decan: Foupe (Fatiti) | Ruler: Mars
Pletho's Calendar: Dichomenia | 8th Month
Attic Calendar & Festivals: Metageitnion 17 | Eleusinia (Festival honoring Demeter).
Roman Calendar & Festivals: A.D. III NON. AVG. (C.C.)
Gaulish Calendar and Festivals: Elembiuos VIIII - PRINNI LAGET
Egyptian Calendar: Thoth - Day 16

17   Saturday

Real Planetary Day: Moon
Moon: Waning Gibbous
Zodiac: Leo (♌︎△)
Decan: 3rd Decan: Foupe (Fatiti) | Ruler: Mars
Pletho's Calendar: Phthiontos 2 | 8th Month
Attic Calendar & Festivals: Metageitnion 18 | Eleusinia (Festival honoring Demeter).
Roman Calendar & Festivals: PRID. NON. AVG. (D.C.)
Gaulish Calendar and Festivals: Elembiuos X - N - INIS R | Offerings to Cissonius (also called Cisonius, Cesonius), God of trade and protector of travelers.
Egyptian Calendar: Thoth - Day 17

18   Sunday

Real Planetary Day: Mars
Moon: Waning Gibbous
Zodiac: Leo (♌︎△)

Decan: 3rd Decan: Foupe (Fatiti) | Ruler: Mars
Pletho's Calendar: Phthiontos 3 | 8th Month
Attic Calendar & Festivals: Metageitnion 19.
Roman Calendar & Festivals: NON. AVG. (E.F.) | Salus: Public offerings (sacrificium publicum) at the Temple of Salus (Goddess of safety and well-being, welfare, health and prosperity).
Gaulish Calendar and Festivals: Elembiuos XI - D - AMB
Egyptian Calendar: Thoth - Day 18

19 Monday

Real Planetary Day: Mercury
Moon: Waning Gibbous
Zodiac: Leo (♌△)
Decan: 3rd Decan: Foupe (Fatiti) | Ruler: Mars
Pletho's Calendar: Phthiontos 4 | 8th Month
Attic Calendar & Festivals: Metageitnion 20.
Roman Calendar & Festivals: A.D. VA.D. III ID. AVG. (F.F.)
Gaulish Calendar and Festivals: Elembiuos XII - D
Egyptian Calendar: Thoth - Day 19

20 Tuesday

Real Planetary Day: Jupiter
Moon: Waning Gibbous
Zodiac: Leo (♌△)
Decan: 3rd Decan: Foupe (Fatiti) | Ruler: Mars
Pletho's Calendar: Phthiontos 5 | 8th Month
Attic Calendar & Festivals: Metageitnion 21.
Roman Calendar & Festivals: A.D. VII ID. AVG. (G.C.)
Gaulish Calendar and Festivals: Elembiuos XIII - D
Egyptian Calendar: Thoth - Day 20

21   *Wednesday*

Real Planetary Day: Venus
Moon: Waning Gibbous
Zodiac: Leo (♌︎△)
Decan: 3rd Decan: Foupe (Fatiti) | Ruler: Mars
Pletho's Calendar: Phthiontos 6 | 8th Month
Attic Calendar & Festivals: Metageitnion 22.
Roman Calendar & Festivals: A.D. VI ID. AVG. (H.C.)
Gaulish Calendar and Festivals: Elembiuos XIIII - D
Egyptian Calendar: Thoth - Day 21

22   *Thursday*

Real Planetary Day: Saturn
Moon: Waning Gibbous
Zodiac: Leo (♌︎△)
Decan: 3rd Decan: Foupe (Fatiti) | Ruler: Mars
Pletho's Calendar: Phthiontos 7 | 8th Month
Attic Calendar & Festivals: Metageitnion 23.
Roman Calendar & Festivals: A.D. V ID. AVG. (A.C.) | Sol Indiges: Public offerings (sacrificium publicum) to Sol Indiges (First Sun God) linked to the Mithraic mysteries.
Gaulish Calendar and Festivals: Elembiuos XV – D | Offerings to the Sun God Belenus (also spelled Belenos, Belinus, Bel, Beli Mawr).
Egyptian Calendar: Thoth - Day 22

23   *Friday*

Real Planetary Day: Sun
Moon: Third (last) Quarter
Zodiac: Leo (♌︎△)
Decan: 3rd Decan: Foupe (Fatiti) | Ruler: Mars

Pletho's Calendar: Phthiontos 8 | 8th Month
Attic Calendar & Festivals: Metageitnion 24.
Roman Calendar & Festivals: A.D. IV ID. AVG. (B.C.)
Gaulish Calendar and Festivals: Elembiuos I of Atenoux - MD - EDRINI
Egyptian Calendar: Thoth - Day 23

---

24   Saturday

Real Planetary Day: Moon
Moon: Waning Crescent
Zodiac: Virgo (♍︎♍︎)
Decan: 1st Decan: Tôm (Athoum) | Ruler: Sun
Pletho's Calendar: Apiontos 7 | 8th Month
Attic Calendar & Festivals: Metageitnion 25.
Roman Calendar & Festivals: A.D. III ID. AVG. (C.C.)
Gaulish Calendar and Festivals: Elembiuos II of Atenoux - MD - EDRINI
Egyptian Calendar: Thoth - Day 24

---

25   Sunday

Real Planetary Day: Mars
Moon: Waning Crescent
Zodiac: Virgo (♍︎♍︎)
Decan: 1st Decan: Tôm (Athoum) | Ruler: Sun
Pletho's Calendar: Apiontos 6 | 8th Month
Attic Calendar & Festivals: Metageitnion 26.
Roman Calendar & Festivals: PRID. ID. AVG. (D.C.) | Hercules Invictus: Offerings to Hercules Invictus, with a libation from the skyphos of Hercules.
Gaulish Calendar and Festivals: Elembiuos III of Atenoux - D - AMB EDRINI

Egyptian Calendar: Thoth - Day 25

---

26   Monday

Real Planetary Day: Mercury
Moon: Waning Crescent
Zodiac: Virgo (♍︎▽)
Decan: 1st Decan: Tôm (Athoum) | Ruler: Sun
Pletho's Calendar: Apiontos 5 | 8th Month
Attic Calendar & Festivals: Metageitnion 27.
Roman Calendar & Festivals: ID. AVG. (E.NP.) | Nemoralia: First day of the three-days festival honoring Diana (Goddess of hunting, the moon, and nature).
Gaulish Calendar and Festivals: Elembiuos IIII of Atenoux – D | Offerings to Apollo Cunomaglus, God of hunting.
Egyptian Calendar: Thoth - Day 26

---

27   Tuesday

Real Planetary Day: Jupiter
Moon: Waning Crescent
Zodiac: Virgo (♍︎▽)
Decan: 1st Decan: Tôm (Athoum) | Ruler: Sun
Pletho's Calendar: Apiontos 4 | 8th Month
Attic Calendar & Festivals: Metageitnion 28.
Roman Calendar & Festivals: A.D. XIX KAL. SEPT. | Nemoralia: 2nd day.
Gaulish Calendar and Festivals: Elembiuos V of Atenoux - D - AMB
Egyptian Calendar: Thoth - Day 27

28   Wednesday

Real Planetary Day: Venus
Moon: Waning Crescent
Zodiac: Virgo (♍♈)
Decan: 1st Decan: Tôm (Athoum) | Ruler: Sun
Pletho's Calendar: Apiontos 3 | 8th Month
Attic Calendar & Festivals: Metageitnion 29.
Roman Calendar & Festivals: A.D. XVIII KAL. SEPT. | Nemoralia: 3rd day.
Gaulish Calendar and Festivals: Elembiuos VI of Atenoux - D
Egyptian Calendar: Thoth - Day 28

29   Thursday

Real Planetary Day: Saturn
Moon: Waning Crescent
Zodiac: Virgo (♍♈)
Decan: 1st Decan: Tôm (Athoum) | Ruler: Sun
Pletho's Calendar: Apiontos 3 | 8th Month
Attic Calendar & Festivals: Metageitnion 30.
Roman Calendar & Festivals: A.D. XVII KAL. SEPT.
Gaulish Calendar and Festivals: Elembiuos VII of Atenoux - D - AMB
Egyptian Calendar: Thoth - Day 29

30   Friday (Opening of the Egyptian Year)

Real Planetary Day: Saturn
Moon: New Moon (●)
Zodiac: Virgo (♍♈)
Decan: 1st Decan: Tôm (Athoum) | Ruler: Sun

Pletho's Calendar: Hene Kai Nea ("the old and the new"); It is a day of self-examination and analysis.
Attic Calendar & Festivals: Boedromion 1.
Roman Calendar & Festivals: A.D. XVI KAL. SEPT. | Portunalia: Festival honoring Portunus (God of keys, doors, livestock and ports).
Dies natalis (founding day) of the Temple of Janus.
Gaulish Calendar and Festivals: Elembiuos VIII of Atenoux - D
Egyptian Calendar: Season Akhet (Month 1 - Thoth) Day 1
New Year (*Opening of the Year* - Birthday of the sun-god Ra-Horakhty)

31   Saturday

Real Planetary Day: Sun
Moon: Waxing Crescent
Zodiac: Virgo (♍▽)
Decan: 1ˢᵗ Decan: Tôm (Athoum) | Ruler: Sun
Pletho's Calendar: Noumenia (Histamenou 1) | 9ᵗʰ Month
Attic Calendar & Festivals: Boedromion 2 | Niketeria: Offerings to Nike.
Roman Calendar & Festivals: A.D. XV KAL. SEPT.
Gaulish Calendar and Festivals: Elembiuos VIIII of Atenoux - D – AMB | Offerings to Apollo Grannos.
Egyptian Calendar: Season Akhet (Month 1 - Thoth) Day 2
HAt rnpt: Day of the front of the year.

SEPTEMBER

6: ☽ 14: ◯ 22: ☾ 28: ●

1   Sunday

Real Planetary Day: Moon
Moon: Waxing Crescent
Zodiac: Virgo (♍▽)
Decan: 1ˢᵗ Decan: Tôm (Athoum) | Ruler: Sun
Celebration and Remembrance: Day dedicated to Agathos Daimon.
Pletho's Calendar: Histamenou 2 | 9ᵗʰ Month
Attic Calendar & Festivals: Boedromion 3 | Plataia: Day of Reconciliation; offerings to Hera.
Roman Calendar & Festivals: A.D. XIV KAL. SEPT. | Vinalia Rustica: Ancient Latin harvest festival, celebrating the grape harvest, vegetable growth and fertility. This festival honors Jupiter and Venus.
Gaulish Calendar and Festivals: Elembiuos X of Atenoux – D | Offerings to Audrinehae, mother Goddesses of destiny.
Egyptian Calendar: Season Akhet (Month 1 - Thoth) Day 3 Ihhy: jubilation.

2   Monday

Real Planetary Day: Mars
Moon: Waxing Crescent
Zodiac: Virgo (♍▽)
Decan: 1ˢᵗ Decan: Tôm (Athoum) | Ruler: Sun
Pletho's Calendar: Histamenou 3 | 9ᵗʰ Month
Attic Calendar & Festivals: Boedromion 4.
Roman Calendar & Festivals: A.D. XIII KAL. SEPT.

Gaulish Calendar and Festivals: Elembiuos XI of Atenoux - D - AMB
Egyptian Calendar: Season Akhet (Month 1 - Thoth) Day 4

---

3   Tuesday

Real Planetary Day: Mercury
Moon: Waxing Crescent
Zodiac: Virgo (♍♅)
Decan: 2nd Decan: Ouestebkôt (Brusous) | Ruler: Venus
Pletho's Calendar: Histamenou 4 | 9th Month
Attic Calendar & Festivals: Boedromion 5 | Genesios: Festival honoring the dead.
Roman Calendar & Festivals: A.D. XII KAL. SEPT. | Consualia/Consuales Ludi: Festival honoring Consus (God of the harvest and stored grain).
Gaulish Calendar and Festivals: Elembiuos XII of Atenoux – D | Offerings to the Healing God Mars Lenus (Ocelus Vellaunus).
Egyptian Calendar: Season Akhet (Month 1 - Thoth) Day 5

---

4   Wednesday

Real Planetary Day: Jupiter
Moon: Waxing Crescent
Zodiac: Virgo (♍♅)
Decan: 2nd Decan: Ouestebkôt (Brusous) | Ruler: Venus
Pletho's Calendar: Histamenou 5 | 9th Month
Attic Calendar & Festivals: Boedromion 6 | Artemis Agrotera: Festival in honor of Artemis the Huntress.
Roman Calendar & Festivals: A.D. XI KAL. SEPT.
Gaulish Calendar and Festivals: Elembiuos XIII of Atenoux - D - AMB

Egyptian Calendar: Season Akhet (Month 1 - Thoth) Day 6

---

5   *Thursday*

Real Planetary Day: Venus
Moon: Waxing Crescent
Zodiac: Virgo (♍︎♋︎)
Decan: 2nd Decan: Ouestebkôt (Brusous) | Ruler: Venus
Celebration and Remembrance: Birth of Cosimo de' Medici (1434)
Pletho's Calendar: Histamenou 6 | 9th Month
Attic Calendar & Festivals: Boedromion 7 | Boedromia: Festival in honor of Apollo Boedromios, the helper in distress.
Roman Calendar & Festivals: A.D. X KAL. SEPT. | Vulcanalia/ Feriae Volcano: Festival honoring Vulcan (God of fire, metalworking, and the forge).
Offerings to Maia (Nymph partner of Zeus and mother of Hermes) and the Nymphs.
Gaulish Calendar and Festivals: Elembiuos XIIII of Atenoux – D | DIVERTOMV
Egyptian Calendar: Season Akhet (Month 1 - Thoth) Day 7

---

6   *Friday*

Real Planetary Day: Saturn
Moon: First Quarter
Zodiac: Virgo (♍︎♋︎)
Decan: 2nd Decan: Ouestebkôt (Brusous) | Ruler: Venus
Pletho's Calendar: Histamenou 7 | 9th Month
Attic Calendar & Festivals: Boedromion 8.
Roman Calendar & Festivals: A.D. IX KAL. SEPT. | Offerings to Luna. Opening of the ritual pit called the mundus cerialis.

Gaulish Calendar and Festivals: Lustre 4: MID AEDRINIOS 4 MATU M EDRINI MAT | Aedrinios I - D - CANTIOS - IVO
Egyptian Calendar: Season Akhet (Month 1 - Thoth) Day 8

---

7 Saturday

Real Planetary Day: Sun
Moon: Waxing Gibbous
Zodiac: Virgo (♍︎♈︎)
Decan: 2nd Decan: Ouestebkôt (Brusous) | Ruler: Venus
Celebration: Day dedicated to Poseidon, son of Zeus.
Pletho's Calendar: Histamenou 8 | 9th Month
Attic Calendar & Festivals: Boedromion 9.
Roman Calendar & Festivals: A.D. VIII KAL. SEPT. | Opiconsivia: Festival honoring Ops/Opis meaning "Plenty," Goddess of agricultural resources and wealth.
Gaulish Calendar and Festivals: Aedrinios II - MD - IVOS
Egyptian Calendar: Season Akhet (Month 1 - Thoth) Day 9

---

8 Sunday

Real Planetary Day: Moon
Moon: Waxing Gibbous
Zodiac: Virgo (♍︎♈︎)
Decan: 2nd Decan: Ouestebkôt (Brusous) | Ruler: Venus
Pletho's Calendar: Mesountos 7 | 9th Month
Attic Calendar & Festivals: Boedromion 10.
Roman Calendar & Festivals: A.D. VII KAL. SEPT.
Gaulish Calendar and Festivals: Aedrinios III - MD - IVOS
Egyptian Calendar: Season Akhet (Month 1 - Thoth) Day 10
Procession of Isis (Late Period).

9   *Monday*

Real Planetary Day: Mars
Moon: Waxing Gibbous
Zodiac: Virgo (♍︎)
Decan: 2nd Decan: Ouestebkôt (Brusous) | Ruler: Venus
Pletho's Calendar: Mesountos 6 | 9th Month
Attic Calendar & Festivals: Boedromion 11.
Roman Calendar & Festivals: A.D. VI KAL. SEPT. | Volturnalia: Festival honoring Volturnus (God of the waters, of the fountains, of the Tiber, and by extension God of all rivers).
Gaulish Calendar and Festivals: Aedrinios IIII - MD | Offerings to Apollo Maponus.
Egyptian Calendar: Season Akhet (Month 1 - Thoth) Day 11

10   *Tuesday*

Real Planetary Day: Mercury
Moon: Waxing Gibbous
Zodiac: Virgo (♍︎)
Decan: 2nd Decan: Ouestebkôt (Brusous) | Ruler: Venus
Pletho's Calendar: Mesountos 5 | 9th Month
Attic Calendar & Festivals: Boedromion 12 | Demokratia (Festival celebrating democracy and offerings to Zeus Agoraios, Athena Agoraia and to the Goddess Themis).
Roman Calendar & Festivals: A.D. V KAL. SEPT.
Gaulish Calendar and Festivals: Aedrinios V – N | Offerings to Visucius, God of trade (usually identified with Mercury).
Egyptian Calendar: Season Akhet (Month 1 - Thoth) Day 12

11   Wednesday

Real Planetary Day: Jupiter
Moon: Waxing Gibbous
Zodiac: Virgo (♍︎▽)
Decan: 2nd Decan: Ouestebkôt (Brusous) | Ruler: Venus
Celebration and Remembrance: Imperial edict (364) orders the death penalty for all Pagans.
Pletho's Calendar: Mesountos 4 | 9th Month
Attic Calendar & Festivals: Boedromion 13.
Roman Calendar & Festivals: A.D. IV KAL. SEPT.
Gaulish Calendar and Festivals: Aedrinios VI - PRINNI LOUDIN
Egyptian Calendar: Season Akhet (Month 1 - Thoth) Day 13

12   Thursday

Real Planetary Day: Venus
Moon: Waxing Gibbous
Zodiac: Virgo (♍︎▽)
Decan: 2nd Decan: Ouestebkôt (Brusous) | Ruler: Venus
Pletho's Calendar: Mesountos 3 | 9th Month
Attic Calendar & Festivals: Boedromion 14 |
Roman Calendar & Festivals: A.D. III KAL. SEPT.
Gaulish Calendar and Festivals: Aedrinios VII - MD - TIOCOBREXTIO
Egyptian Calendar: Season Akhet (Month 1 - Thoth) Day 14

13   Friday

Real Planetary Day: Saturn
Moon: Waxing Gibbous
Zodiac: Virgo (♍︎▽)
Decan: 2nd Decan: Ouestebkôt (Brusous) | Ruler: Venus

Celebration and Remembrance: Death of Dante Alighieri (1265-1321)
Pletho's Calendar: Mesountos 2 | 9th Month
Attic Calendar & Festivals: Boedromion 14 | Eleusian Great Mysteries: First day of the nine-day celebration. A great procession occurs from Eleusis to the Eleusinion in the Agora of Athens.
Roman Calendar & Festivals: PRID. KAL. SEPT.
Gaulish Calendar and Festivals: Aedrinios VIII - MD – TIOCOBREXTIO | Offerings to Melovius, God of the struggle.
Egyptian Calendar: Season Akhet (Month 1 - Thoth) Day 15 Offerings to Hapy and Amun to secure a good flood.

14 Saturday

Real Planetary Day: Sun
Moon: Full Moon (◯)
Zodiac: Virgo (♍︎⏛)
Decan: 3rd Decan: Afoso (Amfatham) | Ruler: Mercury
Celebration: Day sacred to Athena.
Pletho's Calendar: Dichomenia
Attic Calendar & Festivals: Boedromion 15 | Eleusian Great Mysteries: Second day of the nine-day celebration. The head priest inaugurates the festival.
Roman Calendar & Festivals: SEPTEMBER - KAL. SEPT. (F.F.) | Ceremonies for Jupiter Tonans (the Thunderer) and Juno Regina.
Gaulish Calendar and Festivals: Aedrinios VIIII – MD | Offerings to Vesunna, Goddess of water and fertility.
Egyptian Calendar: Season Akhet (Month 1 - Thoth) Day 16

15 Sunday

Real Planetary Day: Moon
Moon: Waning Gibbous
Zodiac: Virgo (♍︎♍︎)
Decan: 3rd Decan: Afoso (Amfatham) | Ruler: Mercury
Pletho's Calendar: Phthiontos 2 | 9th Month
Attic Calendar & Festivals: Boedromion 16 | Eleusian Great Mysteries: Third day of the nine-day celebration. From this day until the 18th, initiates undertake a purification.
Roman Calendar & Festivals: A.D. IV NON. SEPT. (G.F.)
Gaulish Calendar and Festivals: Aedrinios X – MD | Offerings to the God of wine Vinotonus.
Egyptian Calendar: Season Akhet (Month 1 - Thoth) Day 17 Eve of Wag festival.

16 Monday

Real Planetary Day: Mars
Moon: Waning Gibbous
Zodiac: Virgo (♍︎♍︎)
Decan: 3rd Decan: Afoso (Amfatham) | Ruler: Mercury
Pletho's Calendar: Phthiontos 3 | 9th Month
Attic Calendar & Festivals: Boedromion 17 | Eleusian Great Mysteries: Fourth day of the nine-day celebration.
Roman Calendar & Festivals: A.D. III NON. SEPT. (H.C.)
Gaulish Calendar and Festivals: Aedrinios XI - D - AMB
Egyptian Calendar: Season Akhet (Month 1 - Thoth) Day 18 Wag festival dedicated to the death or Osiris and honoring the souls of the deceased on their journey in the afterlife.
Birth of the god Thoth. Day centered on rejuvenation and rebirth.

17   Tuesday

Real Planetary Day: Mercury
Moon: Waning Gibbous
Zodiac: Virgo (♍♓)
Decan: 3rd Decan: Afoso (Amfatham) | Ruler: Mercury
Pletho's Calendar: Phthiontos 4 | 9th Month
Attic Calendar & Festivals: Boedromion 18 | Eleusian Great
Mysteries: Fifth day of the nine-day celebration.
Roman Calendar & Festivals: PRID. NON. SEPT. (A.C.)
Gaulish Calendar and Festivals: Aedrinios XII – MD |
Offerings to Candida, Goddess of luck.
Egyptian Calendar: Season Akhet (Month 1 - Thoth) Day 19
Wag and Thoth festivals.

18   Wednesday

Real Planetary Day: Juupiter
Moon: Waning Gibbous
Zodiac: Virgo (♍♓)
Decan: 3rd Decan: Afoso (Amfatham) | Ruler: Mercury
Pletho's Calendar: Phthiontos 5 | 9th Month
Attic Calendar & Festivals: Boedromion 19 | Eleusian Great
Mysteries: Sixth day of the nine-day celebration.
Roman Calendar & Festivals: NON. SEPT. (B.C.)| Dies
natalis (founding day) of one of the temples to Jupiter Stator.
Ludi Romani (Roman Games): Fifteen-days religious festival
honoring Jupiter It included multiple ceremonies (Ludi).
Gaulish Calendar and Festivals: Aedrinios XIII - MD
Egyptian Calendar: Season Akhet (Month 1 - Thoth) Day 20
Tekh Festival (Feast of Drunkenness) dedicated to Hathor.

19   Thursday

Real Planetary Day: Venus
Moon: Waning Gibbous
Zodiac: Virgo (♍︎♑︎)
Decan: 3rd Decan: Afoso (Amfatham) | Ruler: Mercury
Pletho's Calendar: Phthiontos 6 | 9th Month
Attic Calendar & Festivals: Boedromion 20 | Eleusian Great
Mysteries: Seventh day of the nine-day celebration. On the 20th
and 21st, initiates are initiated in the Telesterion of Eleusis.
Roman Calendar & Festivals: A.D. VIII ID. SEPT. (C.F.)
Gaulish Calendar and Festivals: Aedrinios XIIII - MD
Egyptian Calendar: Season Akhet (Month 1 - Thoth) Day 21

20   Friday

Real Planetary Day: Saturn
Moon: Waning Gibbous
Zodiac: Virgo (♍︎♑︎)
Decan: 3rd Decan: Afoso (Amfatham) | Ruler: Mercury
Pletho's Calendar: Phthiontos 7 | 9th Month
Attic Calendar & Festivals: Boedromion 21 | Eleusian Great
Mysteries: Eighth day of the nine-day celebration.
Roman Calendar & Festivals: A.D. VII ID. SEPT. (D.C.)
Gaulish Calendar and Festivals: Aedrinios XV - MD
Egyptian Calendar: Season Akhet (Month 1 - Thoth) Day 22
Great procession of Osiris; Day sacred to Isis.

21   Saturday

Real Planetary Day: Sun
Moon: Waning Gibbous
Zodiac: Virgo (♍︎♑︎)
Decan: 3rd Decan: Afoso (Amfatham) | Ruler: Mercury

Celebration and Remembrance: Day dedicated to Agathos Daimon.

Pletho's Calendar: Histamenou 2 | 10th Month

Attic Calendar & Festivals: Pyanepsion 3.

Roman Calendar & Festivals: A.D. XV KAL. OCT.

Gaulish Calendar and Festivals: Aedrinios X of Atenoux - +I+ - MD - SINDIV – IVO | Offerings to Brigantia, Goddess of victory.

Egyptian Calendar: Season Akhet (Month 2 - Phaophi) Day 2 (West Europe) | Day 1 (Balkans, Central & East Europe)

OCTOBER

5: ☽ **13** (West Europe) **14** (Balkans, Central & East Europe): ○
21: ☾ **28:** ●

1   Tuesday

Real Planetary Day: Mars
Moon: Waxing Crescent
Zodiac: Libra (♎︎△)
Decan: 1st Decan: Soukhôe (Sfoukou) | Ruler: Moon
Celebration and Remembrance: Death of the Master Marsilio Ficino (1433-1499)
Pletho's Calendar: Histamenou 3 | 10th Month
Attic Calendar & Festivals: Pyanepsion 4.
Roman Calendar & Festivals: A.D. XIV KAL. OCT.
Gaulish Calendar and Festivals: Aedrinios XI of Atenoux - ++I - D – AMB | Offerings to Seixomniai Leuciticai, Celtic goddess, equated with Diana.
Egyptian Calendar: Season Akhet (Month 2 - Phaophi) Day 3 (West Europe) | Day 2 (Balkans, Central & East Europe)

2   Wednesday

Real Planetary Day: Mercury
Moon: Waxing Crescent
Zodiac: Libra (♎︎△)
Decan: 1st Decan: Soukhôe (Sfoukou) | Ruler: Moon
Pletho's Calendar: Histamenou 4 | 10th Month
Attic Calendar & Festivals: Pyanepsion 5.
Roman Calendar & Festivals: A.D. XIII KAL. OCT.

172

Gaulish Calendar and Festivals: Aedrinios XII of Atenoux - MD
Egyptian Calendar: Season Akhet (Month 2 - Phaophi) Day 4 (West Europe) Day of pouring the sand. | Day 3 (Balkans, Central & East Europe)

---

3   Thursday

Real Planetary Day: Jupiter
Moon: Waxing Crescent
Zodiac: Libra (♎♈)
Decan: 1st Decan: Soukhôe (Sfoukou) | Ruler: Moon
Pletho's Calendar: Histamenou 5 | 10th Month
Attic Calendar & Festivals: Pyanepsion 6 | Proerosia (Offerings to Demeter).
Roman Calendar & Festivals: A.D. XII KAL. OCT.
Gaulish Calendar and Festivals: Aedrinios XIII of Atenoux - D - AMB
Egyptian Calendar: Season Akhet (Month 2 - Phaophi) Day 5 (West Europe) Festival of Osiris and the Ennead. | Day 4 (Balkans, Central & East Europe) Day of pouring the sand.

---

4   Friday

Real Planetary Day: Venus
Moon: Waxing Crescent
Zodiac: Libra (♎♈)
Decan: 2nd Decan: Ptekhout (Nefthimes) | Ruler: Saturn
Pletho's Calendar: Histamenou 6 | 10th Month
Attic Calendar & Festivals: Pyanepsion 7 | Pyanopsia: Festival honoring Apollo and Theseus. (olive/laurel branch decoration) Oskhophoria: Festival honoring Sionysos and Athena Skira.
Roman Calendar & Festivals: A.D. XI KAL. OCT.

Gaulish Calendar and Festivals: Aedrinios XIIII of Atenoux - MD
Egyptian Calendar: Season Akhet (Month 2 - Phaophi) Day 6 (West Europe) | Day 5 (Balkans, Central & East Europe) Festival of Osiris and the Ennead.

---

5   Saturday

Real Planetary Day: Saturn
Moon: First Quarter
Zodiac: Libra (ΩΛ)
Decan: 2nd Decan: Ptekhout (Nefthimes) | Ruler: Saturn
Pletho's Calendar: Histamenou 7 | 10th Month
Attic Calendar & Festivals: Pyanepsion 8 | Ogdodia: Festival honoring Theseus and Poseidon.
Roman Calendar & Festivals: A.D. X KAL. OCT.
Gaulish Calendar and Festivals: Aedrinios XV of Atenoux – N | Offerings to the Goddess Sirona, healing deity associated with healing springs.
Egyptian Calendar: Season Akhet (Month 2 - Phaophi) Day 7 (West Europe) | Day 6 (Balkans, Central & East Europe)

---

6   Sunday

Real Planetary Day: Sun
Moon: Waxing Gibbous
Zodiac: Libra (ΩΛ)
Decan: 2nd Decan: Ptekhout (Nefthimes) | Ruler: Saturn
Celebration: Day dedicated to Poseidon, son of Zeus.
Pletho's Calendar: Histamenou 8 | 10th Month
Attic Calendar & Festivals: Pyanepsion 9 | Thesmophoria: First day of a five-day festival honoring Demeter and Persephone restricted to women.

Roman Calendar & Festivals: A.D. IX KAL. OCT. | Dies natalis (founding day) of the rededication of the Temple of Apollo.
Offerings to Latona.
Gaulish Calendar and Festivals: Lustre 4: MID CANTLOS 4 ANMATU M CANTLOS ANM | Cantlos I - MD – AEDRINI | Offerings to the God Grannus, identified to Apollo as a healing or solar deity.
Egyptian Calendar: Season Akhet (Month 2 - Phaophi) Day 8 (West Europe) Local festival of Satet and Anuqet in Elephantine. | Day 7 (Balkans, Central & East Europe)

---

7   Monday

Real Planetary Day: Moon
Moon: Waxing Gibbous
Zodiac: Libra (♎︎)
Decan: 2nd Decan: Ptekhout (Nefthimes) | Ruler: Saturn
Pletho's Calendar: Mesountos 7 | 10th Month
Attic Calendar & Festivals: Pyanepsion 10 | Thesmophoria: Second day of a five-day festival honoring Demeter and Persephone.
Roman Calendar & Festivals: A.D. VIII KAL. OCT.
Gaulish Calendar and Festivals: Cantlos II - D
Egyptian Calendar: Season Akhet (Month 2 - Phaophi) Day 9 (West Europe) | Day 8 (Balkans, Central & East Europe) Local festival of Satet and Anuqet in Elephantine.

---

8   Tuesday

Real Planetary Day: Mars
Moon: Waxing Gibbous
Zodiac: Libra (♎︎)

Decan: 2nd Decan: Ptekhout (Nefthimes) | **Ruler:** Saturn
Pletho's Calendar: Mesountos 6 | 10th Month
Attic Calendar & Festivals: Pyanepsion 11 | Thesmophoria:
Third day (main day) of a five-day festival honoring Demeter and
Persephone.
Roman Calendar & Festivals: A.D. VII KAL. OCT.
Gaulish Calendar and Festivals: Cantlos III - D
Egyptian Calendar: Season Akhet (Month 2 - Phaophi) Day 10
(West Europe) | Day 9 (Balkans, Central & East Europe)

9   Wednesday

Real Planetary Day: Mercury
Moon: Waxing Gibbous
Zodiac: Libra (♎︎)
Decan: 2nd Decan: Ptekhout (Nefthimes) | **Ruler:** Saturn
Pletho's Calendar: Mesountos 5 | 10th Month
Attic Calendar & Festivals: Pyanepsion 12 | Thesmophoria:
Fourth day (main day) of a five-day festival honoring Demeter and
Persephone.
Roman Calendar & Festivals: A.D. VI KAL. OCT. | Dies
natalis (founding day) of the Temple of Venus Genetrix.
Gaulish Calendar and Festivals: Cantlos IIII - PRINNI LAG
Egyptian Calendar: Season Akhet (Month 2 - Phaophi) Day 11
(West Europe) | Day 10 (Balkans, Central & East Europe)

10   Thursday

Real Planetary Day: Jupiter
Moon: Waxing Gibbous
Zodiac: Libra (♎︎)
Decan: 2nd Decan: Ptekhout (Nefthimes) | **Ruler:** Saturn
Pletho's Calendar: Mesountos 4 | 10th Month

Attic Calendar & Festivals: Pyanepsion 13 | Thesmophoria: Fifth day (main day) of a five-day festival honoring Demeter and Persephone.
Roman Calendar & Festivals: A.D. V KAL. OCT.
Gaulish Calendar and Festivals: Cantlos V - +I+ - D - AMB
Egyptian Calendar: Season Akhet (Month 2 - Phaophi) Day 12 (West Europe) | Day 11 (Balkans, Central & East Europe)

---

11   Friday

Real Planetary Day: Venus
Moon: Waxing Gibbous
Zodiac: Libra (Ω♎)
Decan: 2nd Decan: Ptekhout (Nefthimes) | Ruler: Saturn
Pletho's Calendar: Mesountos 3 | 10th Month
Attic Calendar & Festivals: Pyanepsion 14.
Roman Calendar & Festivals: A.D. IV KAL. OCT.
Gaulish Calendar and Festivals: Cantlos VI - N
Egyptian Calendar: Season Akhet (Month 2 - Phaophi) Day 13 (West Europe) | Day 12 (Balkans, Central & East Europe)

---

12   Saturday

Real Planetary Day: Saturn
Moon: Waxing Gibbous
Zodiac: Libra (Ω♎)
Decan: 2nd Decan: Ptekhout (Nefthimes) | Ruler: Saturn
Pletho's Calendar: Mesountos 2 | 10th Month
Attic Calendar & Festivals: Pyanepsion 15.
Roman Calendar & Festivals: A.D. III KAL. OCT.
Gaulish Calendar and Festivals: Cantlos VII – D | Offerings to Mercurio Cimiacinus.

177

Egyptian Calendar: Season Akhet (Month 2 - Phaophi) Day 14 (West Europe) | Day 13 (Balkans, Central & East Europe)

---

13   *Sunday*

Real Planetary Day: Sun
Moon: Full Moon (○) (West Europe)
Zodiac: Libra (ΩΔ)
Decan: 2nd Decan: Ptekhout (Nefthimes) | Ruler: Saturn
Celebration: Day sacred to Athena.
Pletho's Calendar: Dichomenia
Attic Calendar & Festivals: Pyanepsion 16.
Roman Calendar & Festivals: PRID. KAL. OCT.
Gaulish Calendar and Festivals: Cantlos VIII - D
Egyptian Calendar: Season Akhet (Month 2 - Phaophi) Day 15 (West Europe) First day of Ipet[4] festival for Amun that last 11 days (attested in Luxor). | Day 14 (Balkans, Central & East Europe)

---

14   *Monday*

Real Planetary Day: Moon
Moon: Full Moon (○) (Balkans, Central & East Europe)
Zodiac: Libra (ΩΔ)
Decan: 3rd Decan: Kontare (Fou) | Ruler: Jupiter
Pletho's Calendar: Phthiontos 2 | 10th Month
Attic Calendar & Festivals: Pyanepsion 17.
Roman Calendar & Festivals: **OCTOBER** - KAL. OCT. (C.N.) | Ceremonies honoring Fides (Goddess of trust and bona fides "good faith") and the Sororium Tigillum ("sister's beam," wooden beam erected on the slope of the Oppian Hill).

---

4 Also named Opet.

Gaulish Calendar and Festivals: Cantlos VIIII - D
Egyptian Calendar: Season Akhet (Month 2 - Phaophi) Day 16
(West Europe) | Day 15 (Balkans, Central & East Europe) First
day of Ipet[5] festival for Amun that last 11 days (attested in Luxor).

15 Tuesday

Real Planetary Day: Mars
Moon: Waning Gibbous
Zodiac: Libra (ΩΛ)
Decan: 3rd Decan: Kontare (Fou) | Ruler: Jupiter
Pletho's Calendar: Phthiontos 3 | 10th Month
Attic Calendar & Festivals: Pyanepsion 18.
Roman Calendar & Festivals: A.D. VI NON. OCT. (D.F.)
Gaulish Calendar and Festivals: Cantlos X - I++ - D |
Offerings to Annea Clivana, protective Goddess associated with
spirits.
Egyptian Calendar: Season Akhet (Month 2 - Phaophi) Day 17
(West Europe) | Day 16 (Balkans, Central & East Europe)

16 Wednesday

Real Planetary Day: Mercury
Moon: Waning Gibbous
Zodiac: Libra (ΩΛ)
Decan: 3rd Decan: Kontare (Fou) | Ruler: Jupiter
Pletho's Calendar: Phthiontos 4 | 10th Month
Attic Calendar & Festivals: Pyanepsion 19.
Roman Calendar & Festivals: A.D. V NON. OCT. (E.C.)
Gaulish Calendar and Festivals: Cantlos XI - +I+ - D - AMB

---

[5] Also named Opet.

Egyptian Calendar: Season Akhet (Month 2 - Phaophi) Day 18 (West Europe) Local festival of Khnum and Anuqet in Elephantine. | Day 17 (Balkans, Central & East Europe)

17   *Thursday*

Real Planetary Day: Jupiter
Moon: Waning Gibbous
Zodiac: Libra (ΩΔ)
Decan: 3rd Decan: Kontare (Fou) | Ruler: Jupiter
Pletho's Calendar: Phthiontos 5 | 10th Month
Attic Calendar & Festivals: Pyanepsion 20.
Roman Calendar & Festivals: A.D. IV NON. OCT. (F.C.) | Ieiunium Cereris: Day of fasting honoring of Ceres (Goddess of agriculture, grain crops, fertility, and motherly relationships.).
Gaulish Calendar and Festivals: Cantlos XII - D
Egyptian Calendar: Season Akhet (Month 2 - Phaophi) Day 19 (West Europe) | Day 18 (Balkans, Central & East Europe) Local festival of Khnum and Anuqet in Elephantine.

18   *Friday*

Real Planetary Day: Venus
Moon: Waning Gibbous
Zodiac: Libra (ΩΔ)
Decan: 3rd Decan: Kontare (Fou) | Ruler: Jupiter
Pletho's Calendar: Phthiontos 6 | 10th Month
Attic Calendar & Festivals: Pyanepsion 21.
Roman Calendar & Festivals: A.D. III NON. OCT. (G.C.)
Gaulish Calendar and Festivals: Cantlos XIII - D
Egyptian Calendar: Season Akhet (Month 2 - Phaophi) Day 20 (West Europe) | Day 19 (Balkans, Central & East Europe)

19 Saturday

Real Planetary Day: Saturn
Moon: Waning Gibbous
Zodiac: Libra (Ω△)
Decan: 3rd Decan: Kontare (Fou) | **Ruler**: Jupiter
Celebration and Remembrance: Birth of the Master Marsilio Ficino (1433-1499)
Pletho's Calendar: Phthiontos 7 | 10th Month
Attic Calendar & Festivals: Pyanepsion 22.
Roman Calendar & Festivals: PRID. OCT. (H.C.)
Gaulish Calendar and Festivals: Cantlos XIIII - D
Egyptian Calendar: Season Akhet (Month 2 - Phaophi) Day 21 (West Europe) | Day 20 (Balkans, Central & East Europe)

20 Sunday

Real Planetary Day: Sun
Moon: Waning Gibbous
Zodiac: Libra (Ω△)
Decan: 3rd Decan: Kontare (Fou) | **Ruler**: Jupiter
Pletho's Calendar: Phthiontos 8 | 10th Month
Attic Calendar & Festivals: Pyanepsion 23.
Roman Calendar & Festivals: NON. OCT. (A.F.) | Ceremonies honoring Jupiter Fulgur (The God Jupiter of daytime lightning) and Juno Curitis.
Gaulish Calendar and Festivals: Cantlos XV - D - TIOCOBREXTIO
Egyptian Calendar: Season Akhet (Month 2 - Phaophi) Day 22 (West Europe) | Day 21 (Balkans, Central & East Europe)

21   *Monday*

Real Planetary Day: Moon
Moon: Third (last) Quarter
Zodiac: Libra (♎△)
Decan: 3rd Decan: Kontare (Fou) | Ruler: Jupiter
Pletho's Calendar: Apiontos 7 | 10th Month
Attic Calendar & Festivals: Pyanepsion 24.
Roman Calendar & Festivals: A.D. VIII ID. OCT. (B.F.)
Gaulish Calendar and Festivals: Cantlos I of Atenoux - D
Egyptian Calendar: Season Akhet (Month 2 - Phaophi) Day 23
(West Europe) | Day 22 (Balkans, Central & East Europe)

---

22   *Tuesday*

Real Planetary Day: Mars
Moon: Waning Crescent
Zodiac: Libra (♎△)
Decan: 3rd Decan: Kontare (Fou) | Ruler: Jupiter
Pletho's Calendar: Apiontos 6 | 10th Month
Attic Calendar & Festivals: Pyanepsion 25.
Roman Calendar & Festivals: A.D. VII ID. OCT. (C.C.) |
Offerings to the Genius Publicus, Fausta Felicitas, and Venus
Victrix.
Gaulish Calendar and Festivals: Cantlos II of Atenoux - D
Egyptian Calendar: Season Akhet (Month 2 - Phaophi) Day 24
(West Europe) | Day 23 (Balkans, Central & East Europe)

---

23   *Wednesday*

Real Planetary Day: Mercury
Moon: Waning Crescent
Zodiac: Libra (♎△)
Decan: 3rd Decan: Kontare (Fou) | Ruler: Jupiter

Pletho's Calendar: Apiontos 5 | 10th Month
Attic Calendar & Festivals: Pyanepsion 26.
Roman Calendar & Festivals: A.D. VI ID. OCT. (D.C.) | Dies natalis (founding day) of the rededication of the Temple of Juno Moneta.
Gaulish Calendar and Festivals: Cantlos III of Atenoux - D - AMB
Egyptian Calendar: Season Akhet (Month 2 - Phaophi) Day 25 (West Europe) | Day 24 (Balkans, Central & East Europe)

24   Thursday

Real Planetary Day: Jupiter
Moon: Waning Crescent
Zodiac: Scorpio (♏︎♑︎)
Decan: 1st Decan: Stôkhnene (Bôs) | Ruler: Mars
Pletho's Calendar: Apiontos 4 | 10th Month
Attic Calendar & Festivals: Pyanepsion 27.
Roman Calendar & Festivals: A.D. V ID. OCT. (E.NP.) | Meditrinalia: Festival in honor of the new vintage, which was offered as libations to the Gods.
Gaulish Calendar and Festivals: Cantlos IIII of Atenoux - N - INIS R
Egyptian Calendar: Season Akhet (Month 2 - Phaophi) Day 26 (West Europe) | Day 25 (Balkans, Central & East Europe)

25   Friday

Real Planetary Day: Venus
Moon: Waning Crescent
Zodiac: Scorpio (♏︎♑︎)
Decan: 1st Decan: Stôkhnene (Bôs) | Ruler: Mars
Pletho's Calendar: Apiontos 3 | 10th Month

Attic Calendar & Festivals: Pyanepsion 28.
Roman Calendar & Festivals: A.D. IV ID. OCT. (F.C.) |
Augustalia: Ceremony honoring the divinized Augustus.
Offerings to Fortuna Redux (Form of the Goddess Fortuna who
oversaw a return from a long or perilous journey).
Gaulish Calendar and Festivals: Cantlos V of Atenoux - D -
AMB
Egyptian Calendar: Season Akhet (Month 2 - Phaophi) Day 27
(West Europe) 2-day local festival of Montu (Thebes) | Day 26
(Balkans, Central & East Europe)

26   Saturday

Real Planetary Day: Saturn
Moon: Waning Crescent
Zodiac: Scorpio (♏︎▽)
Decan: 1st Decan: Stôkhnene (Bôs) | Ruler: Mars
Pletho's Calendar: Apiontos 2 | 10th Month
Attic Calendar & Festivals: Pyanepsion 29 | Chalkeia: Festival
honoring Athena-Ergani and Hephaestus, protectors of Athens.
Roman Calendar & Festivals: A.D. III ID. OCT. (G.NP.) |
Fontinalia: Ceremony honoring Fontus (God of wells and
springs).
Gaulish Calendar and Festivals: Cantlos VI of Atenoux - D
Egyptian Calendar: Season Akhet (Month 2 - Phaophi) Day 28
(West Europe) Local festival of Satet and Anuket (Elephantine) |
Day 27 (Balkans, Central & East Europe) 2-day local festival of
Montu (Thebes)

27   Sunday

Real Planetary Day: Aether
Moon: Waning Crescent
Zodiac: Scorpio (♏︎▽)
Decan: 1st Decan: Stôkhnene (Bôs) | Ruler: Mars

Celebration: Sacred day of the God Pluto, chief-god of the underworld.
Pletho's Calendar: Hene.
Attic Calendar & Festivals: Maimakterion 1.
Roman Calendar & Festivals: PRID. ID. OCT. (H.EN.) | Dies natalis (founding day) of the rededication of the Temple of the Penates Dei (Household deities, invoked in domestic rituals).
Gaulish Calendar and Festivals: Cantlos VII of Atenoux - D - AMB
Egyptian Calendar: Season Akhet (Month 2 - Phaophi) Day 29 (West Europe) | Day 28 (Balkans, Central & East Europe) Local festival of Satet and Anuket (Elephantine).

28 Monday

Real Planetary Day: Saturn
Moon: New Moon (●)
Zodiac: Scorpio (♏︎♂)
Decan: 1ˢᵗ Decan: Stôkhnene (Bôs) | Ruler: Mars
Pletho's Calendar: Hene Kai Nea ("the old and the new"); It is a day of self-examination and analysis. | 11ᵗʰ Month
Attic Calendar & Festivals: Maimakterion 2.
Roman Calendar & Festivals: ID. OCT. (A.NP.)
Gaulish Calendar and Festivals: Cantlos VIII of Atenoux - D
Egyptian Calendar: Season Akhet (Month 2 - Phaophi) Day 30 (West Europe) | Day 29 (Balkans, Central & East Europe)

29 Tuesday

Real Planetary Day: Sun
Moon Waxing Crescent
Zodiac: Scorpio (♏︎♂)
Decan: 1ˢᵗ Decan: Stôkhnene (Bôs) | Ruler: Mars

Pletho's Calendar: Noumenia (Histamenou 1) | 11th Month
Attic Calendar & Festivals: Maimakterion 3.
Roman Calendar & Festivals: A.D. XVII KAL. NOV. (B.F.) |
Lupinalia: Festival of Wolves.
Gaulish Calendar and Festivals: Cantlos VIIII of Atenoux - D
– AMB | Offerings to the life-giving mother Goddess Sulis, also
effective agent of curses.
Egyptian Calendar: Season Akhet (Month 3 - Athyr) Day 1

---

30   Wednesday

Real Planetary Day: Moon
Moon: Waxing Crescent
Zodiac: Scorpio (♏︎▽)
Decan: 1st Decan: Stôkhnene (Bôs) | Ruler: Mars
Celebration and Remembrance: Day dedicated to Agathos
Daimon.
Pletho's Calendar: Histamenou 2 | 11th Month
Attic Calendar & Festivals: Maimakterion 4.
Roman Calendar & Festivals: A.D. XVI KAL. NOV. (C.C.)
Gaulish Calendar and Festivals: Cantlos X of Atenoux - D
Egyptian Calendar: Season Akhet (Month 3 - Athyr) Day 2

---

31   Thursday

Real Planetary Day: Mars
Moon: Waxing Crescent
Zodiac: Scorpio (♏︎▽)
Decan: 1st Decan: Stôkhnene (Bôs) | Ruler: Mars
Pletho's Calendar: Histamenou 3 | 11th Month
Attic Calendar & Festivals: Maimakterion 5.
Roman Calendar & Festivals: A.D. XV KAL. NOV. (D.C.)

Gaulish Calendar and Festivals: Cantlos XI of Atenoux - D - AMB

Egyptian Calendar: Season Akhet (Month 3 - Athyr) Day 3

NOVEMBER

4: ☽ 12: ◯ 19 (West Europe) 20 (Balkans, Central & East Europe): ☽ 26: ●

1   Friday

Real Planetary Day: Mercury
Moon: Waxing Crescent
Zodiac: Scorpio (♏︎▽)
Decan: 1ˢᵗ Decan: Stôkhnene (Bôs) | Ruler: Mars
Pletho's Calendar: Histamenou 4 | 11ᵗʰ Month
Attic Calendar & Festivals: Maimakterion 6.
Roman Calendar & Festivals: A.D. XIV KAL. NOV. (E.NP.) | Armilustrium: Day honoring Mars.
Gaulish Calendar and Festivals: Cantlos XII of Atenoux - D
Egyptian Calendar: Season Akhet (Month 3 - Athyr) Day 4

2   Saturday

Real Planetary Day: Jupiter
Moon: Waxing Crescent
Zodiac: Scorpio (♏︎▽)
Decan: 1ˢᵗ Decan: Stôkhnene (Bôs) | Ruler: Mars
Pletho's Calendar: Histamenou 5 | 11ᵗʰ Month
Attic Calendar & Festivals: Maimakterion 7 | Maimakteria: Festival honoring Zeus Maimaktes (Blusteing) and announcing the start of winter.
Roman Calendar & Festivals: A.D. XIII KAL. NOV. (F.C.)
Gaulish Calendar and Festivals: Cantlos XIII of Atenoux - D - AMB - IVOS
Egyptian Calendar: Season Akhet (Month 3 - Athyr) Day 5

3   Sunday

Real Planetary Day: Venus
Moon: Waxing Crescent
Zodiac: Scorpio (♏︎▽)
Decan: 2ⁿᵈ Decan: Sesme (Oustikhos) | Ruler: Sun
Pletho's Calendar: Histamenou 6 | 11ᵗʰ Month
Attic Calendar & Festivals: Maimakterion 8.
Roman Calendar & Festivals: A.D. XII KAL. NOV. (G.C.)
Gaulish Calendar and Festivals: Cantlos XIIII of Atenoux - D
– IVOS | DIVERTOMV
Egyptian Calendar: Season Akhet (Month 3 - Athyr) Day 6
Feast of Isis (Late Period)

4   Monday

Real Planetary Day: Saturn
Moon: First Quarter
Zodiac: Scorpio (♏︎▽)
Decan: 2ⁿᵈ Decan: Sesme (Oustikhos) | Ruler: Sun
Celebration: Day dedicated to Poseidon, son of Zeus.
Pletho's Calendar: Histamenou 7 | 11ᵗʰ Month
Attic Calendar & Festivals: Maimakterion 9.
Roman Calendar & Festivals: A.D. XI KAL. NOV. (H.C.)
**Gaulish Calendar and Festivals: Lustre 4: MID SAMONIOS
5 MATU M SAMON MAT** | Samonios I - D - DVMANNI -
IVOS
Egyptian Calendar: Season Akhet (Month 3 - Athyr) Day 7

5   Tuesday

Real Planetary Day: Sun
Moon: Waxing Gibbous
Zodiac: Scorpio (♏︎▽)
Decan: 2ⁿᵈ Decan: Sesme (Oustikhos) | Ruler: Sun

Pletho's Calendar: Histamenou 8 | 11th Month
Attic Calendar & Festivals: Maimakterion 10.
Roman Calendar & Festivals: A.D. X KAL. NOV. (A.C.)
Gaulish Calendar and Festivals: Samonios II - MD – IVOS | Offerings to Rosmerta, Goddess of fertility and abundance.
Egyptian Calendar: Season Akhet (Month 3 - Athyr) Day 8

6   *Wednesday*

Real Planetary Day: Moon
Moon: Waxing Gibbous
Zodiac: Scorpio (♏︎▽)
Decan: 2nd Decan: Sesme (Oustikhos) | Ruler: Sun
Pletho's Calendar: Mesountos 7 | 11th Month
Attic Calendar & Festivals: Maimakterion 11.
Roman Calendar & Festivals: A.D. IX KAL. NOV. (B.C.)
Gaulish Calendar and Festivals: Samonios III - D - DVMMANI EXO - IVOS
Egyptian Calendar: Season Akhet (Month 3 - Athyr) Day 9
Festival of Amun

7   *Thursday (Samhain)*

Real Planetary Day: Mars
Moon: Waxing Gibbous
Zodiac: Scorpio (♏︎▽)
Decan: 2nd Decan: Sesme (Oustikhos) | Ruler: Sun
Celebration and Remembrance: Celebration of the birth and death of Master Plato.
Death of our Past Grand Master Carl L. Weschcke (1930-2015)
Pletho's Calendar: Mesountos 6 | 11th Month
Attic Calendar & Festivals: Maimakterion 12.
Roman Calendar & Festivals: A.D. VIII KAL. NOV. (C.C.)

Gaulish Calendar and Festivals: Samonios IIII - MD
Egyptian Calendar: Season Akhet (Month 3 - Athyr) Day 10

---

8   Friday

Real Planetary Day: Mercury
Moon: Waxing Gibbous
Zodiac: Scorpio (♏︎♐︎)
Decan: 2nd Decan: Sesme (Oustikhos) | Ruler: Sun
Celebration and Remembrance: The Emperor Theodosius outlaws (392) all the non-Christian rituals and names them "superstitions of the Gentiles" (gentilicia superstitio).
Pletho's Calendar: Mesountos 5 | 11th Month
Attic Calendar & Festivals: Maimakterion 13.
Roman Calendar & Festivals: A.D. VII KAL. NOV. (D.C.) | Victory Games of Sulla: Seven days of games for the Roman people.
Gaulish Calendar and Festivals: Samonios V - D - AMB
Egyptian Calendar: Season Akhet (Month 3 - Athyr) Day 11

---

9   Saturday

Real Planetary Day: Jupiter
Moon: Waxing Gibbous
Zodiac: Scorpio (♏︎♐︎)
Decan: 2nd Decan: Sesme (Oustikhos) | Ruler: Sun
Pletho's Calendar: Mesountos 4 | 11th Month
Attic Calendar & Festivals: Maimakterion 14.
Roman Calendar & Festivals: A.D. VI KAL. NOV. (E.C.)
Gaulish Calendar and Festivals: Samonios VI - MD
Egyptian Calendar: Season Akhet (Month 3 - Athyr) Day 12

10   Sunday

Real Planetary Day: Venus
Moon: Waxing Gibbous
Zodiac: Scorpio (♏︎▽)
Decan: 2nd Decan: Sesme (Oustikhos) | Ruler: Sun
Pletho's Calendar: Mesountos 3 | 11th Month
Attic Calendar & Festivals: Maimakterion 15.
Roman Calendar & Festivals: A.D. V KAL. NOV. (F.C.)
Gaulish Calendar and Festivals: Samonios VII - N
Egyptian Calendar: Season Akhet (Month 3 - Athyr) Day 13

11   Monday

Real Planetary Day: Saturn
Moon: Waxing Gibbous
Zodiac: Scorpio (♏︎▽)
Decan: 2nd Decan: Sesme (Oustikhos) | Ruler: Sun
Astral Event: Transit of Mercury (South/West Europe, South/West Asia, Africa, North and South America, Pacific, Atlantic, Indian Ocean, Antarctica)
Celebration: Day sacred to Athena.
Pletho's Calendar: Mesountos 2 | 11th Month
Attic Calendar & Festivals: Maimakterion 16.
Roman Calendar & Festivals: A.D. IV KAL. NOV. (G.C.)
Gaulish Calendar and Festivals: Samonios VIII - D - DVMANNI
Egyptian Calendar: Season Akhet (Month 3 - Athyr) Day 14

12 Tuesday

Real Planetary Day: Sun
Moon: Full Moon (◯)
Zodiac: Scorpio (♏︎♑︎)
Decan: 2nd Decan: Sesme (Oustikhos) | Ruler: Sun
Pletho's Calendar: Dichomenia | 11th Month
Attic Calendar & Festivals: Maimakterion 17.
Roman Calendar & Festivals: A.D. III KAL. NOV. (H.C.)
Gaulish Calendar and Festivals: Samonios VIIII - MD
Egyptian Calendar: Season Akhet (Month 3 - Athyr) Day 15
Fertility festival of Min.

13 Wednesday

Real Planetary Day: Moon
Moon: Waning Gibbous
Zodiac: Scorpio (♏︎♑︎)
Decan: 3rd Decan: Sisieme (Afebis) | Ruler: Venus
Pletho's Calendar: Phthiontos 2 | 11th Month
Attic Calendar & Festivals: Maimakterion 18.
Roman Calendar & Festivals: PRID. KAL. NOV. (A.C.)
Gaulish Calendar and Festivals: Samonios X - MD
Egyptian Calendar: Season Akhet (Month 3 - Athyr) Day 16

14 Thursday

Real Planetary Day: Mars
Moon: Waning Gibbous
Zodiac: Scorpio (♏︎♑︎)
Decan: 3rd Decan: Sisieme (Afebis) | Ruler: Venus
Pletho's Calendar: Phthiontos 3 | 11th Month
Attic Calendar & Festivals: Maimakterion 19.

Roman Calendar & Festivals: NOVEMBER - KAL. NOV. (B.F.)
Gaulish Calendar and Festivals: Samonios XI - D
Egyptian Calendar: Season Akhet (Month 3 - Athyr) Day 17
The lamentations of Isis and Nephthys (New Kingdom).

---

15   Friday

Real Planetary Day: Mercury
Moon: Waning Gibbous
Zodiac: Scorpio (♏︎▽)
Decan: 3rd Decan: Sisieme (Afebis) | Ruler: Venus
Pletho's Calendar: Phthiontos 4 | 11th Month
Attic Calendar & Festivals: Maimakterion 20.
Roman Calendar & Festivals: A.D. IV NON. NOV. (C.F.)
Gaulish Calendar and Festivals: Samonios XII - MD
Egyptian Calendar: Season Akhet (Month 3 - Athyr) Day 18

---

16   Saturday

Real Planetary Day: Jupiter
Moon: Waning Gibbous
Zodiac: Scorpio (♏︎▽)
Decan: 3rd Decan: Sisieme (Afebis) | Ruler: Venus
Pletho's Calendar: Phthiontos 5 | 11th Month
Attic Calendar & Festivals: Maimakterion 21.
Roman Calendar & Festivals: A.D. III NON. NOV. (D.C.)
Gaulish Calendar and Festivals: Samonios XIII - MD
Egyptian Calendar: Season Akhet (Month 3 - Athyr) Day 19

17   Sunday

Real Planetary Day: Venus
Moon: Waning Gibbous
Zodiac: Scorpio (♏︎▽)
Decan: 3ʳᵈ Decan: Sisieme (Afebis) | Ruler: Venus
Celebration and Remembrance: Death of Giovanni Pico della Mirandola (1463-1494).
Pletho's Calendar: Phthiontos 6 | 11ᵗʰ Month
Attic Calendar & Festivals: Maimakterion 22.
Roman Calendar & Festivals: PRID. NON. NOV. (E.C.) | Plebeian Games: Fourteen-day of games for plebeians.
Gaulish Calendar and Festivals: Samonios XIIII - MD
Egyptian Calendar: Season Akhet (Month 3 - Athyr) Day 20

18   Monday

Real Planetary Day: Saturn
Moon: Waning Gibbous
Zodiac: Scorpio (♏︎▽)
Decan: 3ʳᵈ Decan: Sisieme (Afebis) | Ruler: Venus
Pletho's Calendar: Phthiontos 7 | 11ᵗʰ Month
Attic Calendar & Festivals: Maimakterion 23.
Roman Calendar & Festivals: NON. NOV. (F.F.)
Gaulish Calendar and Festivals: Samonios XV - MD
Egyptian Calendar: Season Akhet (Month 3 - Athyr) Day 21
Celebration of Maat.

19   Tuesday

Real Planetary Day: Sun
Moon: Third (last) Quarter (West Europe)
Zodiac: Scorpio (♏︎▽)
Decan: 3ʳᵈ Decan: Sisieme (Afebis) | Ruler: Venus

Pletho's Calendar: Phthiontos 8 | 11th Month
Attic Calendar & Festivals: Maimakterion 24.
Roman Calendar & Festivals: A.D. VIII ID. NOV. (G.F.)
Gaulish Calendar and Festivals: Samonios I of Atenoux - D - DVMANI
Egyptian Calendar: Season Akhet (Month 3 - Athyr) Day 22

20 Wednesday

Real Planetary Day: Moon
Moon: Third (last) Quarter (Balkans, Central & East Europe)
Zodiac: Scorpio (♏︎♑︎)
Decan: 3rd Decan: Sisieme (Afebis) | Ruler: Venus
Pletho's Calendar: Apiontos 7 | 11th Month
Attic Calendar & Festivals: Maimakterion 25.
Roman Calendar & Festivals: A.D. VII ID. NOV. (H.C.)
Gaulish Calendar and Festivals: Samonios II of Atenoux - MD - TRINO SAMONI SINDIV
Egyptian Calendar: Season Akhet (Month 3 - Athyr) Day 23

21 Thursday

Real Planetary Day: Mars
Moon: Waning Crescent
Zodiac: Scorpio (♏︎♑︎)
Decan: 3rd Decan: Sisieme (Afebis) | Ruler: Venus
Pletho's Calendar: Apiontos 6 | 11th Month
Attic Calendar & Festivals: Maimakterion 26.
Roman Calendar & Festivals: A.D. VI ID. NOV. (A.C.)
Gaulish Calendar and Festivals: Samonios III of Atenoux - D - AMB
Egyptian Calendar: Season Akhet (Month 3 - Athyr) Day 24

22   Friday

Real Planetary Day: Mercury
Moon: Waning Crescent
Zodiac: Scorpio (♏︎▽)
Decan: 3rd Decan: Sisieme (Afebis) | Ruler: Venus
Pletho's Calendar: Apiontos 5 | 11th Month
Attic Calendar & Festivals: Maimakterion 27.
Roman Calendar & Festivals: A.D. V ID. NOV. (B.C.)
Gaulish Calendar and Festivals: Samonios IIII of Atenoux - I++ - MD
Egyptian Calendar: Season Akhet (Month 3 - Athyr) Day 25

23   Saturday

Real Planetary Day: Jupiter
Moon: Waning Crescent
Zodiac: Sagittarius (♐︎△)
Decan: 1st Decan: Rêouô (Sebos) | Ruler: Mercury
Pletho's Calendar: Apiontos 4 | 11th Month
Attic Calendar & Festivals: Maimakterion 28.
Roman Calendar & Festivals: A.D. IV ID. NOV. (C.C.)
Gaulish Calendar and Festivals: Samonios V of Atenoux - +I+ - D - AMB
Egyptian Calendar: Season Akhet (Month 3 - Athyr) Day 26

24   Sunday

Real Planetary Day: Venus
Moon: Waning Crescent
Zodiac: Sagittarius (♐︎△)
Decan: 1st Decan: Rêouô (Sebos) | Ruler: Mercury
Pletho's Calendar: Apiontos 3 | 11th Month
Attic Calendar & Festivals: Maimakterion 29.

Roman Calendar & Festivals: A.D. III ID. NOV. (D.C.)
Gaulish Calendar and Festivals: Samonios VI of Atenoux -
++I – MD | Offerings to Damara, Goddess of fertility.
Egyptian Calendar: Season Akhet (Month 3 - Athyr) Day 27

25   Monday

Real Planetary Day: Saturn
Moon: Waning Crescent
Zodiac: Sagittarius (♐△)
Decan: 1st Decan: Rêouô (Sebos) | Ruler: Mercury
Pletho's Calendar: Apiontos 2 | 11th Month
Attic Calendar & Festivals: Maimakterion 30.
Roman Calendar & Festivals: PRID. ID. NOV. (E.C.)
Gaulish Calendar and Festivals: Samonios VII of Atenoux - D
- AMB
Egyptian Calendar: Season Akhet (Month 3 - Athyr) Day 28

26   Tuesday

Real Planetary Day: Saturn
Moon: New Moon (●)
Zodiac: Sagittarius (♐△)
Decan: 1st Decan: Rêouô (Sebos) | Ruler: Mercury
Pletho's Calendar: Hene Kai Nea ("the old and the new"); It is
a day of self-examination and analysis.
Attic Calendar & Festivals: Poseidon 1.
Roman Calendar & Festivals: ID. NOV. (F.NP.) | Epulum
Jovis: Sumptuous ritual feast offered to Jove (Jupiter, God of the
sky and thunder and king of the Gods). The gods were formally
invited and attended in the form of statues.
Gaulish Calendar and Festivals: Samonios VIII of Atenoux -
N - INIS R | Offerings to Nostiluca, Gaulish Goddess of magic.

Egyptian Calendar: Season Akhet (Month 3 - Athyr) Day 29

27 Wednesday

Real Planetary Day: Sun
Moon: Waxing Crescent
Zodiac: Sagittarius (♐︎△)
Decan: 1ˢᵗ Decan: Rêouô (Sebos) | Ruler: Mercury
Pletho's Calendar: Noumenia (Histamenou 1) | 12ᵗʰ Month
Attic Calendar & Festivals: Poseidon 2.
Roman Calendar & Festivals: A.D. XVIII KAL. DEC. | Equorum probation: Cavalry parade.
Gaulish Calendar and Festivals: Samonios VIIII of Atenoux - N - INIS R
Egyptian Calendar: Season Akhet (Month 4 - Choiak) Day 1
Festival of Hathor, celebrating the birth of the Goddess and her blessings.
Festival of Sokar: Making of the new Osiris God mold case.

28 Thursday

Real Planetary Day: Moon
Moon: Waxing Crescent
Zodiac: Sagittarius (♐︎△)
Decan: 1ˢᵗ Decan: Rêouô (Sebos) | Ruler: Mercury
Celebration and Remembrance: Day dedicated to Agathos Daimon.
Pletho's Calendar: Histamenou 2 | 12ᵗʰ Month
Attic Calendar & Festivals: Poseidon 3.
Roman Calendar & Festivals: A.D. XVII KAL. DEC.
Gaulish Calendar and Festivals: Samonios X of Atenoux - MD
Egyptian Calendar: Season Akhet (Month 4 - Choiak) Day 2

29 Friday

Real Planetary Day: Mars
Moon: Waxing Crescent
Zodiac: Sagittarius (♐︎ △)
Decan: 1st Decan: Rêouô (Sebos) | Ruler: Mercury
Pletho's Calendar: Histamenou 3 | 12th Month
Attic Calendar & Festivals: Poseidon 4.
Roman Calendar & Festivals: A.D. XVI KAL. DEC.
Gaulish Calendar and Festivals: Samonios XI of Atenoux - D - AMB - IVOS
Egyptian Calendar: Season Akhet (Month 4 - Choiak) Day 3

30 Saturday

Real Planetary Day: Mercury
Moon: Waxing Crescent
Zodiac: Sagittarius (♐︎ △)
Decan: 1st Decan: Rêouô (Sebos) | Ruler: Mercury
Pletho's Calendar: Histamenou 4 | 12th Month
Attic Calendar & Festivals: Poseidon 5.
Roman Calendar & Festivals: A.D. XV KAL. DEC.
Gaulish Calendar and Festivals: Samonios XII of Atenoux - MD - IVOS
Egyptian Calendar: Season Akhet (Month 4 - Choiak) Day 4

14 Saturday

Real Planetary Day: Mercury
Moon: Waning Gibbous
Zodiac: Sagittarius (♐△)
Decan: 3rd Decan: Komme (Khthisar) | Ruler: Saturn
Pletho's Calendar: Phthiontos 4 | 12th Month
Attic Calendar & Festivals: Poseidon 19.
Roman Calendar & Festivals: KAL. DEC. (G.N.) | Ceremonies honoring Neptune and Pietas (Virtue meaning: duty, religiosity, religious behavior, loyalty, devotion, and filial piety. This virtue has been personified as a Goddess).
Gaulish Calendar and Festivals: Dumanios XI - N - INIS R
Egyptian Calendar: Season Akhet (Month 4 - Choiak) Day 18
Festival of Khoiak: Seventh day of watering the Osiris/relic mold.

15 Sunday

Real Planetary Day: Jupiter
Moon: Waning Gibbous
Zodiac: Sagittarius (♐△)
Decan: 3rd Decan: Komme (Khthisar) | Ruler: Saturn
Pletho's Calendar: Phthiontos 5 | 12th Month
Attic Calendar & Festivals: Poseidon 20.
Roman Calendar & Festivals: A.D.IV NON. DEC. (H.N.)
Gaulish Calendar and Festivals: Dumanios XII - D
Egyptian Calendar: Season Akhet (Month 4 - Choiak) Day 19
Festival of Khoiak: Eighth day of watering the Osiris/relic mold. Censing of the Sokar Figure.
Finding the head of Osiris (according the Jumilhac Papyrus).

16   Monday

Real Planetary Day: Venus
Moon: Waning Gibbous
Zodiac: Sagittarius (♐△)
Decan: 3rd Decan: Komme (Khthisar) | Ruler: Saturn
Pletho's Calendar: Phthiontos 6 | 12th Month
Attic Calendar & Festivals: Poseidon 21.
Roman Calendar & Festivals: A.D. III NON. DEC. (A.N.)
Gaulish Calendar and Festivals: Dumanios XIII - D
Egyptian Calendar: Season Akhet (Month 4 - Choiak) Day 20
Festival of Khoiak: Ninth day of watering the Osiris/relic mold.
Weaving the shroud.
Finding the eyes of Osiris.

17   Tuesday

Real Planetary Day: Saturn
Moon: Waning Gibbous
Zodiac: Sagittarius (♐△)
Decan: 3rd Decan: Komme (Khthisar) | Ruler: Saturn
Pletho's Calendar: Phthiontos 7 | 12th Month
Attic Calendar & Festivals: Poseidon 22.
Roman Calendar & Festivals: PRID. NON. DEC. (B.C.)
Gaulish Calendar and Festivals: Dumanios XIIII - D
Egyptian Calendar: Season Akhet (Month 4 - Choiak) Day 21
Festival of Khoiak: Osiris and relic figures are taken out of molds.
The cloth is woven.
Finding the jaws of Osiris.

18   Wednesday

Real Planetary Day: Sun
Moon: Waning Gibbous
Zodiac: Sagittarius (♐△)
Decan: 3rd Decan: Komme (Khthisar) | Ruler: Saturn
Pletho's Calendar: Phthiontos 8 | 12th Month
Attic Calendar & Festivals: Poseidon 23.
Roman Calendar & Festivals: NON. DEC. (C.F.) | Faunalia: Country festival for Faunus (horned God of the forest, plains and fields) held by the pagi.
Gaulish Calendar and Festivals: Dumanios XV – D | Festival of Epona.
Egyptian Calendar: Season Akhet (Month 4 - Choiak) Day 22
Festival of Khoiak: Search of the sacred lake.
Finding the neck/arm of Osiris.

19   Thursday

Real Planetary Day: Moon
Moon: Third (last) Quarter
Zodiac: Sagittarius (♐△)
Decan: 3rd Decan: Komme (Khthisar) | Ruler: Saturn
Pletho's Calendar: Apiontos 7 | 12th Month
Attic Calendar & Festivals: Poseidon 24.
Roman Calendar & Festivals: A.D. VIII ID. DEC. (D.F.)
Gaulish Calendar and Festivals: Dumanios I of Atenoux - MD - SAMONI
Egyptian Calendar: Season Akhet (Month 4 - Choiak) Day 23
Festival of Khoiak: Burial preparations.
Finding the innards of Osiris.

20   Friday

Real Planetary Day: Mars
Moon: Waning Crescent
Zodiac: Sagittarius (♐︎△)
Decan: 3rd Decan: Komme (Khthisar) | Ruler: Saturn
Pletho's Calendar: Apiontos 6 | 12th Month
Attic Calendar & Festivals: Poseidon 25.
Roman Calendar & Festivals: A.D. VII ID. DEC. (E.C.)
Gaulish Calendar and Festivals: Dumanios II of Atenoux - MD - SAMONI
Egyptian Calendar: Season Akhet (Month 4 - Choiak) Day 24
Festival of Khoiak: The figures of the God of last year are taken out and buried.
Finding the entestine of Osiris.

21   Saturday (Solstice)

Real Planetary Day: Mercury
Moon: Waning Crescent
Zodiac: Sagittarius (♐︎△)
Decan: 3rd Decan: Komme (Khthisar) | Ruler: Saturn
Astral Event: Solstice (8:19 pm PDT)
Celebration and Remembrance: Sol Invictus;
Aurum Solis: Beginning of *Eversionis* (Northern Hemisphere) or *Tempus Messis* (Southern Hemisphere). No initiations are allowed in the Northern Hemisphere during this period of the year.
Pletho's Calendar: Apiontos 5 | 12th Month
Attic Calendar & Festivals: Poseidon 26 | Haloa: Festival honoring Demeter, Dionysus and Poseidon, as the god of seashore vegetation (Poseidon Phytalmios).
Roman Calendar & Festivals: A.D. VI ID. DEC. (F.C.) | Festival for Tiberinus Pater (God of the Riber river) and Gaia (personification of the Earth, ancestral mother of all life).
Gaulish Calendar and Festivals: Dumanios III of Atenoux - D - AMB

Egyptian Calendar: Season Akhet (Month 4 - Choiak) Day 25
Finding the lungs/phallus of Osiris.

22   Sunday

Real Planetary Day: Jupiter
Moon: Waning Crescent
Zodiac: Sagittarius (♐︎△)
Decan: 3rd Decan: Komme (Khthisar) | Ruler: Saturn
Astral Event: Solstice (4:19 UTC)
Pletho's Calendar: Apiontos 4 | 12th Month
Attic Calendar & Festivals: Poseidon 27.
Roman Calendar & Festivals: A.D. V ID. DEC. (G.C.)
Gaulish Calendar and Festivals: Dumanios IIII of Atenoux - D
Egyptian Calendar: Season Akhet (Month 4 - Choiak) Day 26
Finding the thighs/legs of Osiris.

23   Monday

Real Planetary Day: Venus
Moon: Waning Crescent
Zodiac: Capricorn (♑︎▽)
Decan: 1st Decan: Smat (Tair) | Ruler: Jupiter
Pletho's Calendar: Apiontos 3 | 12th Month
Attic Calendar & Festivals: Poseidon 28.
Roman Calendar & Festivals: A.D. IA.D. V ID. DEC. (H.C.)
Gaulish Calendar and Festivals: Dumanios V of Atenoux - D - AMB
Egyptian Calendar: Season Akhet (Month 4 - Choiak) Day 27
Finding the leg/fingers of Osiris.

24   Tuesday

Real Planetary Day: Saturn
Moon: Waning Crescent
Zodiac: Capricorn (♑︎▽)
Decan: 1ˢᵗ Decan: Smat (Tair) | Ruler: Jupiter
Pletho's Calendar: Apiontos 2 | 12ᵗʰ Month
Attic Calendar & Festivals: Poseidon 29.
Roman Calendar & Festivals: A.D. III ID. DEC. (A.NP.) | Offerings to Jupiter Indiges.
Gaulish Calendar and Festivals: Dumanios VI of Atenoux - D
Egyptian Calendar: Season Akhet (Month 4 - Choiak) Day 28 Finding the phallus/arm of Osiris.

25   Wednesday

Real Planetary Day: Aether
Moon: Waning Crescent
Zodiac: Capricorn (♑︎▽)
Decan: 1ˢᵗ Decan: Smat (Tair) | Ruler: Jupiter
Celebration: Sacred day of the God Pluto, chief-god of the underworld.
Pletho's Calendar: Hene
Attic Calendar & Festivals: Poseidon 30.
Roman Calendar & Festivals: PRID. ID. DEC. (B.EN.) | Ceremonies to the God Consus, protector of grains, represented by a grain seed.
Gaulish Calendar and Festivals: Dumanios VII of Atenoux - D - AMB
Egyptian Calendar: Season Akhet (Month 4 - Choiak) Day 29 Finding the heart of Osiris.

26   Thursday

Real Planetary Day: Saturn
Moon: New Moon (●)
Zodiac: Capricorn (♑)
Decan: 1st Decan: Smat (Tair) | Ruler: Jupiter
Astral Event: Annular Solar Eclipse (East of Europe, Much of Asia, North/West Australia, East Africa, Pacific, Indian Ocean)
Pletho's Calendar: Hene Kai Nea ("the old and the new"); It is a day of self-examination and analysis.
Attic Calendar & Festivals: 1 of Poseidon II.
Roman Calendar & Festivals: ID. DEC. (C.NP.) | Compitalia: Festival honoring of the Lares Compitales (household deities of the crossroads).
Lectisternium.6* for Ceres.
Dies natalis (founding day) of the Temple of Tellus (Tellus Mater, Terra Mater mean "Mother Earth." She is a goddess of the earth).
Gaulish Calendar and Festivals: Dumanios VIII of Atenoux - D
Egyptian Calendar: Season Akhet (Month 4 - Choiak) Day 30
Last day of the festival of Khoiak: Burial of figures and raising of the Djed-Pillar.

27   Friday (New Platonic Year 2447)

Real Planetary Day: Sun
Moon: Waxing Crescent
Zodiac: Capricorn (♑)
Decan: 1st Decan: Smat (Tair) | Ruler: Jupiter
Celebration and Remembrance: 1st day of the Platonic Year 2447
Pletho's Calendar: Noumenia (Histamenou 1) | 1st Month
Attic Calendar & Festivals: 2 of Poseidon II.
Roman Calendar & Festivals: A.D. XIX KAL. IAN.

---

6 Propitiatory ceremony, consisting of a meal offered to gods and goddesses.

Gaulish Calendar and Festivals: Dumanios VIIII of Atenoux - N - INIS R
Egyptian Calendar: Season Season Peret (Month 1 - Tybi) Day 1
Neheb-kau festival (called the Beginning of Eternity)

28   Saturday

Real Planetary Day: Moon
Moon: Waxing Crescent
Zodiac: Capricorn (♑︎♅)
Decan: 1ˢᵗ Decan: Smat (Tair) | Ruler: Jupiter
Celebration and Remembrance: Day dedicated to Agathos Daimon.
Pletho's Calendar: Histamenou 2 | 1ˢᵗ Month
Attic Calendar & Festivals: 3 of Poseidon II.
Roman Calendar & Festivals: A.D. XVIII KAL. IAN. | Consualia: Festival in honor of Consus (tutelary deity of the harvest and stored grain).
Gaulish Calendar and Festivals: Dumanios X of Atenoux - D
Egyptian Calendar: Season Peret (Month 1 - Tybi) Day 2

29   Sunday

Real Planetary Day: Mars
Moon: Waxing Crescent
Zodiac: Capricorn (♑︎♅)
Decan: 1ˢᵗ Decan: Smat (Tair) | Ruler: Jupiter
Pletho's Calendar: Histamenou 3 | 1ˢᵗ Month
Attic Calendar & Festivals: 4 of Poseidon II.
Roman Calendar & Festivals: A.D. XVII KAL. IAN.
Gaulish Calendar and Festivals: Dumanios XI of Atenoux - D - AMB

Body and soul in Ancient Egypt

By Andre Dollinger

The ancient Egyptian view of what made up a person is confusing. The main constituents were the body, its ka, and its name which remained always in close proximity to each other even in the tomb, and the shadow, the ba, sahu and akh which were more mobile and independent.

In magical thinking the limits of a person are ill defined: things which we would pay little heed to could be of critical importance to an ancient Egyptian. How much of a person's essence is inherent in an image? Jilted lovers still tear up pictures of their former love, but they know that this cannot hurt anybody. An ancient Egyptian on the other hand believed that he could harm somebody by destroying his image or gain power over him by applying spells to things which had belonged to him.

Some of the terms below were at times (at least in our eyes) almost interchangeable, and they acquired new aspects during the three millennia of their use, changing their meanings. There are no proper unequivocal translations for them, though attempts have been made to equate them with modern psychological terms: The *akh* is referred to as the *Id*, the name as the *Ego* and the *ka* as the *Super-ego*. Only, they are nothing like it.

The body (X.t) and its mummy (saH)

Khnum, *the sculptor who gives lives*, created a child's body, the *khat*, (MdC transliteration X.t) - together with its twin, the *ka* - on his potter's wheel and inserted them with the sperm into the mother's womb. The Egyptian view of the body was, from its conception to its death, mostly magical. The biological aspects of the body's functions, apart from the obvious ones everybody can discern, were largely unknown, instead it was populated and surrounded with spiritual and demonic entities whose evil influence caused the diseases and ailments people suffered from.

The preservation of the body[8] by mummification in order to enable the deceased to enjoy a life after death was at first only performed on the corpse of the divine pharaoh but became widespread as the notion of everybody being capable of having an afterlife took root. This afterlife was a continuation of life in the here and now: Tombs were decorated with scenes of daily life (above all during the Old Kingdom), things the deceased had used were left in their graves, and since the Middle Kingdom they were given servants in the form of little statuettes, *ushabtis* to stand in for them and perform their civic duties in the beyond.

The body, the X.t, after its transformation into a mummy, a saH, had to undergo the Ceremony of the Opening of the Mouth to have its senses restored as it was the body which had to justify itself before the judges of the underworld.

The sahu, (MdC transliteration saH), has been variously described as the spirit-body, as a self-defined psychic boundary or the repository of the soul (Budge). It was seemingly immortal and similar in form to the mortal body it sprang from.

> *Thou goest round about heaven, thou sailest in the presence of Ra, thou lookest upon all the beings who have knowledge. Hail, Ra, thou who goest round about in the sky, I say, O Osiris in truth, that I am the Sahu of the god, and I beseech thee not to let me be driven away, nor to be cast upon the wall of blazing fire.*[9]

---

[8] Rituals were of essence in achieving transfiguration, as is written in pBM 10208, the recitation of this ritual is effective for the one who recites it: *[Ritual for the transfiguration of Osiris in the necropolis, to be performed in the temple of Osiris-Khentamenti], the great god, lord of Abydos at all feasts for Osiris and at all his epiphanies in the land, [which are performed in the sanctuaries, both for the transfiguration of his ba and the permanent preservation of his corpse (and that) his ba] shall shine in the heavens and his corpse endure in the underworld, that he may be rejuvenated at the beginning of the month, that [his son Horus] be constant [on his throne, (while) he is holding his office for all eternity].* from Papyrus BM 10208, 4th century BCE, after a German translation on the Thesaurus Linguae Aegyptiae website.

[9] E. A. Wallis Budge, Papyrus of Ani - The Egyptian Book of the Dead, NuVision Publications, 2007, p.35.

The heart (jb)

A special part of the body was the heart, (MdC transliteration jb), the essence of life, seat of the mind with its emotions, intelligence, and moral sense.

> *My heart, my mother; my heart, my mother! My heart whereby I came into being!* (The prayer of Ani[10]).

The heart gave man's life its direction. Enjoyment was closely tied to the sensations of the body. Following one's heart meant living a full life:

> *The west seeks to hide (i.e. death and its realm is forgotten) from him who follows his heart. The heart is a god, the stomach is its shrine.*[11]

When the heart got tired the body died. When the deceased set out on his journey through the underworld, the jb as a record of his moral past was weighed by Anubis against a feather representing Maat. If found too heavy, the heart was devoured by the monster Ammit, destroying its owner for eternity.[12].

---

[10] Epiphanius Wilson, E. A. Wallis Budge, *The Book of the Dead According to the Theban Recension*, Health Research Books, 1968, p.25

[11] The inscription of Nebneteru, M. Lichtheim, Ancient Egyptian Literature, Volume III, p. 22.

[12] The final judgment was - in theory - not influenced by the social position of the deceased:

The west is the abode of him who is faultless,
Praise god for the man who has reached it!
No man will attain it,
Unless his heart is exact in doing right.
The poor is not distinguished there from the rich,
Only he who is found free of fault
By scale and weight before eternity's lord.
There is none exempt from being reckoned:
Thoth as Baboon in charge of the balance
Will reckon each man for his deeds on earth.

Inscription from the tomb of Petosiris. M. Lichtheim Ancient Egyptian Literature Volume III, pp.45f.

On the other hand, the knowledgable were certainly at an advantage. Magic could protect a person, prevent the heart from disclosing any dark secrets, or bully deities into being lenient. Knowlegde, or the means to acquire a semblance of it, went with social position.

The heart of Osiris hath in very truth been weighed, and his Heart-soul hath borne testimony on his behalf; his heart hath been found right by the trial in the Great Balance. There hath not been found any wickedness in him; he hath not wasted the offerings which have been made in the temples; he hath not committed any evil act; and he hath not set his mouth in motion with words of evil whilst he was upon earth. (Book of the Dead).[13]

During the embalming the heart was not removed together with the other interior organs. A scarab was inserted into the mummy's bindings right above the heart in an attempt to prevent it from speaking out against its owner, *lest my name appear stinking and putrid before the lord of the other world.*

Heart scarabs, the earliest examples of which date to the 17th dynasty.[14], were often inscribed with texts from the 30th chapter of the *Book of the Dead*, but at times other texts were chosen, such as the one below which, with its invocation of Nut, is exceptional:

I have come and I have brought to you. I am your guide Nut. I open my wing and spread it over you. I keep your heart in its place: It will not be removed from your coffin until you come to life again, O blessed Tjatenbastet-tanedjemtjaut.[15]

The name (rn)

The name, (MdC transliteration rn), is the foundation of a being as an individual. Only when it has a name, when it can be addressed and related to, does it begin its proper existence—with its name as its essence. The various aspects of the being are reflected in the different names it is given: In the Book of the Dead, chapter 142, Osiris had one hundred different names.

---

[13] The Egyptian Book of the Dead, 1240 BC, THE PAPYRUS OF ANI Translated by E.A. Wallis Budge
[14] Cooney, Kathlyn M., 2008, "Scarab" in Willeke Wendrich (ed.), UCLA Encyclopedia of Egyptology, Los Angeles.
[15] 22nd dynasty. After Étienne Drioton, Une formule inédite sur un scarabée de coeur, BIFAO 41 (1942), p.100.

Names were closely bound up with magic. Knowledge of somebody's names gave one insight into his being and power over him, but speaking out a name could also be dangerous

It is the king who will judge the dead, accompanied by Hell's chief executioner He-who-must-not-be-named, on the day the revered gods are slaughtered. (Pyramid Texts 273-4.[16])

'True' names were often kept secret. In the Pyramid Texts (# 394) a god is mentioned whose name was not even known to his mother.

An adoration of Ra who rises on the horizon, when he makes his ba, the visible form of his soul, rise like a powerful ghost from the underworld - the shining spectre of Ra that is our physical sun; when he raises himself, rejoicing in the power of his ka; an adoration of Ra, his ba and his ka, when he has the sun-boat's steersman shove off from the east and head out into deep sky while addressed in these words by the Osiris X[17]:
Hail Ra!
Hail to your ba!
Hail to your ka!
The Osiris X knows our name, and the names of your ba and your ka in all their aspects. (Book of the Dead 15a[18]).

An important part of ensuring the continued existence after death was the perpetuation of the name, in accordance with the Egyptian saying *He lives whose name is spoken*[19]. Especially important

---

[16] Jacob Rabinowitz, Isle of Fire, A Tour of the Egyptian Further World in English and Hieroglyphics, Invisible Books 2004
[17] The name Osiris in writings found in tombs can refer to the deceased himself: the person has died and is being resurrected like Osiris.
[18] Jacob Rabinowitz, Isle of Fire, A Tour of the Egyptian Further World in English and Hieroglyphics, Invisible Books 2004
[19] Inscription from the tomb of Petosiris, High Priest of Thoth, Hermopolis:
I built this tomb in this necropolis,
Beside the great souls who are there,
In order that my father's name be pronounced,
And that of my elder brother,
A man is revived when his name is pronounced!

was that inscriptions of offerings crucial for survival in the hereafter, named the recipient.

Inscribing names in stone gave them permanence and obliterating them was a kind of postmortem punishment or revenge: the person was assigned to oblivion. This was the fate post-Amarnan pharaohs had in mind when they erased inscriptions containing the name of Akhenaten.

The ka (kA)

Unfortunately, the ancient Egyptians never defined clearly what was meant by the ka, (MdC transliteration kA), or its female complementary, the *hemset* (Hms.t). The concepts may well have undergone changes over the millennia or had different meanings according to the social settings. kA has been variously translated as soul, life-force, will etc. but no single western concept is anything like it. Being written kA like the word for 'bull', a symbol of potency, the closest to it in English may be a 'life-creating force'.[20]

The ka was a constant close companion of the body in life and death, depicted throughout the pharaonic period following the king and bearing the royal Horus name.

> *The kas of Unas are behind him. His hemesets are under his feet. His gods are above him.*[21]

According to pictures drawn during the 18th dynasty, the ka came into being when a person was born, often depicted as a twin or double, but unlike the body it belonged to, it was immortal provided it received nourishment. Being a spiritual entity, it did not eat the food but seems to have extracted the life-sustaining forces from the offerings, be they real or symbolic.

M. Lichtheim Ancient Egyptian Literature Volume III, pp.45f

[20] This interpretation like the ones that follow it are mostly speculative. They reflect what some Egyptologists think rather than what the Egyptians thought.

[21] Pyramid Texts 273-4. After a transliteration and German translation on the Thesaurus Linguae Aegyptiae website, D. Topmann ed.

The sky-goddess replies

Make your seat in heaven,
Among the stars of heaven,
For you are the Lone Star, the comrade of Hu!
You shall look down on Osiris,
As he commands the spirits,
While you stand far from him;
You are not among them,
You shall not be among them![33]

The gods as embodiments of eternal divine might and magical powers would best be described as akhu.

Shining Ra, in your celestial aspect, as an akh,
you are Atum within the sky,
an old man as you set on the horizon,
a judge within your palace - which is the heavens,
a king enthroned in the sunset,
and when you've sunk west into the underworld, a king down there as
well.
Atum, ancient one, who first dawned from Nun, from the black deep of
her primordial night.[34].

The pharaoh, having a divine nature, had always become an *akh* and joined the stars after the demise of his mortal shell, but from the later Old Kingdom on ordinary mortals too could attain this status when they became transfigured dead.[35].
Akh has been translated as spirit, ghost or as transfiguration.[36].

---

[33] M. Lichtheim. Ancient Egyptian Literature: A Book of Readings. Vol. 1 - Pyramid Texts, Utterance 245.

[34] Book of the Dead, chapter 15a ; Jacob Rabinowitz, Isle of Fire, A Tour of the Egyptian Further World in English and Hieroglyphics, Invisible Books 2004

[35] Mark Smith suggests that commoners probably always had access to glorification spells very much like the ones known from the royal Pyramid Texts (Smith, Mark, 2009, "Democratization of the Afterlife" in Jacco Dieleman, Willeke Wendrich (eds.), UCLA Encyclopedia of Egyptology, Los Angeles.

[36] The verb belonging to the noun Ax, sAx, is just as difficult to pin down. "Glorifying", "making excellent" or "rendering effective" have been used as

translations. In the tomb of Meresankh III at Gizeh the process of embalming is described as *glorification by the embalmer*. The unguent used was one of the means: *I put you (i.e. the unguent) on the forehead of this Unas, so that you will make him comfortable under you, so that you will make him effective, that you will give him control over his body*. The oil used in this case was best conifer oil.

The priests too helped to make the deceased perfect. In the mastaba of Hesi the actions of the lector priest are defined precisely: *May he be glorified by the lector priest with the secret writing of the god's library on New Year's Day, the wag-feast, the sokar-feast, the great feast, the appearance of Min, the rekekh-feast of the month, the half-month and daily*.

The aim of these exertions was to make the deceased fit for the company of the gods. Ra-khuief is described in his mastaba as *made excellent and splendidly furnished by the side of the great god*.

The four kas: Human happiness as a gift from the gods

By Andre Dollinger

The ancient Egyptians strove to live a fulfilled life, happiness in this world and eternal bliss in the next.

> *He who keeps to the road of the god, he spends his whole life in joy, laden with riches more than all his peers. He grows old in his city, he is an honored man in his nome, all his limbs are young as those of a child's. His children are before him, numerous and considered foremost in their city; his sons follow each other from generation to generation... At last he reaches the necropolis in joy, in the beautiful embalmment of Anubis' labor.*[37]

Late in the history of the country these expectations took on a fourfold identity and were referred to as the four kas. In the temple of Ismant el Kharab they appeared in the company of the sphinx god Tutu, the Lord of the Book, who had control over shay (SAj), destiny, the fate of the human being. These ideals which make life worthwhile were a happy and long life, children, riches and a proper burial[38], or–alternatively, as in the Esna inscription–riches, children, burial and eternal life:

> *May you (Khnum) maintain in good shape your son whom you love, king of the South and the North, pharaoh, anywhere, because he is your heir who does as you wish. May the four favours which follow in your wake be granted to him, for you are their master in this role of yours of Tanem.*
>
> *May he have eternal life, for you are the great god, pillar of the heavens*
>
> *May he have a great many possessions, for you are the master of the plain*

---

[37] Tomb of Petosiris, Early Ptolemaic Period; After G. Lefebvre Le tombeau de Pétosiris, Première partie p.39.

[38] Kaper 2003, p.64.

May he have gentle children, for you are the god of revolution
May he have a splendid burial after old age, for you are the god of the
divine shrine, whose power is great among the gods..[39]

The ka, one of those Egyptian terms for which there is no good translation, is generally thought of as a person's life force, coming into existence at birth. Since the Middle Kingdom the plural form kas, Egyptian kaw (kA.w), came to mean the food needed to sustain this force, but not partaken of excessively, as greed and excess were harmful[40]. The kas were offerings, depicted as genii bearing boons[41].

Ordinary people could hope for four kas[42], Re, and his mortal sons, the pharaohs, had fourteen[43]. Many gods were apparently involved with granting these blessings. Ptah, creator of worldly goods, was among the foremost[44], Khnum, shaper of a person's ka at birth, was implored to confer them[45], as was Amen-opet[46] and also Khonsu to whom the Late Period royal scribe and Khonsu priest Hor-nefer prayed:

The four boons which you have granted me, may you accord them to [my]
children (too)..[47]

People, generally less critical of their own faults than of their fellow men's weaknesses, must have felt that they deserved their happiness, having led impeccable, or at any rate nearly impeccable, lives. On a Roman period stela found at Akhmim.[48] the deceased claims to have had a long life because he had been a good son and

---

[39] Esna inscription, Roman era; Sauneron, 1958, p.163.

[40] Traunecker 2001, p.22.

[41] Wild 1954, p.203.

[42] These four kas are to be distinguished from the four kas of the goddess Hathor, who was a fourfold deity and as such she is displayed on the square Hathor columns, each side of which shows one face of the goddess. (Wild 1954, p.202)

[43] Kippenberg et al. 1990, p.97.

[44] Smith 2002, p.24.

[45] Temple of Esna, inscription 319 (Sauneron 1958, pp.163f.).

[46] Statue J.E. 37075 Cairo Museum (Wild 1954, p.202).

[47] Hor-nefer's inscription. Wild, 1954, p.199

[48] Berlin Museum Stele No.22489.

a man who never committed any sacrilege; that he had enjoyed his possessions, having been full of good intentions, instructed in the divine laws and never having abandoned the temple; that he had been rewarded with an agreeable family circle and good descendants because he had been moved by humane sentiments and had not given a bad example to his fellow men; and that he had died a happy death and received a splendid funeral, as he had always faithfully observed the cult of the dead and had never committed an evil deed during his life.[49].

A long life, preferably one lived in material comfort, was in a society. which had little experience with old age as people tended to die quite young, an unmitigated blessing. One hundred and ten years became early on the proverbial life span of the wise old man. In the Precepts of the prefect, the lord Ptah-hotep the Old Kingdom vizier Ptahhotep linked his long life with the favor of pharaoh, which guaranteed a life free of want:

> ... you shall obtain years of life without default. It has caused me on earth to obtain one hundred and ten years of life, along with the gift of the favor of the Pharaoh...

The impression many modern people get from ancient Egypt is that the Egyptians were enamored with death, because they invested so heavily in their tombs, but they did so because they wanted life to last forever and since the Middle Kingdom they sometimes addressed the visitors to their tombs—their resurrection machines—with O you! who love to live and hate to die.[50]. Their hunger for life may well have become more pronounced, as doubts began to grow as to the quality of life after death. Holding on to what they had in this world may have appeared preferable to a possibly shadowy, albeit eternal, existence in the twilight of the underworld.

Interestingly, health is not one of the boons. Maybe it was implied in the wish for long life, as disease was a grim reaper killing most Egyptians before they reached forty, and anybody reaching old

---

[49] Wild 1954, p.205
[50] Maya Müller, "Afterlife" in Redford 2001, pp.32-37.

age must have been pretty healthy; or some physical discomfort was uncomplainingly accepted as part of the deal.

Yet it was never omitted from the good wishes anx, wDA, snb, rendered as L. P. H. (life. prosperity, health), tagged on to the names of pharaohs in written documents. Not that it seems to have helped them much: Ramses II did reach the ripe old age of about ninety but suffered badly from arthritis and cannot have enjoyed his food much, as his teeth had been ground down by attrition.[51].

While a beautiful burial[52] is never omitted from the list of the four kas, an eternal afterlife is not always mentioned. In historical times life after death in Egypt, at least for the upper classes, was conditional on a proper burial and also its consequence: the preparation of the tomb and the body and the offerings necessary for the ka to feed on were sine qua non. The kings were the first to become immortal as early as the Old Kingdom, and their servants saw a burial in their lord's vicinity as the culmination of their lives and as their chance of partaking in their master's immortality, with the king's sponsorship smoothening their path. But already in the Coffin Texts, religious texts inscribed on the coffins of the deceased since the end of the Old Kingdom, there are allusions to a Judgment of the Dead, which since the Middle Kingdom all non-royals had to undergo.[53] to be granted eternal life. Thanks to the precautions taken most people must have expected to pass all the tests in the afterworld and overcome all the obstacles and be granted eternal bliss.

Bibliography:

Sarah Iles Johnston, 2004, Religions of the Ancient World: A Guide, Harvard University Press

Olaf E. Kaper, The Egyptian God Tutu: A Study of the Sphinx-god and Master of Demons with a Corpus of Monuments, Peeters Publishers, 2003

---

[51] Underhill 2003, p.11
[52] Kippenberg et al. 1990, p.88.
[53] Iles 2004, p.515.

Hans G Kippenberg, Yme B. Kuiper, Andy F. Sanders, 1990, Concepts of Person in Religion and Thought, Walter de Gruyter

Serge Sauneron, 1958, "La conception égyptienne du bonheur. À propos des 'Quatre Ka'", BIFAO 57 (1958)

Mark Smith, 2002, On the Primaeval Ocean, Museum Tusculanum Press

Donald Redford, ed., Oxford Encyclopedia of ancient Egypt, Vol. I, Oxford University Press 2001

C. Traunecker, 2001, The Gods of Egypt, Cornell University Press

Henri Wild, 1954, "Statue de Hor-Néfer au Musée des Beaux-Arts de Lausanne", BIFAO 54, (1954), pp.173-222

Sarah Underhill Wisseman, The Virtual Mummy, University of Illinois Press, 2003

Heka: The magic of ancient Egypt

By Andre Dollinger

.....to me belonged the universe before you gods had come into being. You have come afterwards because I am Heka..[54]

All religions have a magical aspect[55], ancient religions like the Egyptian, according to which all of creation was animated to some extent, perhaps more so than many others. Through magic the creation had come into being and was sustained by it. Thus, magic was more ancient, and consequently more powerful, than the gods themselves

I am one with Atum when he still floated alone in Nun, the waters of chaos, before any of his strength had gone into creating the cosmos. I am Atum at his most inexhaustible - the potence and potential of all that is to be. This is my magic protection and it's older and greater than all the gods together![56]

It was also the extraordinary means for acquiring knowledge about one's surroundings - above all the hidden parts of them - and gaining control over them. Gods, demons and the dead could

---

[54] Coffin texts, spell 261, First Intermediate Period to Middle Kingdom.

[55] Theologians belonging to the three monotheistic religions tend to deny this, drawing a clear line between their 'pure' doctrines devoid of superstition and paganism. But there is no real difference in attitude between Christians, Jews and Muslims and followers of other traditions. They all use rituals which only to a believer are not classified as magical. Thus, Jews kiss the mezuzah, a small case attached to the doorpost containing religious texts, Christians cross themselves, and Muslims circle around a stone when performing the hadj. People will claim that it is the thought behind the ritual which counts - which of course is exactly what magic is all about.

[56] Book of the Dead, New Kingdom.

be implored, cajoled or threatened. Their help could be enlisted to avert evil or achieve one's desires.

Magic was accepted by all ancient peoples as a real force. The Hebrew tradition which was strongly opposed to it, did not deny its efficacy, but rather extolled the even greater magical power of its own god:

And the Lord spake unto Moses and unto Aaron saying,

When Pharaoh shall speak unto you, saying, Shew a miracle for you: then thou shalt say unto Aaron, Take thy rod, and cast it before Pharaoh, and it shall become a serpent.

And Moses and Aaron went in unto Pharaoh, and they did so as the Lord had commanded: And Aaron cast down his rod before Pharaoh, and before his servants, and it became a serpent.

The Pharaoh also called the wise men and the sorcerers: now the magicians of Egypt, they also did in like manner with their enchantments.

For they cast down every man his rod, and they became serpents; but Aaron's rod swallowed up their rods..[57]

Egyptian magical thinking continued to influence Europe. Thoth, god of wisdom and learning, was identified with the Greek Hermes Trismegistus. He was thought by the Hermetists to have originated the *Hermetica*, 42 books of magic.[58]

The worship of Isis, of whom the Metternich Stela (4th century BCE) says "I am Isis the goddess, the possessor of magic, who performs magic, effective of speech, excellent of words," became widespread throughout the Roman empire. She was the original mother of god, Isis lactans feeding her son Horus, which Christianity adopted as the Madonna. Her role as protectress is reflected in the Marian cult.

---

[57] Exodus 7 about 6th or 5th century BCE. (The stories in Exodus should not be considered to be historical facts. They reflect the Hebrew traditions which appear to be based on intimated knowledge of the ancient Egyptian society.)

[58] Hermes Trismegistus - The Archaic Underground Tradition. Nine Measures of Magic, Nine Measures of Magic, part 1.

Acquiring magical powers

Magical spell in Coptic, Graeco-Roman Period; Source: Duke Papyrus Archive While its efficiency in the hands of mortal practitioners was perhaps often less than had been hoped for, magic attracted people because it was practical and made sense. Everything had a reason, often hidden to the ordinary person, but revealed to the knowledgeable.

Magic explained the relationships between causes and effects using ideas people could relate to. Analogies and symbolisms were widely used, the sympathetic principle of like affecting like was invoked, associations, be they pure coincidence, were imbued with meaning, and historic occurrences became predictors for the future. There were even prescribed ways for explaining why expected results had not materialized.

It appears that, originally, the Egyptians, like some other peoples who practiced ritual cannibalism, thought that spiritual powers resided in the body and could be acquired by ingestion. There is no evidence, though, that such a view was more than speculative and ever acted upon.

> *The king orders sacrifices, he alone controls them,*
> *the king eats humans, feeds on gods,*
> *he has them presented on an altar to himself,*
> *he has agents to do his will. He fires off the orders!*
>
> ....
>
> *The king eats their magic, he gulps down their souls,*
> *the adults he has for breakfast,*
> *the young are lunch,*
> *the babies he has for supper,*
> *the old ones are too tough to eat, he just burns them on the altar as an*
> *offering to himself.[59]*

Magic was tightly bound up with writing, although there must have been an extensive purely oral tradition which was never recorded and is therefore lost to us. Most practitioners gained

---

[59] Pyramid Texts 273-4, Old Kingdom, translated by Jacob Rabinowitz. Pyramid Texts Utterances 273-274: "The Cannibal Hymn"

magical knowledge by studying ancient scriptures.[60]. Chief among them were the lector-priests, the only clerics who were fully professional since the beginning of recorded history. They were the keepers of the sacred books.

The practitioners of magic

Magical knowledge and power emanated from the gods and was bestowed upon their servants, the kings ...

> *Utterance of all the gods, [to] Amon-Re: "This thy daughter [Hatshepsut], who liveth, we are satisfied with her in life and peace. She is now thy daughter of thy form, whom thou hast begotten, prepared. Thou hast given to her thy soul, thy [...], thy [bounty], the magic powers of the diadem......[61]*
>
> *Come glorious one; I have placed (thee) before me; that thou mayest see thy administration in the palace, and the excellent deeds of thy ka's that thou mayest assume thy royal dignity, glorious in thy magic, mighty in thy strength..[62]*

Ay dressed as High Priest; source: Casson _Ancient Egypt_ ... and their substitutes in the service of the gods, the priesthood. But there were also less exalted magicians who did not deal with life and death, but with more mundane issues like good luck charms, pest control or love potions.

Sometimes spells fell into the wrong hands. Anybody capable of reading could use them.[63], and, at times, some did so with evil intentions.

---

[60] At least in tales hard study could be avoided, possibly at the price of upsetting one's stomach: Prince Naneferptah: *"... called for a new piece of papyrus, and wrote on it all that was in the book before him. He dipped it in beer, and washed it off in the liquid; for he knew that if it were washed off, and he drank it, he would know all that there was in the writing."* Princess Ahura: The Magic Book

[61] The coronation of Hatshepsut, 18th dynasty, Breasted Ancient Records of Egypt Part 2, § 220.

[62] Thutmose I, summoning his daughter to be crowned, 18th dynasty, Breasted Ancient Records of Egypt Part 2, § 235.

[63] The magic itself was the essence, not the magician. In the Pyramid Texts king Pepi threatened the gods with the withholding of all offerings if they did not assist him in rising to the heavens. *It is not this king Pepi who says this against you, it*

Now, when Penhuibin, formerly overseer of herds, said to him: "Give to me a roll for enduing me with strength and might," he gave to him a magic roll of Usermare-Meriamon (Ramses III), L.P.H., the Great God, his lord, L.P.H., and he began to employ the magic powers of a god upon people.[64]

To the ordinary mortal magic could be dangerous and coming into physical contact with the divine deadly. The accidental touching of the royal sceptre even by a sem priest had to be counteracted by the king's spell, and the incident was serious enough to be recorded:

The king of Upper and Lower Egypt Neferikare appeared as King of Lower Egypt on the day of the seizing of the anterior rope of the God's barque. There was the sem priest Rewer before his majesty in his office of sem priest, responsible for the clothing. The ames sceptre which was in the hand of his majesty, touched the foot of the sem priest Rewer. His majesty said to him: "May you be well!" - thus spoke his majesty. Behold, his majesty said: "It is desirable to my majesty that he may be well, without a blow for him." Behold, he is more esteemed by his majesty than any other man. His majesty ordered to have (it) put in writing on his tomb which is in the necropolis. His majesty caused a record to be made about it, written in the presence of the king himself in the district of the palace, in order to write down according to what had been said in his tomb which is in the necropolis.[65]

Practical purposes

Magic had important pragmatic aspects, which were exploited to achieve the aims of humans, dead or alive, spirits, and gods: Creation of the world by Ptah, the self-fertilization of Amen or Khnum's shaping of man from clay were all deeds unachievable by ordinary means.

---

is the charm which says this against you, ye gods. J.H. Breasted Development of Religion and Thought in Ancient Egypt, p. 111.

[64] Records of the Harem Conspiracy against Ramses III, 20th dynasty.

[65] From the tomb of Rewer (5th dynasty).

He (Ptah) gave birth to the gods, He made the towns, He established the nomes, He placed the gods in their shrines, He settled their offerings, He established their shrines, He made their bodies according to their wishes..[66]

The giving of birth was not just miraculous, but also dangerous, and the newly born was especially vulnerable.

Birth bricks on which the woman in labour crouched, were decorated with depictions of Hathor and other goddesses and were believed to bestow protection on the mother and above all her baby, and charms were used to guard children from evil demons. Boys appear to have been favoured by their parents and given better protection, e.g. only boy's names are mentioned on apotropaic wands carved of ivory and decorated with pictures of protective deities.[67].

The dead and their resting place needed protecting too and, as history has proven, ancient curses turned out to be most ineffective

The elder of the house of Meni, he says: A Crocodile against him in the water. A snake against him on land. He will do something against that same one. At no time did I do anything against him. It is God who will judge..[68]

Amulets were worn by the living and given to the dead to empower and ward off evil.[69]. Some mummies had dozens of scarabs packed into their bandages.

---

[66] From the Shabaka Stone, 25th dynasty.

[67] Meskell, *op.cit.*, p.65

[68] Inscription in the tomb of Meni, 6th Dynasty, at Giza

[69] In his 1914 monograph on amulets Petrie distinguished five classes of amulets:

1. Similars, or Homopoeic, which are for influencing similar parts, or functions, or occurrences, for the wearer

2. Powers or Dynatic, for conferring powers and capacities, especially upon the dead;

3. Property or Ktematic, which are entirely derived from the funeral offerings, and are thus peculiar to Egypt;

4. Protection or Phylactic, such as charms and curative amulets;

5. Gods or Theophoric, connected with the worship of the gods and their functions

He (the sun god) created for them magic as a weapon,
to fend off the blows of the happenings..[70]

As diseases were thought to be caused by spirits, healing was a magical science: the giving of medicines and the nursing care were accompanied by spells designed to expel these pathogenic agents.

Get thee back, thou enemy, thou dead man or woman ... Thou dost not enter into his phallus, so that it grows limp. Thou dost not cast seed into his anus (?)....[71]

According to the Bentresh Stela, describing an apparently fictitious medical case in the strange far-off country of Bekhten, when the daughter of the chief fell ill, the statue of Khonsu-the-Plan-Maker, Great God, Smiter of evil Spirits was sent from Egypt:

Then this god went to the place where Bentresh was. Then he wrought the protection of the daughter of the chief of Bekhten. She became well immediately.
Then said the spirit which was in her before Khonsu-the-Plan-Maker-in-Thebes: "Thou comest in peace, thou great god, smiting the barbarians.........
I am thy servant. I will go to the place whence I came, to satisfy thy heart concerning that, on account of which thou comest ....[72]

Physicians, priests and magicians - no clear demarcation line appears to have separated these, to our eyes very different, callings - seemingly worked according to quite strict guidelines as to how the body was to be examined, how the results were to be interpreted and which treatments were to be performed and which were not.

There are vessels in every limb of the body. When some physician, some sakhmet priest, some magician lays his finger on the head, on the back of the head, on the hands, on the place of the heart, on both arms and both

---

[70] The teachings of Merikare, Middle Kingdom; After Jan Assmann Ägypten - Theologie und Frömmigkeit einer frühen Hochkultur, p.72
[71] Gardiner, Theban Ostraca, C 1, p.13-15.
[72] Bentresh Stela, possibly 27th dynasty or later; James Henry Breasted Ancient Records of Egypt Part Three, § 443 f.

legs, then he will feel the heart, as there are vessels in every limb of the body and it (i.e. the heart) 'speaks' at the beginning of the vessels of all body parts.[73]

The more radical cures, like Isis restoring Osiris to life or Khufu's magician Djedi re-attaching cut-off heads belonged strictly to the realms of mythology or fancy.

The acquisition of knowledge concerning spiritual beings or the future enhanced a person's control over his destiny. One path to such knowledge was the interpretation of dreams, which was also used for justifying one's actions or legitimizing one's power:

In year 1, of his coronation as king ...... his majesty saw a dream by night: two serpents, one upon his right, the other upon his left. Then his majesty awoke, and he found them not. His majesty said: "Wherefore [has] this [come] to me?" Then they answered him, saying: "Thine is the Southland; take for thyself (also) the Northland. The two goddesses shine upon thy brow, the land is given to thee, in its length and its breadth. [No] other divides it with thee."[74]

The power attained through magic could serve many purposes, good or evil. It could be used to manipulate people's behaviour or feelings as the many love-spells prove.[75] According to the writings of Pseudo-Callisthenes Nectanebo II used magic to defend his country from outside enemies.

Whenever he was threatened with invasion by sea or by land he succeeded in destroying the power of his enemies, and in driving them from his coasts or frontiers; and this he did by the following means. If the enemy came against him by sea, instead of sending out his sailors to fight them,

---

[73] Ebers Papyrus, col. 99, Middle Kingdom.

[74] Stela of Tanutamen, 25th dynasty, James Henry Breasted Ancient Records of Egypt Part Four § 922.

[75] The little statuette on the right is about 8 centimetres tall, dates to the Graeco-Roman period, and bears an inscription invoking the powers the deceased depicted by the statuette was thought to have: *Rise and bind him whom I look at, to be my lover, (for) I adore his face.* (After Etienne Drioton, Un charme d'amour égyptien d'époque gréco-romaine, BIFAO 41 (1942), p.79). It appears that the constraint of being magically bound to do someone's will could be broken by an encounter with a magician or hearing some auspicious noise like the braying of an ass or the bark of a dog.

he retired into a certain chamber, and having brought forth a bowl which he kept for the purpose, he filled it with water, and then, having made wax figures of the ships and men of the enemy, and also of his own men and ships, he set them upon the water in the bowl, his men on one side, and those of the enemy on the other.

He then came out and having put on the cloak of an Egyptian prophet and taken an ebony rod in his hand, he returned into the chamber, and uttering words of power he invoked the gods who help men to work magic, and the winds, and the subterranean demons, which straightway came to his aid. By their means the figures of the men in wax sprang into life and began to fight, and the ships of wax began to move about likewise; but the figures which represented his own men vanquished those which represented the enemy, and as the figures of the ships and men of the hostile fleet sank through the water to the bottom of the bowl, even so did the real ships and men sink through the waters to the bottom of the sea.

In this way he succeeded in maintaining his power, and he continued to occupy his kingdom in peace for a considerable period.[76]

Through death a person lost his power over his body. In order for him to pass safely through the underworld his mummy's sensual functions had to be restored. This was done in the ceremony of the opening of the mouth. Statues were similarly empowered.

There was no tradition of magic that was evil in itself, what we would refer to as Black Magic, but magic could be abused and was in these instances treated as criminal behavior, though possibly especially abhorrent. Both in the Rollin and the Lee Papyrus the deeds of magicians who had supported a conspiracy against Ramses III were called "great crimes of death", "the abominations of the land" or the like, probably because the victim had been the king himself.

The practice of magic

The [magician Horus-son-of] Paneshe returned [quickly]; he brought his books and his amulets to [where Pharaoh] was. He recited a spell to him

---

[76] E. A. Wallis Budge Egyptian Magic.

and bound an amulet on him, to prevent the sorceries of the Nubians from gaining power over him. He [went] out from Pharaoh's presence, took his offerings and libations, went on board a boat, and hastened to Khmun. He went to the temple of Khmun, [made his] offerings and his libations before Thoth, the eight-times great, the lord of Khmun, the great god. He made a prayer before him saying: "Turn your face to me, my lord Thoth! Let not the Nubians take the shame of Egypt to the land of Nubia! It is you who [created] magic [spells]. It is you who suspended the sky, who founded the earth and the netherworld, who placed the gods with .... Let me know how to save Pharaoh [from the sorceries of the] Nubians!".[77]

Preparations

In order for magic spells to succeed elaborate preparations had to be made at times: It was generally wise not to choose an unlucky day, the time (dusk and dawn were especially auspicious) and place (often a *dark chamber, a dark recess, a clean dark cell* or a *secret dark place*) had to be appropriate, and, as is only proper for such spiritual endeavors, the ingredients, the medium and the magician had to be suitable, which generally meant that they had to be ritually pure: *If it be that you do not apply (?) purity to it, it does not succeed; its chief matter is purity.*

Thus, in one divination spell a *boy who has not been with a woman as medium* was required, in another one could address the moon after *being pure for three days.*

Implements and ingredients too needed to be acceptable, either new or carefully cleansed:

You go to a dark chamber with its [face] open to the South or East in a clean place: you sprinkle it with clean sand brought from the great river; you take a clean bronze cup or a new vessel of pottery and put a lok-measure of water that has settled (?) or of pure water into the [cup] and a lok-measure of real oil pure .....[78]

One's own *semen*, a *new brick* or even *milk of a black cow* were relatively easy to come by, a *two-tailed lizard* on the other hand

[77] From the story Prince Khamwas and Si-Osire.
[78] The Demotic Magical Papyrus of London and Leiden; Roman Period

needed some searching, and *Alexandrian weasels* or *hawks* were becoming quite rare in the late first millennium BCE: in a temple which specialized in mummifying hawks there was a major scandal when it was discovered that the mummies contained anything but hawks.

Spells

The word, spoken or, perhaps even more potent, written down and read out aloud, was the means to influence other beings and bend them to one's will. Speech was often accompanied by actions, precisely prescribed rituals for which there were no obvious reasons and which were frequently repeated:

...... you take a vine-shoot before it has ripened grapes, you take it with your left hand, you put it into your right hand - when it has grown seven digits (in length) you carry it [into your] house, and you take the [fish] out of the oil, you tie it by its tail with a strip (?) of flax, you hang it up to ...of(?) the vine-wood.......[79]

Execration rituals included piercing of a figurine with needles or knives, spitting, or burning. Some pharaohs asserted their dominance over their enemies by symbolically trampling on them: they had their foes' pictures painted on the soles of their sandals. Many spells required the use of special foodstuffs, magical implements, figurines, talismans and the like. During the Middle Kingdom magic knives, sometimes also called apotropaic[80] wands, were made of carved hippo tusks and often decorated with animal depictions. One of them carried the words *Cut off the head of the enemy when he enters the chamber of the children* and the spells were hoped to afford protection from snakes, scorpions[81] and other dangers. Animal figurines were among the equipment of tombs. Very popular were hippo talismans. Hippos are fiercely protective of their young and dangerous to man, the dead were therefore frequently endowed with figurines which had a leg purposely broken off to prevent them from hurting the tomb owners.

---

[79] The Demotic Magical Papyrus of London and Leiden
[80] Apotropaic: averting evil, from Greek apotrepein, turn away.
[81] A-bitjet: Charm against scorpions.

Vessels, lamps, knives and other utensils were used. Blood (of *smun*-geese, hoopoes, nightjars, worms, puppies, humans etc), semen, oil and water were mixed with other animal or plant matter *(shavings from the head of a dead man, hawk, ibis or crocodile eggs, gall of a gazelle, ankh-amu plant, [senepe plant], 'Great-of-Amen' plant, qes-ankh stone, genuine lapis-lazuli, 'footprint-of-Isis' plant).* Myrrh and frankincense were burned as was the *Anubis-plant.* Turpentine and styrax (storax), a fragrant gum, were added to the incense.[82].

In execration rituals figurines were made of wax which could then easily be destroyed by force or by fire

> *This spell is to be recited over (an image of) Apophis drawn on a new sheet of papyrus in green ink, and (over a figure of) Apophis in red wax. See, his name is inscribed on it in green ink ... I have overthrown all the enemies of Pharaoh from all their seats in every place where they are. See, their names written on their breasts, having been made of wax, and also bound with bonds of black rope. Spit upon them! To be trampled with the left foot, to be fallen with the spear (and) knife; to be placed on the fire in the melting-furnace of the copper-smiths ... It is a burning in a fire of bryony. Its ashes are placed in a pot of urine, which is pressed firmly into a unique fire..[83]*

Things were often chosen for their colour. Black, mentioned twenty times in the Demotic Magical Papyrus, and white, twelve instances, dominated: *milk from a black cow, blood of a black dog, a new white lamp etc.*

> *Great importance was attached to the names of the invoked gods or spirits, names which were hidden from the uninitiated. The very knowledge of their true names as opposed to those more widely known (Sarpot Mui-Sro is my name, Light-scarab-noble (?) is my true name), gave one considerable power over them. These appellations had to be pronounced properly, in the right sequence and in their entirety:*

---

[82] The Demotic Magical Papyrus of London and Leiden.

[83] Nine Measures of Magic; Part 3: 'Overthrowing Apophis': Egyptian ritual in practice; Ancient Egypt Magazine Issue Nine - November/December 2001

'........ Io, Tabao, Soukhamamon, Akhakhanbou, Sanauani, Ethie,
Komto, Kethos, Basaethori, Thmila, Akhkhou, give me answer as to
everything about which I ask here to-day.' Seven times..[84]

This invocation was to be repeated seven times. Often a simple
two-fold repetition seemed to suffice, but three-, four- and even
nine-fold reiterations were also frequent. In Ani's Book of the
Dead, the deceased reaffirms his innocence four times:

I am pure. I am pure. I am pure. I am pure..[85]

These magical numbers were also important in other contexts. A
certain love spell required *nine apple-pips together with your urine*,
another a *Kesh...-fish of nine digits and black*. For a vessel divination
three new bricks were needed; and one was supposed to pour an
unsavory concoction of semen, blood and other ingredients *into a*
cup of wine and add three uteh to *it of the first-fruits of the vintage*. Other
numbers like five, six or eight were rarely used.[86]

When the life of a patient was in danger because of a snake bite, a
sekhmet priest might threaten to cause the solar barque to run
aground on a sandbank, describing the dire consequences that
would ensue to the very fabric of the world:

The sun barque is at rest and does not proceed,
The sun is still in the same spot as yesterday.
The nourishment is without ship, the temple is barred,
There the disease will turn back the disturbance
To yesterday's location.
The daemon of darkness is about, the times are not separated.
The shadow's shapes cannot be observed anymore.
The springs are blocked, the plants wither,
Life is taken from the living
Until Horus recovers for his mother Isis,
And until the patient's health is restored as well..[87]

---

[84] The Demotic Magical Papyrus of London and Leiden
[85] Budge, The Book of the Dead, Chapter 125.
[86] The Demotic Magical Papyrus of London and Leiden.
[87] After Jan Assmann Ägypten - Theologie und Frömmigkeit einer frühen
Hochkultur, p.85.

The need of the deceased for magic was perhaps even greater than that of the living. After dying they were completely helpless until their faculties had been restored by the ritual of the Opening of the Mouth and they had been equipped with the knowledge needed to address gods and daemons by their hidden, true names and the spells necessary to ward off the dangers they would encounter.

Homage to thee, O great God, Lord of Maati! I have come unto thee, O my Lord, and I have brought myself hither that I may behold thy beauties. I know thee, I know thy name, I know the names of the Forty-two Gods who live with thee in this Hall of Maati, who live by keeping ward over sinners, and who feed upon their blood on the day when the consciences of men are reckoned up in the presence of the god Un-Nefer. In truth thy name is "Rehti-Merti-Nebti-Maati."[88]

But not all was gloom in the Netherworld. The duties a person had to perform by himself in this world, could be attended to by a stand-in, an *ushabti* (also called *shawabti* at times) in the next, if you knew how to make him do it[89]:

Spell for causing a shawabti to work for its owner in the underworld. To be recited over the shawabti, which will be made either of tamarisk or thorn wood. This shall be carved to resemble its owner as he appeared in life, and placed in the tomb.

Look upon this man, ye gods, transfigured souls and spirits of the dead, for he has acquired force, seized his moment, taken on royal authority, he's a pharaoh, ruling mankind, controlling them like cattle.

They were created to serve him. The gods themselves ordained it.

Now, shawabti:

If, in the world of the dead, X is ordered to perform the yearly stint of public work all Egyptians owe their pharaoh,

be it to move bricks, level off a plot of ground, re-survey land when the Nile-flood recedes or till new-planted fields,

---

[88] The Papyrus of Ani, translated by E.A.W. Budge.

[89] If the eagerness of the ushabtis to do their duty was indicative of the work ethics of Egyptian workers we may begin to sympathize with their employers: the tombs ended up by being filled with statuettes, as each was expected to be active for just one day in the year, and there were overseer ushabtis carrying flails.

*you will say; "Here I am!" to any functionary who comes looking for X
while he is trying to enjoy his meal of funerary offerings.*

*Take up your hoe, shawabti, your pick, your demarcation pegs, your
basket, just as any slave would for his master.*

*O shawabti made for X, if X is called for his obligations to the state you
will pipe up: "Here I am!" whether X is summoned to oversee workers
in the new-planted fields, tend to irrigation, move sand from East to
West or vice versa*

"Here I am!" you will say and take his place..[90]

Addressing supernatural powers

Prayers and offerings

Udjat, late period; Source: UCL In dealing with the gods care was
required. They were powerful and, consequently, highly respected:
Mut carried the epithet *Great in Magic*, the vulture-headed
Heknet[91] [26], the Praiser, was *Mistress of Spirits*[92], the hippo
goddess Taweret was called *Great of Sorcery* and Sekhmet was the
Powerful One. Their nature was often dual: Taweret was a
protectress against Typhonic powers, carrying an ankh or a
burning torch, but she had the form of an extremely dangerous
animal[93]; Sekhmet, a ferocious lion goddess, brought death and
destruction when she accompanied the pharaoh on his campaigns
of war, but was the main support of the healers in their fight
against disease. It was best to treat them with reverence.

Many people today may see practices such as prayers and offerings
to gods as distinct from magic, it was not to the Egyptians. Both
the living and the dead went to great lengths to receive the blessing
of the gods. Hymns of praise were composed and recited, written
down on papyrus and put in the tombs. Offerings of food, real or

---

[90] Coffin Text 472, translated by Jacob Rabinowitz.

[91] W. Max Muller, Egyptian Mythology, Kessinger Publishing, 2004, p.133.

[92] Francis Llewellyn Griffith, Herbert Thompson. The Leyden papyrus: an
Egyptian magical book, Courier Dover Publications, 1974, p.159.

[93] Taweret, Goddess-Demoness of Birth, Rebirth and the Northern Sky.

carved on walls, were supposed to satiate the god's hunger and thirst.

Just as the statue of the god Amen for instance was the god himself, a magician, by identifying himself with a god, was transformed into him

'I will say: "Come to me Montu, lord of the day! Come, that you may put N born of N into my hand like an insect in the mouth of a bird". I am Montu whom the gods adore. I will sever your bones and eat your flesh.'[94]

Invoking and dismissing

Lesser magical beings like demons, spirits or the deceased did not quite warrant the same amount of respect. But they were the main agents of magic and could be invoked by simple means:

Prescription to make them speak: you put a frog's head on the brazier, then they speak.

or

Prescription for bringing the gods in by force: you put the bile of a crocodile with pounded frankincense on the brazier. If you wish to make them come in quickly again, you put stalks (?) of anise (?) on the brazier together with the egg-shell as above, then the charm works at once.[95]

If they did not obey they (even lamps) could be threatened:

I will not give thee oil, I will not give thee fat. O lamp; verily I will give thee the body of the female cow and put blood of the male bull into (?) thee and put thy hand to the testicles (?) of the enemy of Horus.[96]

Once one had received their services it was best to send them away as they could be unpredictable

His dismissal formula: 'Farewell (bis) Anubis, the good ox-herd, Anubis (bis), the son of a (?) jackal (and ?) a dog . . . another volume

---

[94] Ostracon found at Deir el Medine; 19th dynasty; Ancient Egypt Magazine: Nine measures of magic.
[95] The Demotic Magical Papyrus of London and Leiden.
[96] Ibid.

saith: the child of . . . Isis (?) (and) a dog, Nabrishoth, the Cherub (?) of Amenti, king of those of.....' Say seven times.

or

The charm which you pronounce when you dismiss them to their place: 'Good dispatch, joyful dispatch!' [97]

---

[97] Ibid.

Druid Musings

By *Vivian Godfrey White (Melita Denning)*.
6th Grand Master of the Order Aurum Solis.

On an evening that marked no special commemoration, three friends met together for the simple purpose of enjoying one another's company. At the "toasts" stage of their shared meal, one of the three with mock solemnity declared,
The past is past:
The die is cast!
Another of the three countered this at once with,
The present is present:
It's happy and pleasant!
The third member of the party, thus inadvertently placed in a rather tight corner, took up the theme with,
The future's the future –
Concluding (after due pause) with
Let's give it good nurture!
The ancient habit of grouping our ideas into trines has remained fixed in our thinking, so as to be accepted often without question. We need not challenge the trine of primary colours, red, blue and yellow. But the colours of the rainbow were also identified at one time as those three, until research on prismatic colour expanded the accepted number to seven; while Jung points out that people nowadays tend spontaneously to accept 'four' basic colours – red, yellow, green and blue – and that in ancient times the accepted four were red, yellow, black and white. The three phases of the moon are a venerable and enduring trine, and so are the three aspects of time – past, present and future – if we consider them existing, so to put it, simply in one plane. This does not, however, represent their appearance to many people's minds.
The equal reality of past, present and future is not shown, for instance, by the myth of the Three Fates who give the thread of each individual life a beginning, an extension and an end: for the

beginning and the end represent no part of the extension. This frequent view of things sees, in fact, only an ever-changing Present Time moving beyond an "unborn Tomorrow and dead Yesterday" (as a Celtic poet rendered the thought of an Ismaili initiate): it is the view of the sceptic, natural or conditioned. There are others, again, who see the Present as scarcely existing in time at all: as a fragile knife-edge of experience continually menaced between the ravaging Past and the ever-encroaching Future. Alphonse de Lamartine, whose association with Druidry is here revealed to us by Dr. Michel Raoult in The Druid Revival in France and Brittany, expresses this anguished attitude to Time in his exquisite poem Le Lac. There Lamartine writes, not as the philosopher but as the poet almost crushed by a tragic bereavement, of future and past as dark gulfs of eternity which seek to swallow up the precious remembered moments of his love. But in the closing lines of the poem this anguish is mitigated and transcended as he realises the oneness of his experience with the enduring life and beauty of Nature. It is surely that sense of unity with the natural world, with the cosmos even, whether it comes to us in sorrow or in joy, which is one of the great inward gifts of the Druid experience.

But there is a third view of Time, I which Past, Present and Future blend almost indistinguishably into one stream: a stream with its shadows and reflections as well as it currents, its hidden springs and drifting twigs. The visionary knows this aspect of time: the prophet, the diviner, are familiar with it almost to the confusion of their pronouncements. In the family circle of Gilbert Murray, renowned Greek scholar and translator, psychism was a happily accepted fact; and we can catch something of the feeling of "remanence" as the dowsers call it, in the lines in his rendering of Euripides' Hyppolytus concerning the seas Goddess Dictynna –

Who in Limna here can find thee,

For the Deep's dry floor is her easy way,

And she moves in the salt wet whirl of the spray.

The past is not dead, and the future has its voices of promise. To live in continual full consciousness of this unity of all Time would doubtless be perilous in the workaday world, but the knowledge of that unity, and the acceptance of it – many folk experiences it occasionally in dreams – is a part of that enlargement of consciousness which does indeed give us, here and now, "life more abundantly". Another, closely related part of that enlargement of consciousness is that unity and continuity of life expressed in the Song of Amergin, quoted at length for us by Philip Shallcrass in his paper on The Bardic Tradition.

These reflections have been prompted by my first reading of The Druid Renaissance in MS, for through it I have been caught into many areas of past happenings, of present work in the inner as well as outer world, and of eager looking into the future. Some topics are familiar ground to me, some are new; some names have previously been known to me and some not: but, all in all, the book brings the delight and stimulation of exploration in the company of friends.

I met Isaac Bonewits in the American Midwest, back in the seventies. He was always a "live wire" in the Pagan movement, and this presentation of his more recent work, in The Druid Revival in Modern America, is of much interest. "Paganism", to accept a popular word of wide application, is a powerful force in the widespread root0seeking nostalgia of the Americas. Hard-and-fast ethnic or regional boundaries cannot and should not be attempted, but certain focal points can be noted. The People of the Land are rallying to the memory and reconstruction of their own Native American traditions and ceremonies; Santeria, Voudoun and allied forms of belief and ritual find their chief allegiance in the further South; but Druidry, with its strong affinity with the world of Nature, holds – as is demonstrated by Isaac Bonewits, by Erynn Rowan Laurie in The Preserving Shrine, and by Graham Harvey in Passage – the most fertile promise for those of European stock and/or tradition.

Graham Harvey's article is, certainly, not related particularly to the American continents but to the whole human race. Is this nostalgia for a lost earth – for Eden, for Tir na nOg, for Guinee, for the Golden Age – an essential part of human nature? Even the strictest monotheists have their harvest or vintage festival, their feast of Tabernacles or other acknowledgement of participation in the wholeness of life. In the words of Joni Mitchell, 'We've got to get ourselves back to the garden'. Or re-create the garden around ourselves? And within ourselves?

However, being no great believer in labels I would not align Druidry entirely with any label, and with that of Paganism I cannot. There must be many Christians who feel that they would gain much by taking literally the injunction to consider the lilies of the field, or to look upon the fields when they are white (or yellow or golden brown) to the harvest: or, with the Psalmist, to consider the heavens, the moon and the stars, and perhaps even to sleep under them. The rules for the Jewish Feast of the Tabernacles enjoins that one's hut or tent should not be completely roofed over: that there should be some aperture through which the lights of heaven can shine. Sometimes people have asked me what I consider to be the quickest and easiest way of awakening their psychic powers: my answer is, spend at least three nights under the stars. Gautama Buddha received enlightenment beneath the branches of a living tree. The prophet Muhammad said that every prophet had been a shepherd, and he knew what he was talking about.

Relating the subject of Christianity to The Druid Renaissance, hwoever, there are some thoughts that I must utter. Treated more inwardly in Frank Owen's paper Nemeton, more outwardly in Gordon Strachan's And Did Those Feet?, is the enduring legend of the visit of some, or all, of the founding fathers of Christianity to Britain. And it is a most enduring legend. One may ask, why? And if there is truth in it, again why is there? If these famous personages, or at least others of that ilk, came to these shores, how can we account for the matter?

Inwardly, psychologically, there is cause enough why the soul of a believer should cling to such tradition. A person does not wish a dichotomy in the great loves of his or her life: the loved land and the loved faith must in some manner be brought together. But to argue thus is only to show cause why people perpetuate a tradition. It gives no ground for either accepting or rejected the tradition itself in its plain, outer-world interpretation.

The framework of a theoretical visit by a "young Jesus" with Joseph of Arimathea is easily formulated. Phoenician traders, as a historical fact, came to south-west Britain. Joseph was a merchant, and Galilee is next door to Phoenicia; Phoenicia indeed contains the home of the tribe of Dan, which "went down to the sea in ships". Easily, then, one pictures Joseph bringing along on one of his voyages the keen-witted, fearless lad with a taste for mystical debate. But there is more to the epic, for an epic it is. There is a presumption of the departure, after the crucifixion, of all the intimates of Jesus of Nazareth from Palestine. There is the legend that the body of the apostle James, albeit he met his death in Palestine, was brought to Compostela, in the province of Galicia, in north-western Spain. There is the very mysterious legend of the Fisher-King, which evidently belongs to the same corpus of tradition with the rest. There is the legend of the death of Mary Magdalene at Lyons, on the Rhone. And there is the story of the arrival at last of Joseph of Arimathea in Glastonbury, bearing those relics of blood and sweat which afterwards gave rise to the sublimated Grail mythology – for a mythology it surely is.

Not attempting here to piece these fragments together, I come back only to my original question, why should such a journey have been directed to Britain? And I will give my suggested answer before following my reasons for it through the interstices of history. The journey was made, and took the course that it did, because the personages in question were basically Celts and sought to be among Celts.

I will not be pedantic about gathered material, which is after all not very much. But t should enable those who so desire, to verify the matter without it becoming tiresome to other readers. The people of my question were from Galilee, and we can begin there. The western limits of its territory bordered Phoenicia, which was such a narrow strip of coastal land that western Galilee itself was not far distant from the Mediterranean. Always a prosperous region through trade as well as from the fertility of the land, Galilee was never very clearly defined in extent. During some considerable period, it extended so far as to include the Cities of the Plain.

Customarily the Israelites of olden times referred to Galilee as "Galilee of the Nations". This was not a compliment. The Galileans were a mixed people, probably to a considerable extent Pagans, and with a large proportion of Canaanites who were accepted peaceably by their Jewish and other neighbours. In such matters the Galileans were easy, tolerant folk; although throughout their history they had the reputation of being fiercely courageous, inured to war from childhood, and contemptuous alike of bribery and of the fear of death. Honour, and independence of spirit were all to them. Not surprisingly they were also described as changeable, habitually opposed to established authority, and prone to sedition.

These same people, however, were industrious and skilful, pursuing every kind of calling for which their fertile and beautiful land provide the materials. Arbela was renowned for its woollen cloth, Bethshean for its linen. Wine, honey, olives, nuts and a profusion of aromatics made life pleasant for the people of the land and gave them rich goods for commerce. Not only the Mediterranean but the Sea of Galilee enabled the region to provide salted fish for the whole of Judaea. At Megiddo there entered Galilee the great merchant-road which ran via Damascus into Egypt. On contrast to Judaea, at no time was this a poor land or a people burdened by toil.

Nevertheless, Judaea was not eager to appropriate Galilee, Perhaps the Galileans were too independent, their speech too noticeably different, their practice and general attitude in religious matters too irreconcilable with Judaean traditions to make any such approach comfortable. Certain it is that by the commencement of the present era the population of Galilee was even more cosmopolitan than it had been in early times, with Greeks, Arabs and Egyptians noted among the numbers. But it is not, I believe, among these later developments that we must look for an explanation of the matter that I am pursuing. It appears to go back into the early history of the region.

At this point I must explain briefly my attitude to the New Testament as we now have it. Detailed exegesis would be too tedious and too complex. Let us take the document as it stands, with its admixture of history, of myth, of faulty reporting, bias, all flaws we tolerate in other documentation every day of our lives. In spite of these there is, it seems to me, a core of consistent narrative in which one can see truth without thereby being a Christian.

My own opinion is that there really lived in Galilee, at something about the period indicated, the man whose name we have in garbled form as Jesus of Nazareth. His family claimed to be descended from David. We are not told how long they had been settled in Nazareth, but they were evidently altogether at home there. It may have been generations; it was very likely centuries. At any event, I am convinced that the reason why they were there is that Galilee was their ancestral home.

The circumstances stand thus. David was a descendant of Ruth, and Ruth was a descendant of Moab. Certainly, David had other relatives, friends and allies, but he repeatedly showed a partiality fro the Moab folk; we can suppose he felt some particular affinity with them.

Ruth was indeed of the race of Abraham – they all were – but her descent was by a rather distinctive line. When, gleaning in the fields, she was noticed by the landowner Booz who subsequently married her, what caught his attention was that she was different from the other Israelite girl gleaners. Unfortunately, we are not told in what way she was different. She undoubtedly has a different accent, but this is hardly likely to have been in her features, her posture, her colouring: any or all of these. Ruth was a descendant of Abraham's nephew Lot, thereby also of the lady reputed to have turned to a pillar of salt when the cities of the Plain were destroyed. We are not told the name or family of that lady.

As to the Cities of the Plain, it is useless to try to fathom exactly what calamity overtook them. There seems to be no evidence of earthquake or meteorite, but the earth is so rich in bitumen and sulphur that fire might have been involved. A violent whirlwind might have occurred, and there is a mountain of readily fragmented sodium minerals in the region. Certainly, in ancient times cities existed – probably there were five of them, probably Canaanite cities – and then, just as certainly, they ceased to exist. Most likely there was a dearth of surviving witnesses, but there are several such unexplained cataclysms in the course of history and prehistory. The shock and dread caused in that era by the calamity can be measured by the horrendous story woven to explain it, so that good folk might live on, assured that no such fate would overtake them.

But against this background of vague nightmare, one story stands out: the story of the woman who could have survived, but that she must linger for one last look back at her home. A most probable reason presents itself. Lot was a sojourner there, but his wife was surely native to the city. Were her people Canaanites, or perhaps of the stock of those other Galileans who had possessed the region? Does the omission of her name from the story perhaps suggest that?

Lot and his wife had two daughters, neither of whose names or marriages are recorded. The family seemed at this point to have passed out of the annals of Israel. But the elder of these daughters was the mother of Moab, himself a patriarchal character who established a new blood-line in the nation, the "Moabites", even as his younger brother's descendents became known as the "Ammonites". Presumably they all spoke Hebrew, as nothing is recorded to the contrary; but that it was a dialect form of the language seems sure. And Ruth, descendent of Moab, was the grandmother of Jesse, whose youngest son was David: shepherd, warrior, king, harpist, mystical poet.

We are, therefore, discussing people who were somehow distinguishable from the people of Israel as a whole, so that when we come to New Testament times this distinction is not to be considered simply as a prejudice on the part of the Jews of Jerusalem. Besides the matter of accent, there was certainly a matter of colouring; in some individuals at least. David as a boy keeping his father's sheep was, we are told, "ruddy, with fine eyes, and good-looking". Again, in the story of his defeat of Goliath, it is repeated, "he was just a youth, ruddy and fair of countenance". In the Song of Solomon it is generally supposed that the figure of the Bridegroom is a portrait, perhaps a self-portrait, of Solomon, son of David: and here the Bride sings, "My beloved is white and ruddy, outstanding among ten thousand. His head is like pure gold, his locks are curly, and black as a raven." This striking combination of "white and ruddy" skin with black hair is not known, in Ireland for instance, although here the description probably indicates also a golden tan.

In the New testament we have no descriptions of anyone's appearance, but we have a fair amount of related tradition. One of the Roman emperors, I think it was Vespasian, asked to know how Jesus of Nazareth had looked. He was given a jewel with an engraved profile, ands description which included dark reddish hair, slightly curling. That is interesting because the source of that traditional in Rome would hardly have been related to a Byzantine canon which gives rules for painting ikons to depict Mary, the mother of Jesus. She should be shown, it says, with dark red hair, a complexion the colour of ripe wheat, and olive-green eyes.

Later Western artists followed their own imaginations more freely, but some traditions remained. Mary Magdalene, inevitably, is shown with glorious auburn or golden hair. The Christ figure always has reddish hair, probably following the Roman tradition already cited. The hair of Judas is always shown as positively carroty, a tradition which gave that colour a bad name for centuries and probably survives in superstition to the present day. Looking for Celtic traces in the Gospels one curious fact stands out. The story of the lost Mabon, the young son of the Goddess whose disappearance fro three days accounts for the intercalary days of the Celtic New Year – is in different forms given twice. There is the disappearance of the twelve-year-old boy (why twelve?) at Jerusalem, when, though we are told his father and mother sought him and found him in the Temple, it is his mother only who is recorded to have spoken to him reproaching his thoughtlessness. And then there is also the greater and more significant "disappearance" following his crucifixion, when he is absents himself from the material world from Friday afternoon until Sunday sunrise.

This period of absence in the realm of death is of particular significance in Byzantine tradition and also in British tradition, in which it is known as the "harrowing of Hell": the presence of the Lord of Light in the Underworld causing the release of the just who have been imprisoned there, an event which is represented as a symbolic and even an actual coming-forth of the dead from their tombs. The story is of great antiquity: certainly, older than the Egyptian Book of the Dead which contains it, for that book is an assemblage of even more texts and traditions. The twelve hours of the Night-journey are there clearly defined. But there is absolutely no connotation of "three days". We might suppose that this statement in the Gospels has no mythic connotation, were it not for that other story of the three days disappearance of the twelve-year-old boy. Even if we can give no clue as to how this strain of Celtic tradition got there, there it unmistakably is.

One more strand among these thoughts of mine should have its place here, tenuous though it may seem. It has sometimes been remarked, and with good cause, that of all the saint who have modelled their lives and characters upon that of Jesus of Nazareth, none has come near to the original as did Francis of Assisi. In Francis, indeed, the resemblance seemed, and I think truly was, based not so much on "imitation" as on a powerful natural affinity of temperament.

Francis was Italien certainly, but he was minimally Latin. His birthplace, Assisi, is in the region of Perugia: and that is the very region in which Celtic blood and culture are so persistent that James Joyce when he went there felt himself to be among Irish people who happened to speak Italian. Moreover, Francis even at home must have seemed more Celtic than most, for his mother called him her "little Frenchman", hence the name by which we know him.

What particularly Celtic characteristics, then, would I say were shared by Francis of Assisi and Jesus of Nazareth? Certainly, a gift of words and a flair for dramatic presentation. A closeness, too, to the earth, and a tenderness towards the small things of the natural world. A complete fearlessness, with a loyalty to inner truth which could annihilate all prudence. And with this independence of spirit, a subtle humour and intelligence which could in one act both obey authority and mock it.

To return to my beginning upon this theme: when anyone – Phoenecian or Galilean merchants, religious emissaries or refugees, anyone – arrived from Palestine, how did they communicate with the people of northern Spain, of France, of the West Country? Assuredly in Greek. Throughout the lands of the Mediterranean and the North, Greek was a familiar and well-accepted second language. This was particularly true in the Celtic culture, as witness the affinity between the Greek and the "public"

simply perform our rite and depart, for Glastonbury is a place of wonders. There were friends to visit, and the Museum, and the delightful Chalice Well gardens. There, once as we were strolling (how the little things stick in the memory!) a dear Red Admiral butterfly settled on the lapel of Hope Brant's cream-white coat and stayed there long enough for John Brant to be called back from the group ahead and to take a photograph.

There is more that should be said of the Brants, and this is as fitting a place as any to say it. A draughtsman by profession, John designed and painted the symbolic banners for the Groves. He also customarily sounded the trumpet for the Gorsedds, deputised for the Chief on the rare occasions of Nuinn's absence, was secretary and archivist and was in general Nuinn's right-hand man. Hope was treasurer over the whole range of monetary transactions, but also she was keeper of the non-personal regalia and advisor on all matters connected with robes generally. She was MC by instinct, and watchful as a dragon over matters of deportment and the safe-keeping of ritual objects. In their devoted loyalty to each other, to Druidry and to Nuinn, the Brants created a strong knot in the bond which united us.

Glastonbury, like Stonehenge, has besides its deep power an intense fascination. Parliament Hill is an ancient and palpable place of power, but without the same glamour. None the less, it seemed to me that of the two sites, when we held Gorsedd at Parliament Hill it held the more responsive atmosphere. Doubtless this was in part because Parliament Hill was the place of our midnight vigil, ushering in the Summer Solstice, for then the vibrancy of the site was intense: not overwhelming, but enfolding. Of Parliament Hill there are two incidents I must record. The first occurred during one of these midnight vigils, at the Summer Solstice of 1967.

We were in our circle, with torches and lanterns, and the ritual was proceeding, when chancing to look skyward I became aware of a very plainly visible UFO, apparently at that moment coming closer, and almost directly opposite me although at a good height. I had not had many UFO sightings and this was a thrilling spectacle: a brilliant sphere, with wavy bands of various fiery colours following each other rapidly across its surface. It, or its occupants presumably, seemed to be aware of us, for having descended so far the luminous sphere made a circuit of our hilltop, disappearing behind my right shoulder and reappearing above my left and then, once more opposite me, darting off on a swift oblique course, ascending and receding until it seemed simply a brighter star among the stars, then vanishing from view. It would not surprise me if that particular Druid assembly is on record in some far region of the Universe.

Of course, my impulse had been to interrupt the rite and to draw attention of my companions to the happening, but to cry out would have seemed wrong and to distract anyone from their scripts by glance or gesture proved impossible. As for Nuinn himself, he seemed, as he often did when conducting a Druid ceremony, to be in an elevated state of consciousness. Hope at one point glanced upwards and I had the impression that she might have seen the UFO, but as it happened, I had no opportunity to speak to her of it until a week later and then she was not sure what she had witnessed although she felt there had been "something". Certainly she, of all people, would have had all her attention firmly focused on the rite.

The other matter connected with Parliament Hill is an unfinished business, and I lay it here before anyone who will complete it, for I think it belongs to Druidry.

A great reason for the success of the OBOD from its inception, granting the rightness and power of the tradition in which it followed, was surely the wholehearted effort with which every one of us worked for it. We belonged to it, and it to us. We gave our free time to crafting implements for special rites, making garments, designing banners, painting, repairing things, even re-writing documents if required. Sometimes Nuinn would ask for a specific piece of work, sometimes we would simply see that something needed to be done and volunteer for it if it lay within our particular abilities. We were a family, and in his own way Nuinn treated us as such: always reserving his own time and seclusion for his own life and work, but now and then inviting one or another of our number to accompany him on some occasion of interest or significance. They were very miscellaneous occasions. I, for example, accompanied him to a Restoration comedy, a display of very classical Indian dancing, and the funeral of Charles Cammell, whose biography of Annigoni Nuinn had discussed with me on an earlier occasion.

Once in the later sixties, when we were at parliament Hill on a clear sunny day, Nuinn pointed out to us one of the few discoverable things which he had ascertained about that strangely bush-covered mound known as "Boadicea's Tomb". He had found that it, that is the summit of Parliament Hill, and the Pen Ton (the top of Pentonville Hill) and my native Bryn Gwyn form a straight line, which he indicated to us, roughly north-west to south-east. This was interesting and evidently significant, and for my part I took the idea away and digested it. I felt there might be more to be said. I got an Ordnance Survey map and put a ruler across it, through the three points in question. Extending the line to the north-west I found nothing of interest – although nobody ought to take that cursory view of mine as conclusive but extending it to the south-east, I saw that it crossed Blackheath. This was more promising, so I took myself to Blackheah with a compass, looked around, and found myself in a thoroughfare called Maze Road.

Unfortunately, I met nobody there who could tell me anything about this, so I had to put the question aside and, in the course of events, it remained put aside. But I still feel it might be worthwhile to know how Maze Road, Blackheath, got its name.

We made excursions to many sites, and always we earned more than the matter in hand. We went pendulum-dowsing at Cadbury Castle, and as we were on questions of earth-magnetism, Nuinn drew our attention to some stately and magnificent trees in the area and encouraged us to find how we could renew our energies by standing with back pressed closely against the trunk. Elsewhere one might see him as essentially the man of cairns and the standing-stones, but among trees another side of his character emerged and rejoiced. He was Nuinn, the Ash tree, and "woodsman of the woods". Customarily we all went to a piece of woodland which he owned, on a steep hillside near Henley-on-Thames, fro our Lughnasadh rites, and a grand picnic outing it made for us, a last breath of summer freedom as the leaves were beginning to brown. Such experiences of the natural world gave to us town-dwellers a fuller sense of the reality of our Druidry.

This brings me to the closing theme of this Afterword. What does Druidry really offer to humanity? I would answer in one word: Humanity. We can look back to the Song of Amergin, and reflect upon it:

Being a stone, I must crystallise within the womb of Earth,

Being a plant, I must root well in the Earth that I may grow.

Being a fish, I must wash in the waters, swim and be clean.

Being a land-creature, I must set my feet firmly on Earth and look Life in the face.

Being a bird, I must soar to the heights.

Being human, I must live in all worlds fro I am all worlds:

Yet must I lose none of them.

If I do not crystallise I can give no light.

If I lose my roots I cannot grow.

If I do not swim, or walk, or soar, I have lost part of my life.

For a number of years now I have been a student of Qabalah. All teachings concerning humanity, if they teach truth and not fantasy, must come to one point in the end for there is only one human nature. And if you call it Qabalah, or Druidry, or what you will, the truth is that as human beings we are one with all life, and all life is one with us. And we each of us, whether consciously or not, live in the four Worlds – of matter, of feeling, of mind and of spirit – and without that fourfold life no person is complete in himself or herself.

So-called "Western civilisation" has been too clever and is leading the world astray. For various reasons – first religious, then intellectual – "Western civilisation" has cut itself off from it roots. Some people among us, seeing this error, have felt called to separate themselves from our whole heritage to become Buddhists, Taoists, Shamans. If they have found ways of life which bring them peace, then peace let it be. But I believe that our Western tradition – which does not consist in eating trash bread and corrupt meats, nor in trying to find the whole meaning of life shut among city walls – I believe that our Western tradition ahs something better to offer the world, something which the world desperately needs. It is not a matter of religion. It is not even a matter of philosophy, for right human living is needful before a person can find their true choice in matters either of spirit or of intellect.

It is, if you like to call it so, a matter of Alchemy. It has been said, "If you want to put the world right, begin with yourself." In its measure this is true counsel, but it needs a corollary. The Alchemist says, "If you want to work upon your inner self, start working on something outside yourself." Follow your talents. Purify your metals, find and test the virtue of new alloys, and you will find their virtues within yourself. Paint or sculpt beauty and strength, and you will find and refine your inner beauty and strength. If you are an accountant, seek and find absolute integrity in your calculations. If you are a teacher, above all teach your pupils to learn. If you prepare food, prepare it as food truly. Live fully and with a good will, and your inner will shall be good. That, it seems to me, is the meaning of Alchemy, and the meaning of Druidry too.

But the opportunity must be there. Just as we must be able to get out of the towns and look at the stars, live among the trees and all living things, eat decent food, breathe decent air and find time for study, rest and meditation, so we must teach others to seek the same qualities of life. For a Druid, whether a member of a named organisation or a druid in spirit, must by some means teach. But can others do what the Druid counsels? Or will future generations be able to do so? Now, as never before, we need all the power we can gather, that the pendulum may swing, the tide may turn, before too late. That is why, besides our present knowledge and understanding, we need all the wisdom we can gather from the past, to meditate it, pre-digest it, for the aid of the future. "Let's give it good nurture!" Truly in this age, people in many lands are turning more and more to the Mother. For she is not only the Earth-Mother, from who we draw our life and to whom we owe our outmost help. She is also Brighid the all-powerful. She is Mary, and Modron. And she is the Divine Sophia, Holy Wisdom. Wherever we may find her and by whatever name – in the ancient cave-shrines, in the forest groves, upon the mountain, in whatever building or holy place – it is indeed Holy Wisdom whose guidance we need. But guided, the work must be ours.

The Lore of Incenses

By *Vivian Godfrey White (Melita Denning).*
6th Grand Master of the Order Aurum Solis.

The following discourse was delivered as a lecture for the Order at Kingsway Hall in London on October 17th 1967, by a member of the Ovate Og grade, who later became known as the occult writer Melita Denning, who acted as the Order's Presider from 1992 to 1997. Her paper discusses incense ingredients in detail and looks at their planetary associations.

Figure 1: Vivian Godfrey (Melita Denning) on the left lights the Yule Candles.

In the blending of incenses, as I shall show later, substances of animal, vegetable and mineral origin are used: but by far the greater number come from the vegetable kingdom, and the use of aromatic vegetable gums for various purposes goes back to remotest antiquity. In Genesis 43, listed among the substances which the brethren of Joseph took into Egypt to trade for wheat in a time of famine, we find mentioned storax, and stacte, of both of which I shall have something to say later, and terebinth trees, whose wood, we know is full of a fragrant oil. We cannot of course take for granted that these materials were intended for use as incense. The name of storax is used for two substances, one of which is otherwise known as stacte: but since stacte is also named here, we can suppose that the storax in question is the other storax, better named styrax, as the Greeks called it, in order to avoid confusion.

Styrax is a greyish, syrupy liquid, a balsam in fact, obtained from the tree or shrub *Liquidambar Orientalis*. It grows in various parts of Asia Minor but not in Egypt, and the ancient Egyptians valued it as an ingredient in perfumes and sometimes for use in mummification. We know this because it has been found by analysis in the contents of perfume-jars and in embalming materials found in the Egyptian tombs. When used in an incense mixture, it should be mixed with other ingredients such as dried herbs, powdered orris or the like, which will partially absorb it.

The arts of the physician, the perfumer, the incense-blender and the embalmer were closely related in early times, for the same precious aromatic substances were used by each. Many of you, even in this present century, may remember being given some tincture of benzoin on a lump of sugar for a chest- cough, while through the ages the antiseptic and healing properties of powdered myrrh were famous as a dressing for wounds, and only went out in the nineteenth century when the use of the sword began to wane.

Another aromatic gum which I have here to show you is Galbanum. This is a native of Persia: it does not come from a woody plant, but from a group of species in the family Umbelliferae, the same family to which our little cow-parsley belongs. Other members of that same family give us such diverse products as Angelica - when you eat pieces of its candied green stems on top of your iced cake, you can reflect that now no demon will come near you - and Hemlock, the most notable poison of antiquity, which gained a perpetual place in our history by taking Socrates out of this world.

The chief producer of Galbanum, if anyone wants its scientific name, is *Ferula galbaniflua*, and the earliest reference to the gum itself, again Biblical, is, this time, in our first indisputable list of ingredients for use as a sacred fumigant: "The Lord said to Moses: Take aromatic substances, stacte and onycha, galbanum of a good odour, and the clearest frankincense, equal parts..." Exodus 30-34. If you read this passage you will notice that a non-aromatic mineral substance, salt, is to be mixed with the ingredients. The purifying and preserving properties of salt, perhaps its healing value as an antiseptic also, had already acquired a symbolic value: and it was in order to represent or even to induce these qualities on the spiritual level, that the salt was to be added to the mixture. Before I pass on further, I want to say a word about the general difficulty of identifying substances named in ancient documents. Even with the two Biblical references which I have already given you, if you compare two or three different versions of the Bible you will find considerable variations, although to most readers this is of no importance. The main trouble is that many ancient traditions, Biblical and otherwise, have been translated from time to time into different languages on their way to us: and usually at some time they have been translated into Greek. The Greeks fixed a name for various objects and materials which belonged to other cultures than their own. These words became parts of the Greek language, and later, when the first object or material had passed out of use or had found a new name in another language, the disused Greek word would be taken up as a convenient name for a somewhat similar object or material. To make this clearer, I will take as an example the word sappheiros, which was the name given by the ancient Greeks to the semi-precious stone which we call by a mixed Latin and Arabic name, lapis lazuli. The sapphire of the High Priest's breastplate was lapis lazuli. When you read in the prophecies of Ezekiel of sapphire, the word means lapis lazuli. When you read in the legends of our country that St. David of Wales brought back among his treasures from the Holy Land a chalice carved from a single piece of sapphire, it was lapis lazuli, and quite probable. Lapis was a sacred material; the ancient Egyptians ground it to powder for use in writing hieroglyphic inscriptions on the royal sarcophagi, just as the church artists of the Middle Ages ground it to produce the wonderful ultramarine for the Virgin's robe or for the brilliant blue skies in the miniatures in the illuminated books. But when the name lapis lazuli came in, the name sappheiros was forgotten, and today is applied to a another brilliantly blue stone, of greater monetary worth, but with no ancient associations.

Confusion of another kind, confusion not in translation but in transliteration, has done its share in confusing the ancient recipes. Take for instance the Greek word *nitron*, from which, through Arabic, English also has derived *natron*. The first means simple nitre, saltpetre as we call it, or potassium nitrate. Saltpetre is frequently added to substances which do not burn easily, to induce a more ready combustion. It is of no use whatsoever in any process to do with embalming. Natron on the other hand is soda as it occurs in the natural state, usually washing soda with a certain admixture of sodium bicarbonate. The Egyptians used it extensively in embalming. It is of no use whatever in incense, and if you put any sort of soda on a fire you will have unpleasant fumes and may easily put the fire out. Yet these two substances are frequently confused in modern translations of various recipes. You have to use your judgement, according to the purpose of the recipe.

Another difficulty in tracing the ancient history of incense ingredients, is that even if there exists a pictorial representation to help us, it may not in fact help very much. For example: the female Pharaoh Hatshepsut, somewhere about the year 1470 BC, sent off a famous expedition to the Land of Punt. This expedition duly returned, laden with products of that country, amongst which there are enumerated a quantity of trees which yielded incense gums. On the walls of the Queen's mortuary chapel at Deir el Bahari, we see a representation of these trees. They seem to be of two kinds: one kind without leaves, one kind with leaves. But what exactly is the artist trying to show us? This may remind you of one of Kipling's Just-So stories. (Remember that nobody is quite sure where the Land of Punt may be, so we cannot begin by seeing what kind of gum-bearing trees it produces.)

Perhaps [when we see the illustration of a tree without leaves] the artist is saying "Our men, being acquainted with matters of horticulture, knew that to transport deciduous trees from one country to another it is best to take them when they are leafless, but, so that you may know what kind of tree they brought back, I will depict some with their leaves on." [So a similar tree is shown with leaves].

If he meant this, it does not help us very much, because from sheer force of habit he drew the usual little conventional tree that he drew all the time, although in fact, it does look rather like a myrrh-tree. But supposing this is not what he meant? Supposing he meant "Our men brought back trees of two kinds, one kind which has leaves, and another which has none." Now in that case, his evidence becomes very interesting, because there actually is a species of frankincense tree which never at any time of year has more than the merest rudimentary leaves; and this tree grows in Somaliland. Myrrh also is found growing in Somaliland; and many Egyptologists are now accepting the hypothesis that Somaliland was the legendary Land of Punt.

Frankincense, or olibanum, takes first place among the aromatic gums. Those of you who are familiar with the smell of church incense, will recognise this as giving it the distinctive and predominating smell: indeed, the main preoccupation of the blenders of church incense seems to be the preservation and fortification of the smell of olibanum, whilst introducing various other ingredients to lengthen its

time of burning and to reduce the cost. In Egypt, in the temple of Ra at Heliopolis, pure frankincense was the offering at every sunrise. Its use passed to the shrines of Greece and to the temples of Imperial Rome, where one finds it designated as thus. Of its later history I shall have more to say presently.

Before proceeding to the next aspect of my subject, there is one more confusion of names which I should like to mention to you, because it offers us a convenient way out of a practical difficulty. One of the finest incenses of the ancient world, bitter yet attractively fragrant, rather like myrrh or saffron but richer, was that known as Aloes. It was pressed from the leaves of a rare plant of the family Liliaceae [reclassified in 2003 as Asphodelaceae], of which the chief source, perhaps the only source, was the island of Socotra. Like many other incense ingredients, it also had medicinal uses, and these uses are equally well served by the more plentiful and cheaper related species, Barbados aloes and Cape aloes. But these will not do as a substitute for use as incense: when burned, they smell thoroughly unpleasant. Unfortunately, to use the true Socotrine aloes is out of the question: it would be fabulously expensive, in fact I have not for many years seen even a mention of Socotrine aloes as a marketed commodity [ED. *It is now available commercially in 2012*]. But there is an alternative of quite respectable antiquity, a substance named as aloes in recipes dating at any rate from before the time of Christ. This is a kind of fragrant wood, with a smell not unlike that of Socotrine aloes, but sweeter and less pungent. The tree grows in parts of India and the wood was introduced by Arab traders. Sometimes it is known as eagle-wood, perhaps from a peculiar feather-type mottling which appears in the grain, but equally likely, I should think, from a corruption of its Arabic name, Agallocha. The wood of this tree (Aquilaria agallocha), or from a closely related tree which grows in China, is fairly plentiful and not outrageously expensive; so that in any incense recipe which calls for aloes, one should not hesitate which kind to use, but should use eagle-wood. Even here, however, experiment is not to be recommended; both the Indian and the Chinese species of eagle-wood are quite safe, but other species of Aquilaria and of the family Thymelaeaceae may not be.

Incidentally, no substance used in incense is poisonous, even those materials which have an unpleasant smell are non-toxic. I have here, carefully sealed with adhesive tape, a bottle of Asafoetida gum: in the Middle ages it had a great reputation for banishing demons, but unfortunately it tends to banish anyone else with any sense of smell who comes within range of it. I have never ventured to burn any of it: its mere smell unburned is more than enough for me; but here it is, and

any hardy soul who wishes to try it is welcome to remove the tape and take a sniff. But it is quite harmless; in fact, the Romans used it as a flavouring ingredient in their cooking. I have no notion why. In the great temples of various lands, blended incenses of extraordinary complexity came to be used. A famous Egyptian recipe, known as Kyphi, found in a rather late papyrus, is one example of this: it names a number of ingredients, some unidentifiable, others open to more than one interpretation, after the manner of the examples I have given. Many attempts have been made to reconstruct this incense recipe; and one such attempt at any rate seems to me a thoroughly convincing success: I have not brought any with me, because the regulations here forbid me to burn anything, and although I think you can judge something of the quality of single substances by their smell in an unburnt state, this would not be possible with anything so complex as Kyphi. I do not know its exact composition: but olibanum and cinnamon, perhaps with cloves also, seem to predominate.

Another very complex incense undoubtedly was that used at the Temple at Jerusalem. I have a recipe which is claimed to be ancient, and which was certainly made up at one time for a number of synagogues where it was believed to be so, although for various reasons I would not suppose that as it stands it goes back to any remote date. But various substances may from time to time through the centuries have been substituted for others in the recipe, and I am willing to believe that the ancient original was almost, if not quite as complex. If so, then it must have inevitably contained a great proportion of the same ingredients, since the number of aromatic gums available both then and now is not so large as to allow of a very different selection. The ingredients are: Benzoin, cascarilla, balsam of tolu, orris of the valley, vervain, star anise, myrrh, Indian frankincense, Arabian frankincense, potassium nitrate (that is the saltpetre I was talking about, which is added merely to improve combustibility), powdered gold - I shall say more about that in a moment – powdered mint, melilot flowers, orange flowers, bay leaves, patchouli, borax, amber, Sumatra benzoin, white sugar, Chinese myrrh, red sandalwood, and a number of floral essences - rose, jasmine, violet, mignonette, bergamot, musk, oil of cloves and so on – added in liquid form, in small quantity.

Notice amongst all this the powdered gold. Here again, as with the Exodus recipe, we have a non-aromatic mineral substance added to the mixture, from fairly obvious motives: to make a costlier and worthier offering, to emphasise the regal aspect of the deity, and to represent the corporate nature of the community; for as blood is to the body of the individual, so gold is, or was, to the body of the community. If gold used in this way was indeed an ancient ingredient in oriental incenses – and I see no reason whatever to doubt it – then a very interesting consequence follows: the three offerings of the Magi to the infant Christ, the gold as well as the frankincense and myrrh, were all incense ingredients, and may well have been offered as such.

But with these considerations I have begun already to bring in the symbolic values of various substances; and before I review these in detail, it would be suitable to pose the questions: Why are incense ingredients selected to have a symbolic value? Why do some religions use incense and not others? What relation has this to the use of incense by magicians? Why in fact does anyone, anywhere, use incense at all?

Making a general survey of the situation, we see, first, that there are certain forms of religion, and certain forms of magic also, in which incense has no place. Those, if I may again put it in general terms, are the religion which has no magic in it, and the magic which has no religion in it. A God who is seen either as completely transcendental, or as entirely indwelling, is not worshipped with incense. A magician who places complete reliance on his own concentration of mind, again does not use incense.

The domain of incense, then, may be defined as that area of human thought and activity in which magic and religion overlap: where the will of the individual and the will of some external power or powers, alike are recognised as existent, and a bridge of some kind is sought for so as to co-ordinate the two. The use of the sense of smell is important here. The senses of touch and of taste are limited in their scope to the material world. The sense of sight is not quite so limited, if we consider the influence of light as a link with the more spiritual planes, and indeed the use of lamps with glass of a carefully chosen colour has long been known in the more esoteric aspects of both religion and magic; but the science of coloured light, like the esoteric science of sound which also has an important role to fulfil, belong largely to the future; whereas the vibrations of smell, a recognition of which is necessary in work with incenses, have been studied and expertly used for many ages and in many lands.

Even so there is a limitation in the development of this art, which for a long time I failed to understand. This is the limitation of the Table of Correspondences, which I am about to discuss in more detail. Unfortunately I have not yet been able to discover exactly what rules govern the burning of incense in India, for instance, but it is quite evident that there does exist in India a feeling, or perhaps something stronger than a feeling, that some incenses are suitable to the worship of certain gods and some are unsuitable, while to certain gods no incense is suitable. I realise, also, that in practices which we should describe as magical rather than religious, and also in Tantra-Yoga, the prescriptions as to a suitable incense are much more carefully laid down than is the case for ordinary purposes of devotion. I have not made a detailed study of those prescriptions, but I have understood that there is a system which is the closest parallel to what I am going to describe, the system that has developed in the West, where a series of faculties in man's psychic and material composition, are postulated as corresponding to certain beings in the world of the gods: and to these again, certain objects, colours, and odours in the outer material world are found to be in harmony: and the heavenly bodies too, in their astrological significance, are attuned to these various modes or attributes. That sounds as if some vast and complex system underlay it all, but in reality it is all very simple: the range of attributes under consideration, and the range of deities and luminaries under consideration, are limited to those which correspond to the recognised attributes of man.

This limitation may surprise you, but here is an example. Supposing, on one of these winter evenings, I look out at the sky, and follow the line of the belt of Orion upward to the right until I came to the stellar cluster that is the Hyades. I gaze at it, and then every evening I make a habit of glancing up to make sure 'my star', Aldebaran, is still there, but this is not enough. Supposing I am rather a religious-minded person of one sort or another. It occurs to me that some god, if I put it in polytheistic terms, or some angel, if I follow Judeo-Christian ideas, or some aspect of the Divine Mind, if I am a Platonist, must be ultimately concerned with Aldebaran. Obviously, or the star would not be there. And I should like to establish a friendly relationship with that god, or angel, or aspect. To make a beginning, perhaps I should burn a suitable incense. So I consult all my books and I ask all my friends, but I find nothing. It can't be done, and perhaps my friends begin to wonder if I am quite a proper human being to suggest such a thing. Because there is nothing charted in the human personality to correspond with Aldebaran.

This is logical, you see. Incense, as I pointed out, makes a psychic bridge: and it is useless trying to throw a bridge over to that side if you have no solid foundation on this side. In short, if I had picked on one of the planets - say Venus or Mercury or Jupiter - if I had worshipped the sun or cried for the moon - then what I suggested would be feasible because all these planets and the deities associated with them, correspond with something known and charted in the human personality. The bridge would have two ends.

I don't say that I personally accept these limits, because if, as I believe, every human being is a microcosm, a miniature model of the universe, then somewhere in the microcosm there must be something corresponding to Aldebaran, Rigel, Betelgeux, Sirius, and all those other splendours, as well as to the planets. But what it is, remains at present unknown and unrecognised.

I have not been digressing here. I hope that what I have said, makes it more intelligible that incense is not meant to be pleasing only to the gods, while the worshipper goes out for a breath of fresh air: nor is it meant simply to help the magician to achieve some feat of auto-suggestion, although if he believes in no power outside his own personality he may possibly use it for that purpose in a rather illogical fashion. It is a subtle mode of setting up a vibration of the ether which tends to attract certain powers and certain conditions from without, whilst at the same time acting through the sense of smell upon the psychic state of the incarnate person present, so that these persons and those powers may come into a closer unity of purpose and of operation.

Just in order to check up on the validity of this description, I have taken a glance here once more at the accepted religious uses of incense. With regard to Catholic Christianity for instance, a lot of people seem to imagine incense smoke pouring out of the churches at every hour of the day, but in fact its use is strictly limited. It is not offered to God in his transcendent aspects; not to God the Father for instance; it is not offered to any of the saints, not even to the Blessed Virgin: it is offered only to Jesus Christ, the God-Man, in the Holy Eucharist. So, incense is used at Mass and at the Benediction of the Blessed Sacrament; and that is all: in other words, when the emphasis is most clearly on the communion of deity and worshipper. In Islam, the more strict sects do not use incense at all: the less orthodox, or more mystical, do use it. With regard to the Jewish religion, I have no information; I told you earlier in this talk of a very elaborate incense recipe which used to be made up for certain synagogues in France, but how they used it or on what occasions I do not know. Perhaps someone will be able to tell me.

Reverting to the more magical uses of incense, the range of entities and vibrations to be reached is, as I have said, limited to the range of human faculties as represented by the planetary system: but within that range, the table of correspondences, as we call it, can be used in a number of ways.

You will realise that at least in the Indo-European mythologies, a considerable amount of agreement can be found as to the character of the various deities. The stories told about their adventures vary considerably with time, place, and nation, and yet something remains of the essential character. Usually we keep to the Greek and Roman concepts because those are the most closely related to our astrological system. The planets themselves are named from the Roman mythology, so here, to avoid confusion, I will call the deities by their Greek names and reserve the Roman names for the corresponding planets. Here are two very much simplified tables, which nevertheless will give you a good working notion of what I am talking about:

Sun (1)

Divinity: Helios
Resins and plants: Olibanum, Cinnamon, Vanilla, Laurel, Heliotropin
Color: Orange

Moon (2)

Divinity: Artemis/ Pallas
Resins and plants: Camphor, Galbanum, Aloes, Almond, Hazel, all lilies, Bay
Color: White
Jupiter (4)
Divinity: Zeus
Resins and plants: Oak, Nutmeg, Cedarwood, Pine-gum
Color: Deep blue
Mercury (5)
Divinity: Hermes
Resins and plants: Mastic, Lavender, Fennel, Sandalwood, Wormwood. (As psychopomp: Liquid Storax, Spikenard
Color: Yellow
Venus (6)
Divinity: Aphrodite
Resins and plants: Red storax, Benzoin, Amber, Roses, Verbena, Sandalwood, Coral, Saffron
Color: Green
Saturn (8)
Divinity: Kronos/Pa
Resins and plants: Myrrh, Asafoetida, Pepperwort, Violet leaves, Jet, Gaiac wood
Color: Black
Mars (9)
Divinity: Ares
Resins and plants: Opopanax, Tobacco, Aloes wood
Color: Bright red
Neptun (3)
Divinity: Poseidon/ Dionysos
Resins and plants: Olive leaves and oil, Ambergris, Myrrh, Liquid Storax, Iodine crystals, Wine, Ivy
Color: Crimson
Pluto (7)
Divinity: Hades / Serapis
Resins and plants: Olibanum, Jasmine, Poppy, aromatic roots
Color: Violet
Uranus (10)
Divinity: Ouranos/Psyche

Resins and plants: Dittany, Barley, aromatic seeds
Color: Turquoise blue

The first table is solidly traditional: the signs of the seven planets known to antiquity, the numbers traditionally associated with them, the names of the corresponding Greek deities, a selection of the aromatic gums and herbs associated with each, and the generally accepted ritual colours. The numbers as I have said, are traditional, and it never seemed to worry anyone that these did not form a continuous series. This however was the consideration which tempted me to try to fit the missing numbers to the more recently-discovered planets. In fact, what I offer you in the lower part of the table is entirely the result of my own research and has no authority other than the ideas which guided me in making it. But now let me run through the whole table and pick out some interesting points.

Heliotropin - You will see this mentioned among the substances dedicated to Helios, and you will not be surprised. I will pass round a sample of this white crystalline powder: you may detect an odour something like vanilla or bitter almonds, but on being burned this is really pungent. It makes quite a satisfactory ingredient in a sun-mixture, but in fact its traditional presence here is due to a misunderstanding. This substance comes from the delightful little sweet-scented plant that we used to call 'Cherry-pie'. Its official name is heliotrope, and when I was a child, I used to watch it carefully to see when it would turn towards the sun as the sunflowers did, but of course this never happened. The plant is called heliotrope because its blossoms are heliotrope-coloured, that is a mixture of red- purple and blue. What, then, is the true heliotrope, from which the fragrant plant is named?

Those of you who went with the Atlantis society to Brighton a couple of weeks ago, will remember mention being made by one of the speakers there, of 'sun-stones'. Sun-stones are blue stones which were much valued by navigators in ancient times, because even on a clouded day they will turn pink when pointed in the direction of the sun. One of the old names for that stone is Heliotrope, for obvious reasons; and from that stone the mingled red-purple and blue flowers of our little plant were called

Heliotrope flowers. But all the same, the fact remains that their essential oil smells very much like vanilla, which is a true sun-essence, and therefore Heliotropin does very well in the same company. Occultism is full of such happenings, where the scientifically-minded can point out a thousand times some flaw in the reasoning, but the conclusion of the faulty reasoning persists in holding good all the same.

Luna - I think that all I want to point out here is that besides Artemis and Pallas, whom I have named, Luna has also to accommodate the different aspects of the Triple-Goddess. I have not dealt with these in detail, but anyone interested can do it. For instance: all lilies, typical moon-plants, have their parts in threes: three or six petals, three divisions to the seed-pod, three sides to the stem.

Jupiter - Zeus - I think everything here is fairly obvious.

Hermes - Here again we have various aspects of Hermes to accommodate, and as one of them is the Physician we could put in all the medicinal herbs. However, most of these, although highly aromatic in their natural state, when burned smell just like any other burning leaves, so there is not much point in including them. Lavender and fennel are exceptions, and I have included them, both the plant itself and the essential oil are very suitable for use in incense. You all know oil of lavender, but I have brought along some Oil of Fennel because it is worth knowing. Even in these sophisticated days it is still in the British Pharmacopoeia: it can be used as a carminative instead of Oil of Peppermint; but its place in our collection here, as an aromatic oil which is still not too fabulously expensive, is rather more distinguished than its place in the Pharmacopoeia.

Hermes, you will recall, is not only the physician of the living but also the guide of the dead. Liquid Storax and Oil of Spikenard have particular associations here, but if you want to fortify some spiritualistic work with a little incense-burning and you have no Oil of Spikenard handy - I see that even Margaret Bruce has marked it 'No longer available' in her latest catalogue, so my little bottle here is particularly precious - that being so, put a few spots of Oil of Cloves on some charcoal and burn that, or of course add a clove in the natural state.

Venus - Aphrodite - In this list you will notice two substances which are associated with luck and beauty and which come out of the sea: Amber and Coral. Amber is a true aromatic. In the hardened state, in which it is used for beads, it has lost most of its aromatic quality; what one needs to use is the 'young' amber as it is called, which is pale yellow in colour and is not very hard, not having been in the sea for so long. It is washed up on our north-east coasts fairly commonly. Coral, however, is one of those non-aromatic substances, like the gold I mentioned earlier, which are added in a powdered state to incense mixtures entirely for the sake of their magical associations. Pink or white coral is preferred and is recommended especially in work that concerns children.

Kronos - Saturn - There is an unfortunate tendency to put anything which is unpleasant, sinister or worthless under the rulership of Saturn. The picture of Saturn as an avaricious and stony-hearted old man is certainly superficially convincing, but it is by no means the whole story. The Golden Age was the age of Saturn, and he identifies also very closely with Pan: as Kronos he relates to the primal concept of Pan, Kosmos, All; while as Saturn he is the rural Pan, patron of pastoral life. Simplicity is here the key word, and the life of the natural seasons, with abundance of those things which time only takes away in order to restore them new and fresh. Eight is the number of regeneration. Nevertheless, nothing can be reborn without first dying, and the black of mystery and the bitter fragrance of myrrh come in here. Jet, again, is a true incense, and this time the kind which is used for beads is aromatic: it is in fact a form of anthracite. So if you want to do a little ritual for a long and active retirement, you can sacrifice one of Aunt Jane's jet beads instead of upsetting all the neighbours by burning asafoetida.

Mars - Ares - You can smell some Opopanax now, and form your own opinion of its suitability as an incense of Mars. Personally I could wish that its rich strong odour was of a wider application; I don't have much occasion for rites of Mars, though I suppose I might do something in that line to improve my chess. Did you ever realise that tobacco was an incense, and that the tobacco pipe is a particularly ingenious form of thurible? So when the Native American Indian chief invited a former enemy to smoke the pipe of peace with him, he was in effect saying "Take part in my offering to the War-god: henceforth we are not enemies but allies."

Now we come to the second part of the chart, which is to a great extent my own.

Neptune - Poseidon - The moon, as you all know, has continually a masculine as well as a feminine aspect. Since in my general scheme of things the Moon in any case has to do duty for all aspects of the Triple Goddess as well as Luna, Dictynna and Pallas Athene, I felt that this was quite enough, and I welcomed the possibility of unloading the masculine aspect of the Moon on to Neptune. Let me remind you of a couple of points: Poseidon, the sea deity, is brother to Zeus, and those two with Pluto rule all the regions of our universe. Neptune, the planet, insofar as his attributes have yet been discovered by the astrologers, seems to rule the world of dreams, and all that region of psychic life which is symbolised by mist and by fluidity. I allotted the number 3 to him, partly because this is represented by the trident, and partly because of the numbers at my disposal, it was the only one relating directly to the 6 of Aphrodite. I think there were other considerations besides: at all events, I felt it to be a suitable number. I then accorded to Neptune those of the moon-incenses which occur in liquid form. The iodine was an idea of my own, but it seems to go very well. The myrrh is that of Myrrha or Mara, the bitterness of the sea. The colour, crimson, may startle you, but in fact crimson has long been one of the colours associated occultly with the moon; so I left Luna her more conventional white, and took this for Neptune, remembering also Homer's references to seas dark as wine. I have seen that dark wine-red in the ocean myself: I have caught glimpses of it in the Mediterranean, but on one occasion in mid-Atlantic under a brilliant March sky it was most impressive. But then by degrees I realised that under this sign I must make arrangements for Dionysos also. This first came to me in hints, subconsciously. I had to write a description in verse of Manannan, the Celtic Poseidon, and I found myself describing his dark beard against his pale face as being like ivy-leaves against the moon. The image seemed incongruous, but it persisted; the crimson colour, the intoxication of the dream world and its shifting images, the three forms of Dionysos, as man, woman and bull all settled the matter in my mind.

Pluto - The Lord of the Underworld, of darkness and mystery. If the number 3 is allotted to Neptune and 4 to Jupiter, then 7 is appropriate to the third brother of the triumvirate. Again, it is the moment before the 8 of rebirth. But Pluto is not only Hades, he is also Serapis of the mystery religions. I have chosen the plants of the hidden and mysterious things accordingly.

Uranus - The other two unallocated numbers are odd numbers, male: the 10 is an even number, and furthermore the ten is both the end and the origin of a cycle. I found myself thinking of feminine names, Urania the heavenly Muse, and Psyche the daughter of earth and bride of the Divine, and if you like also Cerridwyn [Ceridwen] of the seeds. Proclus, whom as you may remember I am rather fond of, quoting whenever possible, says that the number 10 is of earth as well as of heaven. I am not original in choosing the colour Turquoise for the planet Uranus, but the earlier people who suggested it did not seem for some reason to see its feminine connotations. Others suggest variegated or pied colours, but I will keep to my idea of turquoise for the time being. As to incense plants, there is only one besides of course aromatic seeds, which is a candidate here: Dittany of Crete. This when burned gives off very heavy smoke and was traditionally used in rites of evocation to visible appearance, in which its particles were believed to clothe astral forms, thus rendering them more readily visible. In other words, dittany is a substance which has the power to manifest the hidden, to disclose that which is secret: powers symbolic of divine fruition, of the female principle in nature. This, of course, brings us back to Proclus, where the number 10 is both transcendent and immanent: for that which is manifested on earth has its origin in heaven.

Great is the fascination of research in the incense-lore of the past; however, the requirements of the present age also call forth their own studies. In this regard, the Order of Bards, Ovates and Druids has its own distinctive incense, and this, because the Order is British and works with the spiritual currents of these islands, contains no oriental ingredients but only substances which may readily be found here. The recipe comprises the following items: Dried lavender flowers -20g; Dried red rosebuds - 20g; Saffron - 5g; Pine gum - 50g; Powdered orris (as required); Oil of lavender,10 drops; Oil of roses,10 drops; Oil of anise, 15 drops.

This Celtic incense has a fine fragrance and burns long and steadily. To compound it, a particular technique is required, owing to the semi-fluid and highly adhesive condition of fresh pine gum. Before proceeding with the other ingredients, the pine gum is first blended with the powdered orris-root until it forms a mass of crumbling granules which, if not subjected to undue pressure, can be handled without inconvenience.

To familiarise oneself with the exquisite incense materials and with their correspondences is a most interesting study; and it is a true alchemy, in which the substances are realised as participating in the qualities they represent.

Neoplatonist and Pagan views in the late Byzantine era

By Orestis Sakellaropoulos

Gemistus Pletho was a renown philosopher, intellectual pioneer and a public figure of the late byzantine era. He was born in Istanbul between 1355 and 1360 AD and died in Mystras of Peloponnese at June 26, 1452. Little is known of his early years, his family or his teachers. Gennadius Scholarius, also a Byzantine philosopher and theologist and later Ecumenical Patriarch of Constantinople, was his main ideological rival and a source of scarce information about his past. According to Gennadius he was an apprentice of a polytheist from Judaea by the name of Elisha. He spent his early years in the court of the Turkish sultan in Adrianopolis (Edirne). This is where he studied Aristotle philosophy and was initiated in Zoroaster spiritual system. Surely, he also studied general philosophy, history, mathematics, astronomy, law and music; the basic educational set of the times. He appeared in Constantinople later teaching philosophy. He was accused of paganism and heresy and emperor Manuel II Palaiologos dispatched him to Mystras of Peloponnese. Mystras was considered "the spiritual and political center of the rebirth of the Hellenic world". Gemistus attracted a talented group of students and soon was considered a wise teacher and man of letters. Gemistus was honored with many titles: protector of the fatherly law, protector of the Greek court of law and Senator. Land titles were directly offered to him and his offsprings, a proof of the nobles' favor towards him.

He had a considerable influence on the politics of the Byzantine empire. He wrote letters to the emperor himself to advise him on ways to avoid the Turkish conquest and fall of the empire. The emperor's brother visited Gemistus in Mystras to ask for advice concerning the reunion of the orthodox and catholic church. A proof of Gemistus' liability in matters of faith is that he was a part

The Moon within the Hermetic Tradition

By Mark Todd

Within the western hermetic tradition there are seven celestial spheres that influence the fate of each individual. They are Saturn, Jupiter, Mars, the Sun, Venus, Mercury and the Moon. Out of these seven celestial influences, it is only the moon that is in the unique position of being our closest celestial neighbor. No doubt, this position of prominence within the evening sky instigated the development of various explanations connecting the moon to daily life.

One of the earliest cultures to make use of the moon to organize daily life occurred in the time of the Chaldean's, when the lunar month was divided into four parts, each composed of seven days each (De Biasi, 2011, p. 41). Moving a little forward in time and in a similar manner, the Egyptian also associated the moon with time. More specifically with the week, month and year. This was particularly important as the lunar cycle divided their seasons and as such helped to organize their agricultural practices.

Apart from the mundane aspects of the lunar cycles, the moon has also played an important role in the development of cultural mythologies and religious practices. Egypt provides a excellent example of this where the moon was commonly used to denote the specific times of the year when various events to celebrate the Gods and Goddesses occurred (De Biasi, 2011, p. 39). More than this however the moon played a pivotal role in the theology, philosophy and ritual praxis of the Egyptians.

For the Egyptian priests the moon expressed an array of symbols and meanings that could allow for the exploration of the spiritual aspects of life. Hidden within the mythologies of the moon lay the hermetic understanding which was only available to those initiated to its mysteries. Arguably, one of the most significant expression of the hermetic power of the moon was expressed by the god

Thoth. Thoth is an integral part of the Egyptian pantheon and the ritual and theological traditions of Egypt.

In Egypt Thoth was referred to as the "Lord of time" and the "king of eternity" (https://www.aurumsolis.us). Thoth was a god existing outside of time, while simultaneously being responsible for some aspects of time such as the length of a person's life. For the Egyptian priests, Thoth was considered to be the original source of occult powers present in ritual as well as being the founder of the cosmic order (De Biasi, 2014). This clearly places Thoth as a lunar god in a position of importance within the context of ritual practice and the theological beliefs of the Egyptians.

Thoth's particular responsibilities generally included overseeing temple rituals, ceremonies, writing and magic. Thoth being also associated with the moon and its cycles, the ritual practices in Egypt tended to center on the cycles of the moon. This pattern was similarly replicated in Hellenistic Greece and the practice has continued as a tradition until modern times. One of the reasons for organizing rituals in this way, stems from the idea that from a new moon and while the moon is waxing, ritual actions connected to our energetic bodies are more efficient and rituals are more easily able to deeply affect our invisible bodies. In addition to this, deactivation and blessing should occur during the waxing moon while activation and invocation should occur during the waning moon (De Biasi, 2014, p. 175).

Of course, there are many more aspects to the role of the moon within ritual other than its cycles. Depending on the school of hermetic tradition followed, working with the moon may call for specific ritual tools, prayers, invocation or evocations, gestures and offerings etc. All of these aspects of the ritual work together to help build an atmosphere as well as a conscious change upon the magician that assists in making contact with spiritual forces. There are of course many other associations with the moon that are beyond the scope of this article. A few of note however are the Goddesses Hecate, Selene and Artemis, the incense camphor, pearls, silver, the hazel tree, the wood alder, and abilities such as divination, the control of dreams and oniromancy.

As we can see from this brief outline, the moon has always been and will continue to be, an object that captivates the hermetic imagination. The moon is an ever present symbol of our hermetic heritage, one that has helped generations of initiates to perceive and understand the spiritual world. As a symbol used to express deep spiritual experience, the moon ties us closely with the Egyptian god Thoth. Who in turn through the use of ritual, theology and philosophy can help us in the process as we seek the path of return.

References

De Biasi, J. L. (2011). The Divine Arcana of the Aurum Solis (1st Edition). United States, Llewellyn.

De Biasi, J. L. (2014). Rediscover the Magick of the Gods and Goddesses (1st Edition). United States, Llewellyn.

Ordo Aurum Solis, (2018), The Special Function of Thot as a Lunar Divinity, https://www.aurumsolis.us/topic/teaching-3-the-special-function-of-thot-as-a-lunar-divinity/)

Harmonization with the planetary days

By J.L. de Biasi

One of the most important periods in the history of the Hermetic Tradition occurred in Florence, Italy, during the years 1438-1439. Several Greek scientists, including the Neoplatonist Georgius Gemistus Plethon (or Pletho), traveled to Florence and lived in the accommodations there for the duration of the Council of Florence, which gathered together all the Churches of the East and the West.

This great philosopher Pletho, whose work was an inheritance of the Platonic Academy, contacted Cosimo de' Medici and transmitted a corpus of philosophical and hermetic texts which were unknown until then. Marsilio Ficino received an order from Cosmo to translate them, starting with the books of Hermes. A group was formed around this venture and was placed in the continuity of the old school of Plato. Cosmo made a gift of the Careggi Villa to them, which became the headquarters of this new Platonic Academy.

All the followers of Plato gathered to "practice philosophy". These were, first and foremost, philosophical discussions in the spirit of the "Platonic Agape". But far from limiting itself to this intellectual aspect, the Hermetic tradition expanded to include many rites and practices of a Theurgic nature. The astrological magic developed by Ficino was based on the tradition of the signatures and on the affirmation of the Emerald Tablet: "That which is above is like that which is below, and that which is below is like that which is above, for the performance of the miracles of the One."

Using these rites, hymns, music, colors and all the correspondences resulting from the laws of Universal fellowship, the members of the Academia Platonica tried to elevate themselves toward the spiritual world. They demonstrated that happiness is possible here below, by re-harmonizing the inner planes of the individual.

Theurgic work implies three aspects:

- a moral process of internal purity, fraternity and love;
- a philosophical training which is the expression of a religious mind/spirit or Religio Mentis;
- a ritual and aesthetic work based on astrology. The rites in this book are inspired by this aspect of the ancient teachings.

The Cosmos is governed by a pattern of order and an original state of harmonic balance. The planets which move in the celestial sphere take part in this harmonic pattern. A specific character, attached to a specific Divinity, is allocated to each one of the planets. Astrology in its initiatory dimension, and, as it was gradually developed by the initiates who studied the origins of mankind, became the source of an important system of correspondences that demonstrate a vital connection among everything that exists in the universe. Each planet, each sign, corresponds to an entire grouping of symbols including a sound, a color, a perfume, etc... These associations (correspondences) include Psychological character archetypes. Thus, the universe we are part of does not consist of cold, dead stars. Rather it consists of powerful Divine archetypes which influence us by their position in the Cosmos and by their movements in that sphere.

Be aware that this is literally true: "That which is below is like that which is above". Thus, our being is a true cosmos in miniature. We consist of several influences and natures, at the same time psychological and vibratory. Some, more Martian, are marked by intense energy, strength, courage and anger, while others, more Jupiterian, are recognizable by their nature or affinity for justice and sometimes pride. We are occultly constituted by these stars or interior powers. Their harmonious balance establishes health, serenity and peace within us. It is easy to realize that this happiness of the heart and this health of the body are not often a reality. Unfortunately, imbalance, anguish and ills are more often present in our daily human lives.

However, the correction and balance of these instabilities requires an understanding of our true nature. The interior characters of our characters (of which we are formed) are closely related to the order of the entire cosmos. Astrology thus becomes the means of understanding the powers which make up our personality. Celestial magic enables us to act in a way that recreates whatever harmony we have lost in the process of living. Rites based on this knowledge have thus been an established practice from earliest antiquity.

The principles are simple:

- using symbols and signatures we recreate the cosmos in a ritual space;
- we establish a link between the external and celestial archetypes and the inner powers of our psyche;
- then we restore our inner balance using a prescribed ritual with specific components (aesthetics, music, etc.)

The initiatic Order of the "Aurum Solis," is still using the most advanced theurgic technics to help each initiate to harmonize with the planets and ascend to the divine. Seven rituals have been published in my book "Rediscover the magick of Gods and Goddesses." In this book the Seven Planetary Rituals are based on the Hellenistic archetypal powers. The powers of the planets are represented in these rites by the Deities of Greek mythology: Apollo, Artemis, Ares, Hermes, Zeus, Aphrodite and Kronos. They constitute powerful personalities, who are able to have an in-depth effect on our being. Each personality (Gods or Goddesses) corresponds to a planet and a day of the week. As I explained in the first part of this almanac, these planetary days are not chosen randomly. Consequently, they are not linked to the days of your usual calendar which have absolutely no connection with any astral reality. In my book, I unveiled for the first time the original roots of these planetary days and the way to find the real ones. This almanac gives you the real days for this current year.

Besides advanced theurgic processes, you can place your planetary day under the protection and the blessing of the deity of the day by using prayers and hymns. You can find below the seven adorations coming from the Aurum Solis tradition. You can use also a specific translation of the Orphic hymns published by Theurgia. We recommend using these texts when you wake up on the morning as a way to be connected with the specific divinity.

Other elements strengthening this bond can be found in the Aurum Solis Tarot.

Kronos (Saturn)

Adoration

Sublime and shadowed one, austere awakener of high aspiration and mystic hope! Thou art giver of the silent will to endure, thou art patron of the spirit's creativity and of the forces of preservation and of renewal. In thy keeping are alike the scythe of the reaper and the instruments of the builder in stone; thine too is the open scroll of the past, and thine the sealed scroll which holds the mysteries of the future. Hail to thee

Helios (Sun)

Adoration

Far-riding ruler of days, all-seeing arbiter of the planetary powers! Thine is the wisdom of prophecy, the rapture of music and poesy, the upward surging force of mystical endeavor. Thine is the vision which sees beyond all change and chance, and the clear perception of truth which dispels all shadow. In the rising and in the incomparable luster of the Day-Star thou givest a sacred image to magical ascendence, even as thy power enkindles a glory within us and elevates us to accomplish that which we seek. Hail to thee!

Selene (Moon)

Adoration

O shining and sure guide through the illimitable realm of dreams, most gracious opener of the way to those who venture into worlds unseen! Thou maker and destroyer of illusion, thou who knowest the tides of ocean, the furthest distances of the Mind and the dark places of unreason: hail to thee!

Ares (Mars)

Adoration

All powerful defender of justice and truth, thou noble inspirer of courage and endurance and of bold resolve! Inculcator of loyalty, giver of the joy which springs from shared endeavor. thou divine patron of fruitful debate and of good order, thou who dost confirm the steadfast heart and the unfaltering hand! Thou mighty adversary of the powers adverse, hail to thee!

Hermes (Mercury)

Adoration

O thou swift and unconstrained traveler in the ways between the Worlds, divine imparter of secret tidings to gods and to humankind, bountiful bestower of aid in Art Magick! Knowledge and skill, rite and high result are thine to impart! Thine are the Tongues and the Numbers, thine the Signs and the Sigils and the words of Power. Thine it is to heal, and to teach, and to watch upon the way. Hail to thee!

Zeus (Jupiter)

Adoration

Royal and magnanimous giver of abundance from a cup unfailing, Shepherd of the golden Stars, Lord of the tides of fortune! Glorious dispenser of mercy, divine patron of paternal and filial love! Thou dost bless peace and amity between all beings: thou great Father of benevolent rule and of priesthood, and of that loving wisdom which sublimates authority! Hail to thee!

Aphrodite (Venus)

Adoration

O thou radiant giver of love, ruler of the forces of life, divinely robed in light and girded with invincible beauty! Perfect harmony and concord are as the perfumes of thy presence, and thou it is who dost create the rhythms whose pulsings call into life the sacred dance. O thou who ever sendest forth all delight, hail to thee!

Note:

The Orphic Hymns usable for individual invocations and harmonization have been published in a book called: "Pagan Prayer Book."

The numinous experience and the archetype of the *teophoros*

By Pedro Mouro

The numinous experiences shape a distinctive group of spiritual experiences that are described by those who live them as a particular kind of spiritual summit experience. Because their characteristic qualities and the function they fulfill within the process of spiritual unveiling, these experiences have a constructive and special meaning for the adept and the initiate.

Analyzing the numinous experience, we can discover various distinctive characteristics:

- First, the numinous experience breaks without warning, apparently alien to all causality, unstoppable and irrepressible. Characteristic of this experiences is, so, to receive them in the middle of the daily life, when the conscious mind is embedded in the daily tasks. Either cooking, or attending the work's responsibilities, or in the middle of the leisure time, without knowing why the spirit widens without warning, the soul inflames itself with the secret fire and the person is dragged by the passional divine fury without being able to prepare himself to the experience he is about to receive.

But, of course, the numinous experience does not occur without any reason. It is the product of a continuous and sincere spiritual practice, and of a daily effort for achieving moral purity and integrity.

- The second characteristic of the numinous experience manifests its difference with the spiritual experiences. And is that while a spiritual experience needs the personal consciousness for participate consciously in the spiritual practice, so the spiritual experience can begin and maintain during the time of the spiritual practice; in a numinous experience, if the person tries to participate of the experience, retiring himself from the daily life and take advantage of the numinous moment by performing the spiritual practice, this numinous experience will cease completely. One of the teachings of this particular kind of experiences is that both its origin and its goal are far beyond the personal consciousness. What began without the intercession of the conscious mind, does not need the conscious mind to end.

- The third characteristic of this experiences is closely related to their attribute of inevitability, because it is common to them that, after have crossed that first part of spiritual expansion, the individual that goes through the experience is sunken into a space of disquietude, atavistic fear and even terror without cause.

Some could explain that this is caused by the irruption of the experience, which leads to a fear caused by the inability to control the experience, and even if they could have part of reason, I think this characteristic fear of the numinous has its origin is other cause.

A numinous experience is, at the end, a breaking into the psyche by the sacred Other without warning. Once the initial stage of the experience is passed, characterized by the approach of the divine passional fury to the adept, the true summit experience begins when the person starts to feel that he is surrounded by an irrational terror, accompanied by a fascination and attraction to the experience itself; and all of this is because is then when the sacred Other breaks fully into the subtitle bodies of the initiate.

This atavistic fear, almost biological, is the instinctive and unconscious fear of the personality in the face of its dissolution, and it is a characteristic of psychological irruption of the Other in the psychic world of the person.

This part of the experience is truly the summit moments, because is now when the initiate must discover what is found on the other side of this ancient fear, and dare to cross the doors of knowledge, controlling his emotions and feelings and opening himself to the perception of the huge blessing this moment will suppose to his inner life.

The Mysteries, in my humble opinion, are closely related to the numinous experience, and the construction they perform is intimately related to the inner ability of the initiate to give space in himself to the passional fury of his spirit.

The magical personality and the built of the Témenos could be seen as the two faces of the same coin. By building the Témenos as inner temple, formed with the mortar of the spiritual bodies of the initiate, is prepared the place where the magical personality will be born. This new conscience, which is the initiate, is born in the inner space consecrated to the Mysteries as if the initiate will carry with him for now on the image of himself in his divine perfection.

The initiate transforms himself in the recipient of his own inner God, as the archetypal image of the Teophoros, literally "the carrier of Gods". The opening of this inner space is what will allow the opening to the spiritual transcendence, this is, the way to the other side of the limitations of the personal conscience, and the reception of the spiritual forces that are far beyond him

The Decans

Decans have an important role in theurgic practices and astrology. We can find names of these decans in medieval books, grimoires and other books. We indicate below the two most important names that can be found in the early western tradition. The first one provided below is coming from Hephaestion of Thebes, Hellenized Egyptian astrologer. The second one in brackets is coming from the Hermetic texts.

Aries - Bélier
1- Χονταρέ (Χενλαχωρί) – Khontare (Khenlakhôri)
2- Χονταχρέ (Χονταρέτ) – Khontakhre (Khontaret)
3- Σικέτ (Χικέτ) - Siket (Khiket)

Taurus - Taureau
1- Χώου (Σώου) – Khôou (Sôou)
2- Ερω (Ἀρῶν) – Erô (Arôn)
3- Ρομβρόμαρε (Ῥωμενώς) – Rombromare (Rômenôs)

Gemini - Gémeaux
1- Θοσόλκ (Ξοχά) – Thosolk (Kokha)
2- Ουαρε (Οὐαρί) – Ouare (Ouari)
3- Φούορι (Πεπίσωθ) – Fouori (Pepisôth)

Cancer - Cancer
1- ΣωΘίς (ΣωΘείρ) – Sôthis (Sôtheir)
2- Σίτ (Οὐφισίτ) – Sit (Oufisit)
3- Χνουμίς (Χνοῦφος) – Knoumis (Khnoufos)

Leo - Lion
1- Χαρχνούμίς (Χνοῦμος) – Kharkhnoumis (Khnoumos)
2- Ἤπη (Ἴπι) – Êpe (Ipi)
3- Φούπη (Φάτιτι) – Foupe (Fatiti)

Virgo - Vierge
1- Τώη (Ἀθουμ) – Tôm (Athoum)
2- Οὐεστεβκώτ (Βρυσούς) – Ouestebkôt (Brusous)
3- ΑΦόσο (Ἀμφαθάμ) – Afoso (Amfatham)

Libra - Balance
1- Σουχωέ (Σφουκοῦ) – Soukhôe (Sfoukou)
2- Πτηχούτ (Νεφθίμης) – Ptekhout (Nefthimes)
3- Χονταρέ (Φοῦ) – Kontare (Fou)

Scorpio - Scorpion
1- Στωχνήνε (Βώς) – Stôkhnene (Bôs)
2- Σεσμέ (Οὕστιχος) – Sesme (Oustikhos)
3- Σισιεμέ (Ἄφηβις) – Sisieme (Afebis)

Sagittarius - Sagittaire
1- Ῥηουώ (Σέβος) – Rêouô (Sebos)
2- Σεσμέ (Τεῦχμος) – Sesme (Teukhmos)
3- Κομμέ (Χθισάρ) – Komme (Khthisar)

Capricorn - Capricorne
1- Σμάτ (Τάιρ) – Smat (Tair)
2- Σρώ (Ἐπίτεκ) – Srô (Epitek)
3- Ισρώ (Ἐπιχναῦς) – Isrô (Epikhnaus)

Aquarius - Verseau
1- Πτιαῦ (Ἰσυ or Θρώ) – Ptiaou (Isu or Thrô)
2- Αεύ (Σοσομνῶ) – Aeu (Sosomnô)
3- Πτηβυού (Χονουμοῦς) – Ptêbuou (Khonoumous)

Pisces - Poissons
1- Βίου (Τετιμώ) – Biou (Tetimô)
2- Χονταρέ (Σοπφί) – Kontare (Sopfi)
3- Πτιβιοῦ (Συρώ) – Ptibiou (Surô)

Hermes

By Sophie Watson

Myths and Folklore: Hermes is the messenger of the Gods. A trickster and a thief, he is also the Divine patron of healers, wise men and women, and of the Hermetic Tradition. He is the son of Zeus and Maia, and the father of Hermaphroditus and Pan. Keryx, the first herald of the Mysteries at Eleusis, is sometimes considered his offspring, as are many local heroes across Greece. Myths tell us Hermes was born in Arcadia on Mont Cyllene. On the day of his birth, he killed a tortoise and made a lyre with its shell. Later on the same day, he secretly stole fifty cows from Apollo in order to make offerings to the Immortal Olympians. Apollo later found out, but Hermes gave him his tortoise lyre to appease him. Recognizing Hermes' wits and talents, Apollo bestowed great powers upon him.

A popular myth featuring Hermes in classical times is the story of the murder of Argus. The nymph Io, who was loved by Zeus, had been changed into a heifer. The Father of the Gods transformed her so as to protect her from the wrath of Hera. However, Zeus was later tricked into giving the heifer to his wife. Hera decided to put Io in Argus' care. The latter was a herdsman with a hundred eyes all over his head. Argus never lost sight of the nymph. Displeased at his beautiful lover's captivity, Zeus asked Hermes to kill Io's monstrous keeper and free her from Hera. The messenger of the Gods, equipped with winged feet, a helmet, and his caduceus, went in search of Argus. On the way he stole a herd of goats to disguise himself. Walking by with his caduceus as a shepherd's crook, and playing the reed pipe, he found Argus on the slopes of a hill.

Hermes tried to charm Argus to sleep with his music, but it was of no use as the herdsman resisted every song he knew. As Hermes was singing about the invention of the reed pipe, Argus finally drowsed, and Hermes cut off his head. Free, Io wandered to Egypt where Roman poets claim she became the great Goddess Isis. As for Argus, Hera took his hundred eyes and put them on the peacock's colorful tail. The latter part of the story has since been understood by alchemists to signify the extraordinary succession of colors crowning the Great Work.

The name 'Hermes' most probably comes from 'herma', a very old Greek word meaning 'pile of stones'. Piles of stones assembled in various ways were used early on in ancient Greece to mark important social and religious spaces. In Plato's time, one would often encounter later versions of such markers. Rectangular stone pillars decorated with an erect phallus and a sculpted head of Hermes could be seen at crossroads, in the agora, next to doors, in a house's vestibule, and on the threshold of sacred spaces (sanctuaries, temples, and cemeteries). Such pillars were called "Hermae," and were mostly used as boundaries and markers of space they were thought to magically protect.

From the Ptolemaic era onward, especially in Khmun (Hermopolis), Hermes was identified with the Egyptian God Thoth with whom he had much in common. Not only was Thoth the messenger of the Gods and Goddesses, but he ruled over the magical and sacerdotal arts, and was the God of understanding, language, and the judgement of individual souls. Works with Hermes in the Ogdoadic Tradition carry, to this day, this important association between Egyptian religion and Greek Mysteries.

Invocation: Hermes is the wise and volatile God associated with Mercury. He is the patron of magic, prophecy, divination, alchemy, the healing arts, and secrecy. He is also associated with speech, music, numbers, good luck, travels, exchanges, transmissions, translations, and mediations, be they inside one's being (the nervous system), with other individuals (communication and affects), or between the physical and the spiritual realms (in theurgy).

Hermes should be invoked in matters connected to the learning, teaching, and practice of magic and theurgy. The same could be said of alchemy and astrology. His influence is paramount in matters of divination and healing, but also, in any work involving passages from the visible to the invisible and vice versa. Hermes' influence should be sought in all matters related to intellectual and mental activities and processes as well as the transmission of knowledge. Hermetists wanting to develop their focus, a clarity of mind, wit, memory, vision, and awareness should work with him. He can also be invoked, along with Selene, to develop dream-consciousness and empathy in general.

Symbols: You can decorate your lararium (a traditional altar to the divinities and to one's ancestors) according to certain symbols when invoking Hermes. A list is given below. These symbols can also be used when making talismanic images, furniture, or jewelry for the God. Drawing from these specific symbols in your work will ensure harmonious and propitious contacts with Hermes. They can be used as materials (wood, rocks and gems, magical objects), or as images. The shapes, patterns, and colors of leaves, fruits, rocks, and gems should inspire your creations:

In the vegetal realm: Angelica, anise, basil, buttercup, carrot, celery, citronella, coltsfoot, dill, endive, fennel, fern, flax, garlic, gentian, harefoot, hawthorn, hazel, hop, lavender, liquorice, magnolia, mandrake, marjoram, mercury flowers, mint, mulberry tree, myrtle, oak tree, oats, orange, oregano, parsley, parsnip, pistachio, poplar tree, poppy, valerian, and wormwood.

In the animal realm: Baboon, birds in general, cheetah, fox, gazelle, giraffe, ibis, jackal, mule, rooster, snake, wolf, zebra and from mythology: Sphinx, unicorn, winged snake, three-headed snake, and hermaphrodite.

In the mineral realm: Abalone shell, banded agate, alexandrite, cinnabar, opal, rhinestone, quicksilver, and topaz.

Other symbols include coins, shells, pebbles, dice, winged hat, broad-rimmed felt hat, winged boots, caduceus, syrinx (reed pipe), lyre, shepherd's crook, sandals, sacred wand, papyri, stylus, hood, and alchemist's vessel.

Offerings and perfumes: When working with Hermes, one should draw from the symbols of the vegetal realm above for food offerings. Beer, and in some cases mead, or anise scented liquors such as Arak Razzouk, are the best all-around beverages used in rites and prayers to the God. The burning of perfumes should precede offerings when working with the divinities. You can either use a thurible or a cauldron for these incense offerings. You can experiment with the perfumes of some of the plants and seeds mentioned above (be careful to distinguish between roots and leaves in your notes) but should also familiarize yourself with age-old perfumes associated with Mercury: mastic, liquid storax, spikenard oil, lavender flowers and oil, poppy seeds, and yellow sandal, either as wood or oil. I personally use a mix of mastic, oliban, and lavender for works with Hermes as the Divine Patron of Hermetism, and a recipe with fair amounts of spikenard oil and poppy seeds for works involving Hermes' proximity with death, dreams, and the pilgrimages of the Soul.

With time, your relationship with Hermes will develop, and allow you to properly recognize the perfumes associated with him. You will then be able to explore and discover new perfumes related to Mercury and try out different incense recipes of your own creation. Symbols, offerings, and perfumes are there for you to discover the God's role in nature, as well as in yourself. Have fun experimenting with these and discovering your own divinity.

May Hermes be with you.

The Mysteries

By Klaytonus Silvanus

The English word "mystery" is derived from the Greek word *"musterion"* (plural: *musteria*). The closest word in English would be "sacraments," though they're not equivalent. The word *sacrament* is derived from the Latin word *sacramentum*, a sign and what is <u>seen</u>. *Mustērion*, in contrast, refers to something <u>hidden</u> and stresses the power of the Good as made manifest in an unseen way through their holy rites.

There were plenty of mysteries across the Hellenic world, and Julian the Philosopher is known to have at least been in three. The intended effects of the mysteries are to lead practitioners from a state of ignorance and occlusion to *gnosis* and *henosis* through the measured steps appropriate to each soul. It is through the mysteries the human soul can escape the confines of fate and more fully participate in the providence of the divine. Likewise, it is through the mysteries that the One makes itself known to the cosmos through the soul of humanity.

A mystery is a sacred rite that has hidden within it the power and providence of the One. These rites are both mysterious and hieratic, containing the sacred and hidden powers of the unseen world. Tradition holds that hieratic (proper) rites were originally instituted by *Julian the Chaldean* and his son, *Julian the Theurgist*. As theurgic rites, however, they have their origins in the *One*, the *Celestial Demiurge*, and the *divine intelligibles*. They were fully brought into by the divine Iamblichus, who himself first applied the term "hieratic" to theurgic rites. It is a two-fold allusion:

- First to that which is sacred and priestly
- Second to ancient Egyptian sacred writings

Initiates into Mysteries don't have a sense that non-initiates are following a "false" religion, even though they themselves were in possession of some higher truths. There are <u>many</u> paths to the divine truth.

How they function

All Mysteries tended to be incredibly varied, but most held certain traits in common:

- **Initiation**: Membership that was required to enter the mysteries.
- **Hierarchy**: The secrets of the sect were revealed in successive stages, with only a select number ever reaching the highest stages.
- **Fellowship**: Among initiates there was a sense of brotherly solidarity.
- **Promise of spiritual benefits**: Initiates tend to expect, for example, a happier status in the afterlife.

They also, by large, never let most of their information leak. However, we can gather some rather broad information on how they function.

Firstly, one must be in a proper spiritual state to both give and receive a mystery if there are any hopes of the intelligible rites having success. Both the *giver* of the mystery *and* the *receiver* of a mystery must commit to several spiritual preparations, such as contemplation, purification and potentially some sacred rites. If a mystery is received in an unprepared state, at best, nothing happens. At worst, however, the mystery may have the opposite of its intended result; moving the soul farther away from the Good instead of closer via antipathy.

By large the efficiency of a mystery would depend on the person administering it. The administer of a mystery isn't merely a conduit for divine power, but rather a participant in that power. Without proper participation, a mystery can only be performed in its outer form with an absent inner power.

If performed by a fully purified and illuminated soul a mystery will always produce the desired result. However, since these souls being few are far between, it's possible for mysteries to fail depending on the state of the soul performing it and the capacity of the soul receiving it. If both souls are in a properly prepared state, a mystery will always be successful, to varying degrees, depending on the differing states of those involved.

The Afterlife

By Klaytonus Silvanus

Belief in the afterlife is prevalent in many religions and varies widely, even among followers of the same religion. This is particularly the case in Hellenism, where views on life after death can vary widely, ranging from a paradise the Gods would send the righteous to reside in, to terrifying scenes of punishment for those who had sinned in this life, to a more or less benign state of being that followed after death but was secondary to this life. So what is the truth? Here the doctrines of Plato and Iamblichus, the nature of the Gods, and our very own existence will be examined to find out the universal divine truth.

Upon death, our souls are released from our bodies and see judgment by Lord Serapis, Lord of the Gods of the underworld, who are the guardians and rulers of souls. It is here that one of two things can happen to the person.

Metempsychōsis

Metempsychōsis (μετεμψύχωσις), also sometimes called *Palingenesía* (Παλιγγενεσία), is the process of reincarnation. Reincarnation of the soul is directed by the Gods into successive bodies to fulfill divine order, as we are born into bodies, and thus we can deduce it is the duty of souls to do their work in a body, and not remain idle after death. This is what most people endure through. Here, upon death the soul is separated from the body and punished, "some wandering among us, some going to hot or cold places of the earth, some harassed by spirits. Under all circumstances they suffer with the irrational part of their nature, with which they also sinned. For its sake there subsists that shadowy body which is seen about graves, especially the graves of evil livers" (Sallustius, XIX). Eventually, the Irrational Soul, a Shade, is sent by the divine Serapis to undergo punishment in Tartarus, which is actually a process of purification impure souls go through for the next time the Irrational Soul is joined with the Rational Soul. After purification, the soul will descend again to be reincarnated into a new body.

In our corporeal life, people will develop identities built around things such as their wealth, profession, appearance, nationality, family, and possessions. None of these, however, will last beyond our deaths. Underneath our conscious minds, there lies subliminal memories which have formed from endless impressions and traits which have been formed from a countless number of life experiences, which all spring from the Rational Soul, our highest and truest divine selves, which holds the power of memory (*mneme*/μνήμη). These are the seeds which we carry into our next life that explain our character, such as why we have innate talents, why we have certain tendencies, and why our personalities have various unique qualities. In this relentless circle of births, we may have been male or female, rich or poor, lawgivers or criminals. We can often detect the remnants of past life experiences, such as when we experience déjà vu, the familiarity of having already performed something previously, love at first sight, and so on. We have subtle clues that somewhere deep within ourselves we carry the imprints of another time.

Metempsychōsis happens because the Celestial Demiurge, Zeus-Helios, who is perfect, created the universe perfectly, with all things that could be created having been created– thus meaning the number of souls in the universe is fixed. Birth is therefore never the creation of a soul, but only a transmigration of a soul from one body to another. If souls didn't enter into new bodies again, they must either be infinite in number or God must constantly be making new ones. But there is nothing infinite in the world, for that which is infinite can never exist in that which is finite. Neither can new souls be made, for everything in which something new goes on being created, must be imperfect. And the universe, being made by a perfect author, ought to naturally be perfect (Sallustius, XX).

Spirits will always be reincarnated into the body of a similar creature. It is impossible for a human, which has a rational soul, to be reincarnated into the body of an animal, which is an irrational creature. This is because it's absurd to speak of reason in connection with irrational animals. God didn't create a superfluous creature since He created the world perfect, and thus He did not put a rational soul into cattle or wild beast, seeing that it would never have the opportunity to exercise its proper function. Instead, if the soul migrates to an irrational creature, it follows the body outside, similar to how a Personal Daimon follows a man (Sallustius, XX).

The cosmic journey our souls go through involves sampling and experiencing all aspects of the beauty incarnated in life, and although we experience much beauty, the mortal condition, where we are reborn continuously and time and time again experience death either through old age, sickness, or violence, is also inherently painful, and our Rational Soul longs for union with the divine.

Henosis

If one is stuck in the permanent loop of reincarnation because of the impurities surrounding their soul, then the ultimate goal is to purify oneself– to reach perfection, as a means of breaking free of that cycle. The one who breaks this cycle frees themselves from such corruption and is able to bear witness to the divine realm. Upon the death of the body, the soul is freed to its immortal life. Living is being dead and after death we, our soul, come to truly live. This process is called *henosis* (ἐνωσης) meaning "divine union" or "unity with the divine." In this case, Lord Serapis breaks our corporeal bonds and lifts us upwards towards divine union. The Rational Soul is brought into union with the World Soul, and the Irrational Soul separates from the body and becomes a Shade in Hades' Realm. A good index here is the case of Heracles, whose Shade is said to inhabit Hades' Realm, while another part of His immortal Soul resides among the divine Olympians, and has been married to Hebe, been adopted by Hera, and so on. This part of Heracles is a wholly perfected soul, and hence does not undergo reincarnation.

Henosis is union with the divine, from the Personal Daimon to the highest reality in the universe, the One, which is what from which everything else proceeds from. Henosis is the ultimate goal in life, and a soul who has attained henosis and returned to the One achieves union with the World Soul and does not descend again, at least, not in this world period– even theurgic sages such as Empedocles and Pythagoras recall previous incarnations and expect future ones.

Even though breaking the cycle of infinite reincarnation is one of the results, it is a lesser important goal. The true end goals of achieving henosis are (Theourgia.com Catechism, 88):

− Withdrawal from alien things
− Restoration of one's own essence
− Perfection
− Fullness
− Independence of will
− Ascent to and unification with the creative cause
− The demiurgic activity of conjoining of parts with wholes
− Contribution from the wholes to the parts of power, life, and activity

Henosis is a universal liberation; an experience of perfect understanding. Henosis is a true ascent, when the soul rejoins the bliss, wisdom and eternal perfection of its source, participating in the divine intelligibles, and through purification being gradually assimilated into the divine. The ultimate end goal of henosis is happiness. Only through restraint, virtue, and realization can we hope to achieve salvation. This is accomplished through theurgy. Absolute union with the One is impossible. The soul is unique and individual, coming from and participating in Nous (The Divine Mind/Celestial Demiurge). The soul is distinct from the One and is somewhat locked in its ontological position as the lowest of divine beings, though it can rise, practically if not actually, to Angelhood.

Henosis isn't the obliteration of the *psyche* (the soul/the self) in union with the One. The soul is always itself: a particular soul with unique Being (Ousia), Powers, and Activities. Simultaneously the soul isn't solitary; it's still one part of a greater whole that it participates in. Thus henosis isn't the merging of the soul into all this, but rather through rituals of purification that allows the soul to realize its own divine self, it is to find its place within it. Furthermore, this act isn't an act of subjugating itself to the whole. By remembering its unique self, the soul both comes to understand the activity proper to it and willfully engages in demiurgy in alignment with its natural place in existence.

Quotes

"The whole of theurgy presents a double aspect. On the one hand, it is performed by men, and as such observes our natural rank in the universe, but on the other, it controls divine symbols, and in virtue of them is raised up to union with the higher powers, and directs itself harmoniously in accordance with their dispensation, which enables it quite properly to assume the mantle of the Gods. It is in virtue of this distinction, then, that the art both naturally invokes the powers from the universe as superiors, inasmuch as the invoker is a man, and yet on the other hand gives them orders, since it invests itself, by virtue of the ineffable symbols, with the hieratic role of the Gods."

Iamblichus Chalcidensis

"The choice of souls was in most cases based on their own experience of a previous life… Knowledge easily acquired is that which the enduing self-had in an earlier life, so that it flows back easily."

Plato

"You are everywhere at once; in the earth, in the sea, in heaven. You are not yet born, you are in the womb, you are old, a youth, dead, in an afterlife. Realise all of these things simultaneously, all times, places, things, qualities, and you can realize God."

Plotinus

Christian Persecutions against Pagans

(Summarised from Vlasis Rassias' book "Demolish them," published in Greek, Athens 1994, Diipetes Editions, May 1999)
(All dates "era vulgaris" = Christian Era)

314- Immediately after its full legalization, the Christian Church attacks the Pagans (Gentiles): The Council of Ancyra denounces the worship of Goddess Artemis.

324- Emperor Constantine declares Christianism as the only official Religion of the Roman Empire. In Dydima, Minor Asia, he sacks the Oracle of the God Apollo and tortures the pagan priests to death. He also evicts all the Pagans (Gentiles) from Mt. Athos and destroys all the local Hellenic Temples.

326- Emperor Constantine, following the instructions of his mother Helen, destroys the Temple of the God Asclepius in Aigeai of Cilicia and many Temples of the Goddess Aphrodite in Jerusalem, Aphaca, Mambre, Phoenice, Baalbek, etc.

330- Emperor Constantine steals the treasures and statues of the pagan Temples of Greece to decorate Nova Roma (Constantinople), the new capital of his Empire.

335- Emperor Constantine sacks many pagan Temples of Minor Asia and Palestine and orders the execution by crucifixion of "all magicians and soothsayers". Martyrdom of the Neoplatonist philosopher Sopatrus.

341- Emperor Flavius Julius Constantius persecutes "all the soothsayers and the Hellenists". Many Gentile Hellenes are either imprisoned or executed.

346- New large-scale persecutions against the Pagans (Gentiles) in Constantinople. Banishment of the famous orator Libanius accused as "magician".

353- An edict of Constantius orders the death penalty for all kind of worship through sacrifices and "idols."

354- A new edict orders the closing of all the pagan Temples. Some of them are profaned and turned into brothels or gambling rooms. Executions of pagan priests.

354- A new edict of Constantius orders the destruction of the pagan Temples and the execution of all "idolaters." First burning of libraries in various cities of the Empire. The first lime factories are being organized next to the closed pagan Temples. A major part of the holy architecture of the Pagans (Gentiles) turns to lime.

357- Constantius outlaws all methods of Divination (Astrology not excluded).

359- In Skythopolis, Syria, the Christians organize the first death camps for the torture and executions of the arrested Pagans (Gentiles) from all around the Empire.

361 to 363- Religious tolerance and restoration of the pagan cults declared in Constantinople (11th December 361) by the pagan Emperor Flavius Claudius Julianus.

363- Assassination of Emperor Julianus (26th June).

364- Emperor Flavius Jovianus orders the burning of the Library of Antioch.

364- An Imperial edict (11th September) orders the death penalty for all Pagans (Gentiles) that worship their ancestral Gods or practice Divination ("sileat omnibus perpetuo divinandi curiositas"). Three different edicts (4th February, 9th September, and 23rd December) order the confiscation of all properties of the pagan Temples and the death penalty for participation in pagan rituals, even private ones.

365- An Imperial edict (17th November) forbids the Gentile officers of the army to command Christian soldiers.

370- Emperor Valens orders a tremendous persecution of the Pagans (Gentiles) in all the Eastern Empire. In Antioch, among many other Pagans (Gentiles), the ex-governor Fidustius and the priests Hilarius and Patricius are executed. Tons of books are burnt in the squares of the cities of the Eastern Empire. All the friends of Julianus are persecuted (Orebasius, Sallustius, Pegasius etc.), the philosopher Simonides is burned alive and the philosopher Maximus is decapitated.

372- Emperor Valens orders the governor of Minor Asia to exterminate all the Hellenes and all documents of their wisdom.

373- New prohibition of all Divination methods. The term "pagan" (pagani, villagers) is introduced by the Christians to lessen the Pagans (Gentiles).

375- The Temple of God Asclepius in Epidaurus, Greece, is closed down by the Christians.

380- On 27th February, Christianism becomes the exclusive Religion of the Roman Empire by an edict of Emperor Flavius Theodosius, requiring that "all the various nations which are subject to our clemency and moderation should continue in the profession of that religion which was delivered to the Romans by the divine Apostle Peter". The non-Christians are called "loathsome, heretics, stupid and blind". In another edict Theodosius calls "insane" those that do not believe to the Christian God and outlaws all disagreements with the Church dogmas. Ambrosius, bishop of Milan, starts destroying all the pagan Temples of his area. The Christian priests lead the hungry mob against the Temple of Goddess Demeter in Eleusis and try to lynch the hierophants Nestorius and Priskus. The 95 years old hierophant Nestorius ends the Eleusinian Mysteries and announces the predominance of mental darkness over the human race.

381- On 2nd May, Theodosius deprives of all their rights the Christians that return back to the pagan Religion. In all the Eastern Empire the pagan Temples and Libraries are looted or burned down. On 21st December, Theodosius outlaws even the simple visits to the Temples of the Hellenes. In Constantinople, the Temple of Goddess Aphrodite is turned to brothel and the Temples of Sun and Artemis to stables.

382- "Hellelu-jah" (Glory to Yahweh) is imposed in the Christian mass.

384- Emperor Theodosius orders the Praetorian Prefect Maternus Cynegius, a dedicated Christian, to cooperate with the local bishops and destroy the Temples of the Pagans (Gentiles) in Northern Greece and Minor Asia.

385 to 388- Maternus Cynegius, encouraged by his fanatic wife, and bishop ("Saint") Marcellus with his gangs scour the countryside and sack and destroy hundreds of Hellenic Temples, shrines and altars. Among others they destroy the Temple of Edessa, the Cabeireion of Imbros, the Temple of Zeus in Apamea, the Temple of Apollo in Dydima and all the Temples of Palmyra. Thousands of innocent Pagans (Gentiles) from all sides of the Empire suffer martyrdom in the notorious death camps of Skythopolis.

386- Emperor Theodosius outlaws (16th June) the care of the sacked pagan Temples.

388- Public talks on religious subjects are also outlawed by Theodosius. The old orator Libanius sends his famous Epistle "Pro Templis" to Theodosius with the hope that the few remaining Hellenic Temples will be respected and spared.

389 to 390- All non-Christian date-methods are outlawed. Hordes of fanatic hermits from the desert flood the cities of the Middle East and Egypt and destroy statues, altars, Libraries and pagan Temples and lynch the Pagans (Gentiles). Theophilus, Patriarch of Alexandria, starts heavy persecutions against the Pagans (Gentiles), turns the Temple of Dionysos into a Christian church, burns down the Mithraeum of the city, destroys the Temple of Zeus and burlesque the pagan priests before they are killed by stoning. The Christian mob profanes the cult images.

391- On 24th February, a new edict of Theodosius prohibits not only visits to pagan Temples but also looking at the vandalized statues. New heavy persecutions all around the Empire. In Alexandria, Egypt, the Pagans (Gentiles), led by the philosopher Olympius, revolt and after some street fights, they lock themselves inside the fortified Temple of God Serapis (The Serapeion). After a violent siege, the Christians take over the building, demolish it, burn its famous Library and profane the cult images.

392- On 8th November, the Emperor Theodosius outlaws all the non-Christian rituals and names them "superstitions of the Pagans

(Gentiles)" (gentilicia superstitio). New full-scale persecutions against the Pagans (Gentiles). The Mysteries of Samothrace are ended and the priests slaughtered. In Cyprus the local bishop ("Saint") Epiphanius and "Saint" Tychon destroy almost all the Temples of the island and exterminate thousands of Pagans (Gentiles). The local Mysteries of Goddess Aphrodite are ended. Theodosius' edict declares: "the ones that won't obey pater Epiphanius have no right to keep living in that island". The Pagans (Gentiles) revolt against the Emperor and the Church in Petra, Aeropolis, Rafia, Gaza, Baalbek and other cities of the Middle East.

393- The Pythian Games, the Aktia Games and the Olympic Games are outlawed as part of the Hellenic "idolatry". The Christians sack the Temples of Olympia.

395- Two new edicts (22nd July and 7th August) cause new persecutions against the Pagans (Gentiles). Rufinus, the eunuch Prime Minister of Emperor Flavius Arcadius directs the hordes of the baptised Goths (led by Alaric) to the country of the Hellenes. Encouraged by Christian monks the barbarians sack and burn many cities (Dion, Delphi, Megara, Corinth, Pheneos, Argos, Nemea, Lycosoura, Sparta, Messene, Phigaleia, Olympia, etc.), slaughter or enslave innumerable Gentile Hellenes and burn down all the Temples. Among others, they burn down the Eleusinian Sanctuary and burn alive all its priests (including the hierophant of Mithras Hilarius).

396- On 7th December, a new edict by Emperor Arcadius orders that paganism be treated as high treason. Imprisonment of the few remaining pagan priests and hierophants.

397- "Demolish them!" Emperor Flavius Arcadius orders all the still standing pagan Temples to be demolished.

398- The Fourth Church Council of Carthage prohibits to everybody, including to the Christian bishops, the study of the books of the Pagans (Gentiles). Porphyrius, bishop of Gaza, demolishes almost all the pagan Temples of his city (except 9 of them that remain active).

399- With a new edict (13th July) Emperor Flavius Arcadius orders all the still standing pagan Temples, mainly in the countryside, to be immediately demolished.

400- Bishop Nicetas destroys the Oracle of the God Dionysus in Vesai and baptises all the Pagans (Gentiles) of this area.

401- The Christian mob of Carthage lynches Pagans (Gentiles) and destroys Temples and "idols." In Gaza too, the local bishop (also a "Saint") Porphyrius sends his followers to lynch Pagans (Gentiles) and to demolish the remaining 9 still active Temples of the city. The 15th Council of Chalkedon orders all the Christians that still keep good relations with their gentile relatives to be excommunicated (even after their death).

405- John Chrysostom sends hordes of gray dressed monks armed with clubs and iron bars to destroy the "idols" in all the cities of Palestine.

406- John Chrysostom collects funds from rich Christian women to financially support the demolition of the Hellenic Temples. In Ephessus he orders the destruction of the famous Temple of Goddess Artemis. In Salamis, Cyprus, the "Saints" Epiphanius and Eutychius continue the persecutions of the Pagans (Gentiles) and the total destruction of their Temples and sanctuaries.

407- A new edict outlaws once more all the non-Christian acts of worship.

408- The Emperor of the Western Empire Honorius and the Emperor of the Eastern Empire Arcadius order together all the sculptures of the pagan Temples to be either destroyed or to be taken away. Private ownership of pagan sculpture is also outlawed. The local bishops lead new heavy persecutions against the Pagans (Gentiles) and new book burning. The judges that have pity for the Pagans (Gentiles) are also persecuted. "Saint" Augustine massacres hundreds of protesting pagans in Calama, Algeria.

409- Once again, an edict orders Astrology and all methods of Divination to be punished by death.

415- In Alexandria, Egypt, the Christian mob, urged by the bishop Cyrillus, attacks a few days before the Judaeo-Christian Pascha (Easter) and cuts to pieces the famous and beautiful philosopher Hypatia. The pieces of her body, carried around by the Christian mob through the streets of Alexandria, are finally burned together with her books in a place called Cynaron. On 30th August, new persecutions start against all the pagan priests of North Africa who end their lives either crucified or burned alive.

416- The inquisitor Hypatius, alias "The Sword of God," exterminates the last Pagans (Gentiles) of Bithynia. In Constantinople (7th December) all non-Christian army officers, public employees and judges are dismissed.

423- Emperor Theodosius B declares (8th June) that the Pagan religion (Religion of the Gentiles) is nothing more than "demon worship" and orders all those who persist in practicing it to be punished by imprisonment and torture.

429- The Temple of Goddess Athena (Parthenon) on the Acropolis of Athens is sacked. The Athenian pagans are persecuted.

435- On 14th November, a new edict by Emperor Theodosius B orders the death penalty for all "heretics" and Pagans (Gentiles) of the Empire. Only Judaism is considered a legal non-Christian Religion.

438- Emperor Theodosius B issues a new edict (31st January) against the Pagans (Gentiles), incriminating their "idolatry" as the reason of a recent plague (!)

440 to 450- The Christians demolish all the monuments, altars and Temples of Athens, Olympia, and other Greek cities.

448- Theodosius B orders all the non-Christian books to be burned.

450- All the Temples of Aphrodisias (City of Goddess Aphrodite) are demolished and all its Libraries burned down. The city is renamed Stavroupolis (City of the Cross).

451- New edict by Emperor Theodosius B (4th November) emphasises that "idolatry" is punished by death.

457 to 491- Sporadic persecutions against the Pagans (Gentiles) of the Eastern Empire. Among others, the physician Jacobus and the philosopher Gessius are executed. Severianus, Herestios, Zosimus, Isidorus and others are tortured and imprisoned. The proselytiser Conon and his followers exterminate the last Pagans (Gentiles) of Imbros Island, Norheast Aegean Sea. The last worshippers of Lavranius Zeus are exterminated in Cyprus.

482 to 488- The majority of the Pagans (Gentiles) of Minor Asia are exterminated after a desperate revolt against the Emperor and the Church.

486- More "underground" pagan priests are discovered, arrested, burlesqued, tortured and executed in Alexandria, Egypt.

515- Baptism becomes obligatory even for those that already say they are Christians. The Emperor of Constantinople Anastasius orders the massacre of the Pagans (Gentiles) in the Arabian city Zoara and the demolition of the Temple of local God Theandrites.

528- Emperor Jutprada (Justinianus) outlaws the "alternative" Olympian Games of Antioch. He also orders the execution (by fire, crucifixion, tearing to pieces by wild beasts or cutting to pieces by iron nails) of all who practice "sorcery, divination, magic or idolatry" and prohibits all teachings by the Pagans (Gentiles) ("...the ones suffering from the blasphemous insanity of the Hellenes").

529- Emperor Justinianus outlaws the Athenian Philosophical Academy and has its property confiscated.

532- The inquisitor Ioannis Asiacus, a fanatic monk, leads a crusade against the Pagans (Gentiles) of Minor Asia.

542- Emperor Justinianus allows the inquisitor Ioannis Asiacus to convert the Pagans (Gentiles) of Phrygia, Caria and Lydia, Minor Asia. Within 35 years of this crusade, 99 churches and 12 monasteries are built on the sites of demolished pagan Temples.

546- Hundreds of Pagans (Gentiles) are put to death in Constantinople by the inquisitor Ioannis Asiacus.

556- Emperor Justinianus orders the notorious inquisitor Amantius to go to Antioch, to find, arrest, torture and exterminate the last Pagans (Gentiles) of the city and burn all the private libraries down.

562- Mass arrests, burlesquing, tortures, imprisonments and executions of Gentile Hellenes in Athens, Antioch, Palmyra and Constantinople.

578 to 582- The Christians torture and crucify Gentile Hellenes all around the Eastern Empire and exterminate the last Pagans (Gentiles) of Heliopolis (Baalbek).

580- The Christian inquisitors attack a secret Temple of Zeus in Antioch. The priest commits suicide, but the rest Pagans (Gentiles) are arrested. All the prisoners, the Vice Governor Anatolius included, are tortured and sent to Constantinople to face trial. Sentenced to death they are thrown to the lions. The wild animals being unwilling to tear them to pieces, they end up crucified. Their dead bodies are dragged in the streets by the Christian mob and afterwards thrown unburied in the dump.

583- New persecutions against the Gentile Hellenes by the Emperor Mauricius.

590- In all the Eastern Empire the Christian accusers "discover" pagan conspiracies. New storm of torture and executions.

692- The "Penthekto" Council of Constantinople prohibits the remains of Calends, Brumalia, Anthesteria, and other pagan / Dionysian celebrations.

804- The Gentile Hellenes of Mesa Mani (Cape Tainaron, Lakonia, Greece) resist successfully the attempt of Tarasius, Patriarch of Constantinople, to convert them to Christianity.

850 to 860- Violent conversion of the last Pagans of Laconia by the Armenian "Saint" Nikon.

Note: We will be happy to add new dates and references to this list. This is will be integrated in the next edition of the Almanac. You can send an email to secretary@theurgia.us. Thank you!

An interpretation of Plato's Cave

By John White

Though many of the materials and sources of the Hermetic tradition can be traced to the very beginnings of our civilization in Mesopotamia and ancient Egypt, the Hermetic tradition proper takes form in Graeco-Egyptian Alexandria (4th century BCE) and, over the centuries, spreads generally into the Hellenic world. Wherever Hellenism spread, originating with the empire of Alexander, the Hermetic tradition also spread.

The spread of the Hermetic tradition is in part attributable to the emergence of a body of people who called themselves "philosophers." Indeed, the Hermetic tradition was originally developed and taught only among the philosophers: though not every philosopher was a Hermetic practitioner, every Hermetic practitioner was a philosopher (de Biasi, Rediscovering the Magick of the Gods and Goddesses). We therefore learn something about the original Hermetic tradition from understanding the ancient conception of the philosopher. Among the best known of the Greek philosophers are Plato and Aristotle (both of whom were also initiates) and, later, among the Romans, Cicero. These figures became prominent in Hellenic and, later, in Roman culture, both for their work (as teachers and politicians) and for their writings.

Yet, while the philosophy of these figures is much discussed in exoteric scholarship, their interest for esoteric practitioners has less to do with their ideas than the kind of personality they represented. Whereas in our time we might term someone a "philosopher" because of his or her academic credentials or writings, the philosopher for the Ancients represented a specific kind of person, with specific practices and habits (Scheler, "On philosophy's self-constitution," in On the Eternal in Man). The well-known etymology of "philosopher" (philia – love; sophia – wisdom) suggests a person whose basic life-orientation is defined through the search for and love of wisdom.

The philosopher

The Ancients therefore called a "philosopher" someone who's very being and personality were formed in a basic drive and desire for wisdom, a wisdom which was neither only nor primarily knowledge, but characterized by a way of life and a specific formation of character. The ancient philosophers understood that the seeking after wisdom is something only attainable through a constant process of expanding self-knowledge and self-improvement. The primary concept used to describe this improved self-knowledge and character was arete, which is usually translated into English either as "excellence" or, more traditionally, as "virtue."

Hence the philosopher is not primarily a person seeking knowledge or still less a person seeking academic credentials and notoriety. The philosopher, on this ancient model, is a person seeking wisdom through (1) the ongoing process of deepening self-knowledge, e.g. the awareness of both one's strengths and weaknesses, leading to a recognition of how one's vices (the opposite of virtue) lead one astray in one's experience, judgment, and social interaction; hence (2) the philosopher seeks to change his or her own character, through habitual mastery of both inner thoughts and passions and outer behavior, thus developing virtue, i.e. positive habits of character, where previously vice existed. Thus, philosophy was inherently ethical in nature and was above all a practice, because it was both a habitual attitude and a program of how to live (Hadot, What is Ancient Philosophy?). The proof is in the pudding: the philosopher or wisdom-seeker is a person who not only knows but who first and foremost lives the wisdom that he or she attains, thereby bearing witness in his or her life to the fundamental truth in the wisdom discovered.

While exoteric scholarship usually talks of the ancient "schools" of philosophy as if they are primarily defined by their ideas, in fact these schools were much more than educational organizations propagating ideas, especially those associated with Iamblicus and with the later Platonic schools. For these, the first principle of their communities was the celebration of the Mysteries, where the "students" were in fact communal worshippers of the gods. Secondarily, these were also schools of philosophy, but this should not be understood on the model of the modern classroom. Instead, in the hands of a competent master, one learned to think carefully, first about the material cosmos, and then rise to an understanding of the spiritual cosmos, something which, if undertaken successfully, carried with it a certain experience I will call "Illumination" (more on this below). Further, the training was always also a training in virtue, with the understanding that the development of virtue was essential to living and flourishing in community. Indeed, not only the development of virtue but practices we might nowadays associate with both psychotherapy and spiritual direction were also a part of these practices (Hadot, What is Ancient Philosophy?).

While there is much that could be said concerning each of these points, Plato himself offers perhaps the most succinct and profound articulation of this vision in the form of an image, the Parable (sometimes called the "Allegory") of the Cave. I will describe the Parable in my own words and offer some comments by way of interpretation.

The Cave

Plato, speaking through the character of Socrates in his Republic, imagines an underground cave where a number of people are locked and chained into position, facing a wall, unable to move their heads in any other direction. We can quite rightly call these people "prisoners," though, in a way, they are even worse off than prisoners because they are not only locked and chained but are also unaware that they are locked and chained. On the wall they face there are a number of shadows moving which, unbeknownst to them, are produced by people behind them, using cutouts of figures (e.g. cutouts of animals and plants) to cast shadows via the light from a fire. These people also make sounds and noises correlating to the movements among the shadows. Since the prisoners are locked in and can see nothing but the wall in front of them, they understandably assume that what they see is the whole of reality. For example, any sounds they hear they attribute to the shadows, not knowing of any other source from which the sounds might have originated. Consequently, since the shadows appear to be the whole of life, the prisoners compete with each other in contests to see who can name what each shadow is, and they offer prizes to those who succeed at the contest.

This, Plato thinks, is an apt metaphor for the way most people live and of what life without philosophy looks like: it is a life which confuses the shadow of things for reality, which leaves one open to profound deception concerning both oneself and the world, and which has an almost addictive tendency to draw people into its basic illusion, namely, that the shadows constitute the primary part or indeed even the whole of reality.

Plato then imagines that some mysterious and unnamed force loosens the chains on one of these prisoners. This prisoner, suddenly realizing he is no longer locked in and that he is in some sense liberated from what he previously took to be a necessity, turns and looks first from side to side and then, ultimately, behind him. This gesture on his part forces him to recognize things he did not previously think possible. Among them (1) that there is more to life than the shadows he took to be the whole of reality; (2) that the shadows, though in some sense real, are the least real of all things; and (3) that there appear to be interested parties manipulating the prisoners into thinking that the shadows are the entirety of life.

Plato describes those manipulating the masses in other contexts as "sophists," a term Plato uses less to refer to the actual people of his time who called themselves "sophists," than to a certain state of soul that anyone may have. And what is that state of soul?

The sophist is like the philosopher in that the sophist has some sense for wisdom; but the sophist is also the opposite of the philosopher because he or she only recognizes wisdom to the extent that it can be used for power, money and/or material gain. Furthermore, the sophist understands enough of wisdom to recognize and even to partake of this game of shadows occurring in the cave and is willing to leave others in their state of imprisonment, as long as the sophist benefits from it. It is therefore a body of sophists who are in practice keeping these prisoners enchained, i.e. people with just enough of wisdom to know how to make the prisoners the moving pieces of their game. For this reason too, we know that the mysterious and unnamed force that released the prisoner was not someone from among this group of sophists, for the latter seek their own gain through the ongoing deception, whereas this mysterious force released the prisoner and gave the latter the opportunity to recognize that he was imprisoned.

Once the liberated prisoner recognizes he has been deceived and also – and this is the far more painful part – that he himself has actually colluded in the deception by asking no questions, he begins to question the nature of things both inside and outside himself. He is no longer a prisoner not only because he was released but because he learns how to question. Indeed, he now realizes not only that he can question, but that it is his responsibility to question: only through questioning can the liberated prisoner continue the work of the mysterious and unnamed force which released him. Given this situation, we can see why Plato's student Aristotle would say "philosophy begins in wonder." One can only sincerely question what one wonders about. Indeed, we might even say that the point of the game of shadows the sophists play is to tempt the prisoners to be satisfied enough with banal pleasures that they avoid any questioning, since the latter might bring the discomfort of questioning those pleasures too.

However, the liberated prisoner, having learned to question, is not satisfied simply with understanding the deception of the sophists, in part because he recognizes a further point: the cutout figures being used to cast the shadows, though not themselves shadows, are also not the real thing. Analogously, the sophists who are doing the deceiving are acting as if they are wise; yet they, too, are not the real thing. The cutouts of the animals are not themselves animals and the sophists are more "wise guys" than "wise men." Consequently, the liberated prisoner begins to question even the bits of wisdom to be found in the sophists, because it seems as if there must be a fuller and a higher wisdom on which it is based, one which the sophists represent only vaguely, but which must stand behind even their ability to deceive.

Thus, through his questioning, the liberated prisoner begins to move beyond the sophists, the fire and the cutouts. He undertakes a difficult journey and one difficult to comprehend, given his background: he ascends from the underground cave and seeks the higher light. Plato indicates that this journey is arduous and fraught with dangers, not only internal (such as the destruction of our usually inflated self-images) but also external (the sophists can be ruthless in their will to control and, if necessary, in their willingness to destroy their opponents). Furthermore, like the original liberation from the chains, that same mysterious force also continues to pull the liberated prisoner as he makes his way out of the cave, toward the higher world.

The most striking thing that first occurs for the liberated prisoner – or we might just call him a philosopher – as he transitions out of the cave is that he moves from the darkness of the cave to the light of the outer and, indeed, higher world. He is at first blinded, a symbol of what happens when one finds oneself in the presence of the Divine Light, and thus he can't yet look upward. With what tools he has been given, how is he to see what the outer world really is or interpret it in some reasonable way? Only if he develops new organs of perception will he be able to adjust to the new situation. At first, therefore, he can only see the forms that were being imitated by the cutouts, such as real plants, real animals, and so forth. After some time of contemplating these real entities, however, his eyes begin to adjust and so he can also look upward toward the light and recognize the Sun, the symbol of the Origin and Fount of all things and the Highest Good. Once his eyes adjust, in fact, he can recognize the basic principle of wisdom, namely, that whether or not one looks directly at the Sun, it is only in its light that one sees. Even the fire back in the Cave is a mere imitation of the Sun and has its source in realities which exist only by virtue of the action of the Sun. Hence, once the philosopher can in some limited measure understand the Sun, he can also at least in principle understand other things in its light. Yet it is only through that process – the experience of liberation from the cave, from being blinded by the Sun, and by adjusting to participation in the Sun's Light – that one recognizes something of the true nature of things. This is, in its essence, the meaning of Illumination.

Illumination

Let's pause for a moment before continuing with Plato's story, to reconsider what this image tells us about Illumination.

First of all, it should be noted that Plato sees Illumination as a process. It is not something that happens, for example, in the twinkling of an evangelical eye, as if one is suddenly more or less wholly illuminated. Rather, Illumination is an ongoing process which, for heuristic purposes, we could divide into two basic steps: first, being released from the shadows and, second, climbing out of the cave into the authentic Light.

Traditionally, these two steps in Plato's analysis have sometimes been called "moving from double ignorance to single ignorance" and "moving from single ignorance toward wisdom." "Double ignorance" describes the prisoners locked and chained in the cave: they are ignorant, but do not know they are ignorant. They are, as I mentioned above, in some ways worse off than being prisoners, because they are ignorant twice-over: they both mistake the shadows for the whole and the best of reality and, further, imagine that, by virtue of that belief, they are not ignorant.

The first release of the prisoner, therefore, is not a release into wisdom proper; it is first a release from the ignorance of thinking that one knows to the realization that one does not. The destabilizing effect of this first liberation impacts the liberated prisoner greatly, because it widens his horizons but it also humiliates him in some fashion, through his having to acknowledge that he actually does not know all – or perhaps anything – that he thought he did. But when the liberated prisoner can recognize his situation and can see its value, he moves from double ignorance to single ignorance: that is to say, he moves from knowing nothing but thinking he knows all (double ignorance) to the recognition that, in fact, he knows nothing – but at least he knows that (single ignorance). And the recognition that he does not know is the beginning of seeking wisdom.

This first step might appear like it is a small gain, but it is in fact a great gain indeed. Plato's analysis here suggests that most people live in the state of double ignorance, deceived by sophistic influences and, worse, by allowing themselves to be so deceived. Plato values this first movement so highly, in fact, that many of his greatest dialogues (his philosophical texts were mostly written in dialogue form) end precisely at this point, where the philosopher (usually Socrates) has proved to his interlocutor who thought he knew how things worked that he in fact understood nothing of what he claimed to know. Further, in many of these dialogues, this revelation to the dialogue partner which brings the latter from double to single ignorance is not welcomed. All too often, people experience such insight as a humiliation, rather than as a call to humility. Most people, Plato believed, are content to live in the prison of double ignorance, providing their instinctual needs are satisfied: liberation to a deeper and richer wisdom brings with it both the painful loss of one's cherished self-deceptions and also a certain level of responsibility to aid others in their liberation. We will return to this problem below.

But we also need to see that, as painful, destabilizing, and humiliating as the move from double to single ignorance can be, it is the unavoidable first step toward wisdom and Illumination.

We cannot be generally wise until we have sufficiently freed ourselves of what we might call "the Great Deception," i.e. the various ways in which we are being deceived and allowing ourselves to be deceived. Every age has had its various ways of producing the deception that keeps prisoners enchained at the level of soul, whether through false religions, false patriotisms, false nationalisms, and other sources. In our time entire industries dedicated to mass deception, such as advertising, entertainment, and a "news industry" and "political process" modeled precisely on the advertising and entertainment industries are also examples. This is not to say that these industries might not have some level of value; sometimes their content has some definite value – just like there are bits of wisdom among the sophists. But the intent of the industries highlights the problem: on the one hand, they maneuver one into total dependence on their "information" and into an emotional indifference and complacency about seeking higher Light and, on the other, they aim to turn one's desires toward purely instinctual gratification. After all, it is not easy to turn the higher Light into a commodity for sale.

If one can be sufficiently freed of the game of shadows, one can in principle move to the second step, the movement from single ignorance – recognizing that I know nothing – toward wisdom. One cannot seek wisdom in truth unless one clearly recognizes that one does not already possess it. If Plato's analysis is basically on target, most people cannot seek wisdom because they cannot countenance the insight that they in fact know little and they cannot stomach the humiliation of recognizing that what they took for wisdom was basically only "winning the prize among the shadows," i.e. by happening to be the best at working with the materials of deception already given. Illumination, in contrast, requires being willing to give over even one's pet "prizes" in the game, such as social status, money, power and similar commodities, if the latter are also obstacles to seeking after wisdom. Indeed, some of the characters in Plato's dialogues get to the point of single ignorance but, like the rich man in the Gospel, "go away sad," because they wanted a wisdom that did not demand that, at times, they give up some of their "prizes" for something better.

Yet, as the Parable suggests, there is a mysterious, invisible force which also pulls on us to make this movement from double ignorance toward wisdom. This pull is invisible and unnamed because it is a divine movement that impels the soul in the direction of wisdom. The ancient philosophers typically described the divine as "pulling" on the soul, drawing the soul toward wisdom and the participation in the divine and divine things. Aristotle's concept of the divine as the "final cause" drawing all of being toward itself is only the most famous example of a set of symbols that runs throughout the ancient philosophers (Voegelin, "Reason: the classic experience," in Anamnesis). But while those in double ignorance can be drawn by this divine pulling – whether it is understood to be God or a god or one's holy guardian angel or what have you – they do not yet have the experiences by which to understand it. Only in the movement toward wisdom, toward understanding the ultimate principles – or what Plato, Carl Jung, and many esoteric traditions call the "archetypes" – can one manage to recognize something of the nature of the divine impulse which tugs on the soul.

Consequently, the person who undertakes this pursuit is not only after a wisdom that looks like knowledge; rather, he or she seeks a wisdom that consists in an attunement to the divine and to divine things. Hence it is really a way of life, a way of being, and consists in large measure in the development of the virtues conducive to living a life of wisdom. On this model, the divine becomes the primary ordering principle of the soul, which entails not only a knowing but a releasing of the latent Divine Spark within.

Returning to the Cave

Plato's narrative does not end therefore with the attainment of wisdom for, having a soul more and more ordered to the divine through the process of Illumination, the philosopher feels an increased connection to and concern for those who are still locked up in the cave, gazing at the shadows. Some of kind existential philia, i.e. a profound and general love of one's fellow human beings, drives the philosopher to enter back into the cave, though he would much rather remain outside it, in the hope of aiding those who remain enslaved by the game of shadows, the Great Deception. Yet, as Plato notes, when the philosopher does this, he will typically be ignored, ridiculed, or even killed as a nuisance. Just as Socrates was killed for "corrupting the youth" though in fact he was simply highlighting the deceptive ways and culture of the Athens of his time, so Socrates' death will be a paradigm case for philosophers throughout the ages, some of whom will pay a high price for seeking wisdom and for attempting to aid others in the process of Illumination. Both the commitment to purely sensuous pleasures on the part of the prisoner and the interests of the sophists generating the shadows may result in an unwillingness to listen to the philosopher and even in a boundless fury at the philosopher for trying to awaken the prisoners from their mindless slumber.

Philosophy and esoteric practice

Seeking wisdom and Illumination, on Plato's account, is an arduous – indeed, it can even be a bloody – business, not made for the weak of heart. Yet it was not without reason that the Hermetic practitioners were also philosophers in Plato's tradition. Here are some reasons why.

1. Knowledge of self is the Alpha and Omega of esoteric practice. Yet there are in fact many ways of knowing oneself that are essential to esoteric practices and one of those ways is exemplified in the Parable of Cave: the recognition of where one is self-deceived. Any movement toward wisdom and Illumination requires a prior effort to free oneself from self-deception.

How does one do that? The Parable hints that the portal to liberation is through recognizing where the divine "pulls" at the soul. Wherever one feels the impulse towards wonder or questioning with an eye toward expanding one's intellectual, moral or spiritual point of view or wherever a dissatisfaction with the status quo leads one not just to complaining and cynicism but to recognizing a potentially higher life behind what one sees, one should assume that there is a divinely-inspired impulse there. This is not so much a movement toward a general skepticism concerning the world as a recognition that appearances can only be understood in the light of higher planes of Being. Following such impulses, carefully and thoughtfully, can give one a context in which to understand the Great Deception and thereby in some measure leave the game of shadows, in the direction of single ignorance.

That this step of the process is important for esoteric practitioners should be clear. For example, since esoteric practices as a rule increase one's power to achieve ends as well as evoke certain powers of the psyche not typically in use by contemporary humanity, being caught in the game of shadows will at best lend confusion and at worst lead to unintended and damaging effects – or to discovering that one's practice has implicitly been intensifying rather than mitigating the sophistical game of shadows.

2. The movement out of the cave, i.e. the movement from single ignorance toward wisdom and Illumination, should be understood as correlating to the release of the Divine Spark within. This second stage of the illuminative process suggests an ever-deepening participation in divine life and being, to the point of experiencing all things in the divine light. This too is a kind of self-knowledge. It is not merely the knowledge of self-deception and of the vices which arise in its wake, however, something characteristic of the first stage of illumination. It is rather a knowledge and experience of the Higher Self within.

One can easily see how this stage of the process correlates in some ways to theurgic practices. If we image the latter as in some way a "descent" of the divine into us, the philosophical work is the correlating "ascent" from the cave into the light. Similar symbols have been used for illumination in other traditions. For example, St. Bonaventure offers a Christian version of this duality of illuminative descent-ascent in terms of the image of Jacob's ladder, on which the angels both descend and ascend. These first two steps reveal why a philosophical attitude is crucial for Illumination and also something of why theurgy should have a primacy over other kinds of esoteric practice.

3. The movement back into the cave, the third step, suggests a re-engaging with the shadows, but from the new, more illuminated point of view. An important piece of this movement is the love for humanity which impels one back into the cave, a symbol of the responsibility for the well-being of others that comes with philosophy and also with adepthood. A further dimension of this movement is that it suggests that the philosopher becomes an agent of the divine, through the participation in the light of the Sun. The genuine philosopher, one might say, collaborates with the invisible divine movement which is always attempting to release others from the shadows of the cave, by using his or her experience of both life within the cave and life without it to persuade others to follow the divine pulling.

This third step suggests that a genuine philosopher and the genuine adept does not seek the power associated with Illumination only for his or her own purposes, but also for the aid and liberation of the world.

4. However, though the image gives a more or less linear description of illumination, as if it is simply a three-step process, in practice it is more properly an ongoing and cyclical process. That is to say, this movement back into the cave is not just for others but also for oneself: it is a re-descending into places in our own soul where there are still lurking shadows and undertaking anew the illuminative process with respect to those things. One is never just illuminated or not illuminated; it is always a question of degrees and further illumination is also always possible.

This being the case, it should be clear why the community of philosophers was the natural place for Hermetic practices. The practices associated with philosophy, including the seeking after a wisdom to be lived, the contemplation of the cosmos, and the practice of the virtues are all deeply beneficial to Hermetic practices. Philosophy in its ancient sense both stabilizes and supplements all esoteric practices, by aiming to realize the highest excellences in human nature.

Creed of the Ecclesia Ogdoadica

By Gemistus Pletho

Here are the Ogdoadic Principles of the Creed which are the most essential to everyone who wishes to live as a wise human being.

1. I believe that the Goddesses and the Gods really exist.

2. I believe that, by their providence, the Goddesses and the Gods sustain and guide human destiny for the good. They accomplish this directly, by themselves, or through the Divinities of the lower planes, but always in accordance with the Divine laws.

3. I believe that the Goddesses and the Gods are never the origin of any evil, neither for us, nor for any being. On the contrary, they are, by their essence, the origin of every good.

4. I believe that the Goddesses and Gods act to bring about the best possible result, according to the laws of an immutable fate, which is inflexible and emanates from the Supreme Divine Principle.

5. I believe that the Universe is eternal. It did not begin at some point in the past and it will never end. It is composed of many parts that are organized together and harmonized into a unique whole. It was created to be the most perfect it can be and there is nothing to add that would make it more perfect. It always remains steadily the same- in its original state- and it continues to be eternally immutable.

6. I believe that our soul shares the same essence as the Divinities; it is immortal and eternal. The Immortal Divinities

direct the soul, sometimes in one body, sometimes in another, according to the laws of universal harmony and from the perspective of what is needed for that being to ascend to the Divine. This union between the mortal and the immortal contributes to the unity of everything.

7. I believe that, in order to be in harmony with our Divine nature, we must consider Beauty and Goodness to be the most essential aspects of what exists, and the highest aspirations of our lives.

8. I believe that, in determining the laws that govern our existence, the Immortal Divinities have put our happiness into the immortal part of our being, which is also the most important part of us.

Hymn to the Gods

By Proclus

Hear me, O Gods, you who hold the rudder of sacred wisdom. Lead us mortals back among the immortals as you light in our souls the flame of return. May the ineffable initiations of your hymns give us the power to escape the dark cave of our lives and purify ourselves.
Hearken, powerful liberators!
Dispel the surrounding obscurity and grant me the power to understand the holy books; replace the darkness with a pure and holy light. Thus, may I truly know the incorruptible God that I am.
May a wicked spirit never keep me, overwhelmed by ills, submerged in the waters of forgetfulness and far away from the Gods and Goddesses.
May my soul not be fettered in the jails of life where I am left to suffer a terrifying atonement in the icy cycles of generation. I do not want to wander anymore.

O you, sovereign Gods of radiant wisdom, hear me! Reveal to one who hastens on the Path of Return the holy ecstasies and the initiations held in the depth of your sacred words!

Orpheus

By Vivian Godfrey White (Melita Denning).
6ᵗʰ Grand Master of the Order Aurum Solis.

I
I seek a token
Higher than death with breath of fire can abate,
Greater than plant's enchantment, than secret spoken,
Sweet as song, strong as fate.

II
Grief's passion to purpose turning
Lingered the Thracian, musician fingers ever for the dead
Questing upon the strings, un-resting, never discerning
The sounds that from those quivering seven bled:
Music whose skill had he willed, from the walls of the hills a voice
Had called of human tears, or the mirth of earth to rejoice:
Music that held in its power each hour of the planets' burning:
When suddenly his mind heard, and its burden shed.
He knew his way to tread.

III
How travels living man to the land where Death is king?
Some unquestioning, no heed giving, sightless go.
But of those who know, there are few that sing
The journeying of the terrible road to show.
In the chasm where the traveller descends,
Half down the riven pit, on the steep
Crumbling cliff where drift of the daylight ends
A tree is rooted deep,
Reaching its mere bare greyness towards the air:
And the twigs that are nearest the day are called Despair.
As far beneath, where breathing is pent by wraiths of night,
With ravelled shadow closed about, the traveller goes

In doubt of living, perceiving without sight:
And there it is the silent river flows
Oblivious venomous mist for ever weaving:
And there it is, the history truly vouches,
With changeless gaze the triple horror couches:
Lip-slavering hate, fear whimpering, howling, grieving,
And leaden jaws that close.
But here the harper safely passed, nor greatly heeded:
Clear in his heart was the remembered day
When trees entranced had danced to hear him play.
Not yet to win his way a greater art he needed.

IV
Solemn splendour of Hades' hall!
Sombre columns with golden capitals crowned,
And jewelled throngs attending, languid all,
Pallid as candle flames by the noonday drowned:
Where the dark king with his consort virginal
Still smiles as if he frowned.

V
O Hades, here at thy throne
In homage the doom I sing of kingdoms of man.
Ringed be a land with pride, or of wider span
Than can in a season ripen what spring beyond spring has sown.
Though high cities besides with store of gold have shone,
Yet when, O king, thou dost but call thine own,
Man's government is done.
Or shall I sing the fate of ancient things?
Wherever the power, the honour of age is won
And treasure of measured time has greatly grown.
There, when some hour thy pleasure's message brings –
O strings, falter and moan —
At once all is gone.
Shall learning be our boast?
Short time, a life, for that unearthly reaping!
Nor ever shows some frail earth-questing ghost
More grant of all his hoarded knowledge keeping

Than strife of stuttered words his life could have uttered sleeping.
The wise who learn to die, their prize avails the most.

VI

So sang, so played on the seven strings' sweetness and pain
The stranger, every hope laying low at Hades' feet:
Broken, plaintive every tone was made.
Whether of good or of pride, to Death was the gain:
The faithful sailor lost, the trader by storm betrayed,
Glory of courage in war outpoured, vainly scorning retreat.
Then to a stronger cry the music leading
His inmost grief he told.
Of the bride from his long gaze torn — from his tortured pleading
—

Beauty that vied with morning, borne alone to the cold
Skyless night of Hades' hold.
And with his love his life's harsh overturning.
Not, he sighed, that I sought; although awhile
In her smile I caught more joy than the Fates allow:
But one doom waits, however we make its trial.
Where Zeus has struck, a vine may deck the barren bough
But Hades' victim is smitten beyond denial
And past adorning.

VII

But mark, O king: hear and heed a deed of mine!
See, my harp has a new thing, the new, the eighth string!
Thine is power on the dower of earth, but this is divine.
Freedom I cry, the birth of freedom I sound and sing:
Greater than fate, the eighth string: O king, do you know its
worth?

VIII

Seven sounds ring for all the earth has seen.
Weave and change the player may, aspiring
Beyond that range: but the leaping fire of his lay
Falls back, back as if tiring
In mortal weariness its bonds between:

For all the sun has seen is indeed thy prey
But the eighth string makes thy power its mirth.
This is the octave: gate that closes
By opening onward: end that suspends all end.
Here then, O king, is my token:
Phoenix, the scale as a stair of fire to ascend
Where ever higher she hovers, never reposes.
By this, the one thing free in a world at thy feet,
I bid thee behold at last thy sovereignty broken.
My own I claim, not entreat.

IX
So thus his music earned the unheard-of boon
To bring his bride again to sight of the skies:
But how to tell
His faith's one flaw, one doubt that all was well,
Doubt of ill chance, that glanced about too soon?
She faded from his eyes:
But thus far wise, he knew, though his heart had failed,
The mystery was true and had prevailed
Though never his should be the blissful prize.

X
How lives the lover by love and by death forsaken?
He lives to rove as if blind to time and place,
But the beloved finding in every face
To a life beyond his life he must awaken.
The harper his way has taken
To slopes of rock and grass where slow flocks move,
Now bent on solitude his sorrow's bond to sever,
Now with the herd-boys met, matching in mock endeavour –
As if the novice-power of his harp to prove –
Their music's wild grace shaken,
Their wine-ripe fruit-sweet fluting to the river:
But death was ever present though absent ever,
And never present, never absent was love.

XI

Listeners came,
Guessing his name revered, to tell, and bear
Of his fame a listener's share:
But not the old clear praises could they frame,
So strange the maze he traced from his song's beginning:
The bride gained yet denied to him, lost yet closer than air,
And death's gate unbarred, ajar for the winning.
But he welcomed them with laughter, and wrought a splendour of
sound —
The sport of after echoes around the mountain meadow —
And the women danced, their spirit seeming as his unbound
And the earth but shadow.
Nearer whirled the dancers, one tossed glance seeking
From him who played of heart's desire, eyes lost in light of vision:
Till a girl sped to his side, from height of the frenzy breaking,
Grasped his wrist resistless away from the strings, and cried
'Darkness and nothing is this, or day and the kiss of your bride?
Singer, give proof of the truth of your song: give us life, O
magician!'

XII

So the first hands smote: the crowd so loudly calling and shrieking
His own throat's cry he doubted, or if he panted dumb.
He saw his arm unplanted
His no more to raise though breath were granted.
Then to his neck, death-consented, one struck:
And night was come.

XIII

They strewed him to the sobbing winds, to the rain
That dropped on the hills, his head to the flooding river.
And all the land was shrill with shuddering pain.
But so the doom was past:
Day serene has smiled from darkness flying:
One with his love is that child of the lords undying.
Blest at last:
And earth has his song for ever.

Tradition of the Aurum Solis

Early ages

It is fair to say that Sumer was the birth of all civilization, where the invention of writing took place, as well as maybe one of the first elaborate forms of religion. Some of the most important esoteric principles and practices were passed into Egypt, where they became associated with the Magical knowledge of the early Egyptians. This is how really started what we can call the Western Tradition which eventually spread in the countries around the Mediterranean Sea.

Birth of the "Gold Chain" (the chain of the adepts)

The God Thot and the Goddesses Isis are the real founders of the hermetic and theurgic traditions. The "Sacred Mysteries" and the "Cult of Isis" became better known than the Theurgic and Hermetic Traditions that were derived from the teachings of Thoth. It is obvious that this part of the heritage constituted the roots of what has been called hundreds of years later "Theurgy," the "divine work."

Until the 5th century this fascinating tradition continues to develop in several steps that will be explained in more details on other parts of this website.

The first main aspect has been the development of the cult of Thoth in Hermopolis. Based on the founding story of the creation of the world, the priests elaborated rites and sacred mysteries. The same happened for the Goddess Isis who was also linked to magic.

During the Hellenistic period of Egypt known as Ptolemaic period from the name of its founder Ptolemy I, this very ancient tradition became associated to the Greek Mysteries. This is the time when philosophy and theurgy were taught in Alexandria. This period and place should be seen as the birth place of the tradition we are referring to

Egypt, birth place of the Western Tradition

The first famous figure to travel to Egypt in order to learn the secrets of this ancient religious and Magical Tradition, was Pythagoras, in the 5th century. He spent a long time there and obviously received the teachings and training that were available in the Temples of this country.

Just as Pythagoras had done, Plato travelled to Egypt in order to receive the teachings from priests who were part of the clergy of Heliopolis. Then back in Athens (Greece) after years of learning, he founded the Academy. Today scholars agree on the fact that this Academy maintained the organization of the Pythagorean School by the publication of books, and with oral and private teachings. It is startling to realize that this Academy was active from the 5th century BCE until 6th century CE, so for over 10 centuries!

Porphyry of Tyre (233-305 CE) who was the Scholarch (chief) of the Platonic Academy of Athens was one of the masters of Iamblichus. It is very likely that he passed on his philosophical heritage and initiations (from Plato and Pythagoras) to him. Iamblichus additionally learned all the platonic texts, enacted several ancient Mysteries and ultimately received what became a real revelation, the full revelation of the "Chaldaean Oracles."

Iamblichus discovered the sacred science that was inherited from the Chaldeans and the Egyptians: Theurgy!

Of course, Magic existed prior to this period, but Iamblichus unified these different doctrines, all of which originated from Egypt and Chaldea, upon the theological and ritual foundation of the Chaldaean Oracles. It was really at this moment that this spiritual family found its axis and homeland. Iamblichus taught in Apamea throughout the entire first quarter of the 4th century.

The dark days

Meanwhile during the period when Iamblichus was teaching, Christianity was rising rapidly, imposing its absolute and intolerant view. Unfortunately, and as is very often true in the history of humanity, it was not the moderate participants who shaped this new religion...

The Ptolemaic dynasty ended in 30 BCE. The school of Alexandria continues to exist until the 5th century. Hypatia was savagely murdered by Christians while the library of Alexandria was destroyed by the rising rage of Christianity. Initiates, theurgists, philosophers, and scientists flew to other countries such as Italy, Greece, Syria, etc.

Keeping these elements in mind, it is possible to say that the Hermetic and Theurgic Tradition was maintained in Byzantium, Greece, and Italy. First of all, I would like to highlight the names of Leon the Mathematician, Michael Psellos, and Michael Italikos. All of these men respectfully learned the "Chaldaean oracles" and wrote extensively about these texts. Italikos was even named the "second Plato." It is indubitably the case that Magic and even Theurgy were used by many scholars.

During the early days of the Christian religion, the Emperor Justinian declared that the Orthodox Nicene Christian faith was the official (and only permitted) religion that could be practiced in the Empire. The Emperor's Codex contained two statutes which mandated the total destruction of all pagan practices, even in private life.

In 529 the Neoplatonic Academy of Athens was closed by order of the Emperor. From that day forward, Paganism was actively suppressed, as were all related pagan creative works (books, art, etc.) by fanatical monks, encouraged by the authorities of the Empire.

As a result of that decree, an uncounted number of male and female initiates were captured, tortured and killed in the name of "pure Christian love". The secrecy of our Tradition and beliefs became an obligation, a simple matter of survival.

The Renaissance

In the fifteenth century, the Theurgic Neoplatonic tradition (also called in modern times "Ogdoadic tradition") reappeared. Gemistus Pletho (1355–1452) met Cosimo de Medici in Florence and influenced the latter's decision to create a new Platonic Academy there. Cosimo subsequently appointed Marsilio Ficino as head of the newly formed Academy. He proceeded to translate all Plato's works into Latin, including the Enneads of Plotinus, and various other Neoplatonic writings.

The group that met at the Villa Careggi perpetuated both the initiatic mysteries of the Neoplatonist tradition and the Theurgic initiation.

Besides this main philosophy, other parts of the western tradition were known by some members of the Academy. Giovanni Cavalcanti was an initiate of the "Fideli d'Amore" and Pico della Mirandola was a specialist of Qabalah. The tradition of the "Fideli" have been created by French troubadours of the Middle age, while Qabalah was coming from the Hebrew religion. Both were progressively incorporated to the main beliefs and tradition of the Academy. We have also to keep in mind that close contacts existed between other Academies in Italy, such as the academy of Venice and Naples (Academy of Secrets).

This group's remarkable activities marked the rebirth of this ancient pagan tradition that changed the western world on many fundamental aspects including philosophy, theology, art, and many more

Modern times

The period between the Italian Renaissance and the rebirth of the Order in 1897 has been well documented by the Grand Master Jean-Louis de Biasi in his book "Rediscover the Magick of the Gods and Goddesses," Llewellyn Publications. We invite you to go deeper on the subject by reading the historic section of this book.

After the period of the Renaissance, the Theurgic Neoplatonic tradition continued to exist. We should mention an interesting group called "the Fratelli Obscuri" which was active in Italy during the 16th and 17th centuries. This secret organization concealed the laudable object of propagating the Sciences and the love of Virtue. The Fratelli Obscuri had been established in imitation of an older Society which had existed since before the fall of the Grecian Empire in the towns of Constantinople and Thessalonica. It was divided into three Grades.

Antonio Pizzalleti, Grand Officer of this organization came to London and installed the new Society under the name of "the Tavern of the Muses. A few years later William Sedley and Thomas Smith established two new Taverns, one at Oxford and the other at Cambridge." Another tavern was opened at York and many more also opened at the time John Selden was head of the Fratelli Obscuri in England. Eventually, the Fratelli Obscuri in England transformed their society into the Tobaccological Society. The tobaccologist (named Priseurs or Nicotiates in France) were known as the "Children of Wisdom." Remember that the Neoplatonicians were called "Friends of Wisdom," and philosophers.

Freemasonry, and which seem related to this tradition. Perhaps the most significant is the "Academy of the Sublime Masters of the Luminous Ring" (Académie des Sublimes Maîtres de l'Anneau Lumineux).

According to the oral tradition of the Aurum Solis, an "Order of the Helmet" was established in England during the reign of Elizabeth I. This Order could have combined the Fideli d'Amore and Careggi successions. Francis Bacon, Edmund Spenser, Christopher Marlowe and many other notables were among its initiates. Deeply involved with the beginnings of this Order was the "Italiante" movement of the early years of Elizabeth's reign. She herself had, during her sister's reign, been tutored by a Platonist scholar and had avidly studied the works of Castiglione, an intimate of the Medici. Under her personal patronage were Giacomo Aconcio, an initiate of the Ogdoadic Guild Mysteries and Bernardino Ochino, a Sienese. Ochino, it may be mentioned, before traveling (by way of Geneva) to England, had narrowly escaped the trials of the Inquisition in Rome through the timely warning of another initiate, Cardinal Contarini.

During the 20th century druidic and shamanic traditions were incorporated in the Aurum Solis under the name "Green flame of Albion." It was also the time when the past Grand Masters Denning and Phillips created the expression "Ogdoadic Tradition" to talk about this hermetic and theurgic lineage that eventually became the Aurum Solis. Specific sections of this website provide more details about the various parts of this heritage.

Today the Aurum Solis presents all these parts of its heritage in a clear and well-structured curriculum accessible to all serious student. Besides this main corpus of teachings and practices, several main components have been organized in organizations working under the auspices of the Aurum Solis. This is a way to offer to the public all the main aspect of our heritage.

Then, the amazing history of this tradition can continue to be well alive, providing ancient keys very adapted to the modern world.

To learn more

You can learn more about the Aurum Solis, its degrees, curriculum, etc. at: www.aurumsolis.org

NOTES

Discount

Every year, a new "Ultimate Pagan Almanac" is published with an update of the dates and new articles.
As reader of this Almanac 2019, you can take advantage of a discount to order the Almanac 2020. The only thing you need to do is register for the "Theurgia Almanac list." Then we will send you a coupon as soon as the new almanac is available, sometime in Summer 2019.
The address to the list is:
https://www.theurgiauniversity.com/the-ultimate-pagan-almanac/
or: https://goo.gl/JFh3fU

Submissions

If you want to be published in the next almanac, you can send your submission to secretary@theurgia.us. The deadline for these submissions is June 30th.

Press

If you are in charge of presenting books in a magazine, you can send us a request for a free preview of the next almanac either by email or postal mail at: secretary@theurgia.us
or: 2251 N. Rampart Blvd #133, Las Vegas, NV, 89128, USA

THEURGIA - AMAZON

https://goo.gl/RP4RdJ

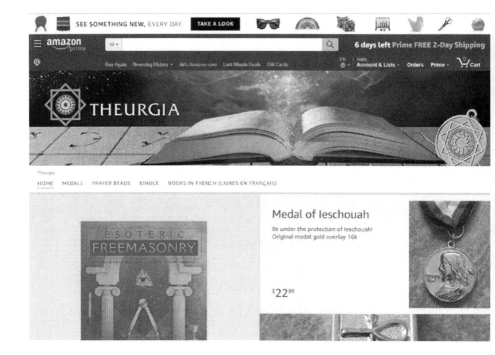

THEURGIA UNIVERSITY

www.theurgiauniversity.com

Home   **Courses**   Bookstore   Store Theurgia ⌄   Contact ⌄   Login   English ⌄   🛒

Home / Cours sur internet / Initiation to Theurgy

Initiation to Theurgy

Includes:

– 170 min video of lectures and practices
– Duplication of these videos in audio
– 160 min of Video-Documents
– Articles
– Full lifetime access
– Access on computer and any mobile device
– Certificate of Completion

[Add to cart]

♡ Add to Wishlist

362

ONLINE STORE THEURGIA

www.theurgia.us

Home   Courses   Bookstore   Store Theurgia ⌄   Contact ⌄   Login   English ⌄   🛒

Store Theurgia

Livraria em Português

Ritual Clothes

Prayer Beads

Medals and Amulets

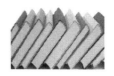

Magic Tools

Magic Squares

Jewels

Incenses

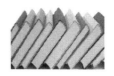

Paperback

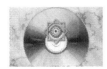

Printed in Great Britain
by Amazon